Additional Praise for *Teaching F*

"*Teaching Fiercely* is a joyful, collegial invitation to incorporate our whole powerful selves into teaching for justice so that we may invite students to engage and learn with their whole powerful selves. As a most beautiful bonus, this invitation comes with guidance for teaching for justice in meaningful, transformative ways from an author who is known to walk her justice talk."

Paul Gorski,
Founder of the Equity Literacy Institute

"Kass Minor has crafted a glorious literacy love letter to all educators committed to bringing 'joy and justice' to life in the company of children. Her words are the gentle nudge we need to envision the HOW so that we may assume an active role toward the diverse, equitable, and inclusive schools our children deserve."

Dr. Mary Howard,
Literacy Consultant and Author

"In a landscape heavy with the weight of increasing WHYs about the urgency for remedying injustices, Kass Minor provides a wise, insightful, and joyful guide for educators about HOW to move forward day to day in the work of justice with a ferocious heart."

Ashley Lamb-Sinclair,
Author, Educator & National Geographic Explorer

"For educators who are striving to engage in justice-centered work and align values to equitable classroom practices, this book will nourish your soul and well-being during these complex times in education. Kass Minor beautifully blends scholarship, teacher activism, and her wealth of educational experiences to emphasize how we build and sustain a sense of connection and belonging in school communities out of love for youth and humanity."

Erica Buchanan-Rivera,
Educator and Author of *Identity Affirming Classrooms: Spaces that Center Humanity*

"*Teaching Fiercely* is exactly what you need right now whether you are a new or veteran teacher. Kass Minor's voice is strong and clear – teaching must be joyful and just. At the heart of this book is love and respect for children, families, communities, and teaching as an art. This book will be your anchor to living a teaching life in which you bring your whole self, and which is steeped in reflection and action."

Dr. Laura Ascenzi-Moreno,
Professor of Bilingual Education, Brooklyn College,
City University of New York

Teaching Fiercely

Teaching Fiercely

Spreading Joy and Justice in Our Schools

Kass Minor

JB JOSSEY-BASS™

A Wiley Brand

The longest road you will ever walk is the journey from your head to your heart.

—Phil Lane

Contents

Work Alongs and Reflections

For an active reading experience, Work Alongs and Reflections are placed at several junctures throughout the text. Readers may wish to refer to these activities directly as they are working in school communities, participating in study groups, and/or other types of professional learning.

Author's Note

Ten percent of the author's royalties from this book will be donated to organizations that work toward the healing of Indigenous peoples within the United States, and BIPOC-owned organizations that work to strategize for equitable, inclusive futures.

Foreword

To know Kass Minor is to have lived experiences where you simultaneously feel a bolt of the universe's energy enter your mind, body, and soul. A connector of hearts, a creator, a community organizer, and really, just such a rad human.

To be a reader of professional texts—of this professional text—is to sit between words and lines and pages, in conversation. In conversation with the author, with far-away and close-by readers reading in the exact moment you are, and, most importantly, in conversation with yourself. This book kindly hands you a mirror to hold up to an evolving you: illuminating reflections of validation, observation, interrogation, and that nudge to try something new. It brings back old-school professional text vibes of deep research, and deep knowledge, requiring the reader to think acutely about their practice. The mirror-holding Kass models for us is honest and steady, as she claims she has specific identity markers and doesn't have all the answers, but does have community and conviction. And we all need those things: community, conviction, and a healthy nudge toward continuing to construct justice for kids. And not for the future, *for right now*.

So, Kass's nudge is loving and fierce, with a sense of urgency. Just like Kass.

Teaching Fiercely is designed to match the demands of today's educators. Though it is highly comprehensive, Kass mentions early on to engage with the chapters the way we coach kid-inquirers to find what they are researching for—read with your questions and identity markers in mind, clear eyes, and your heart wide open. I tried it this way and went down an empowered and individualized pathway—curated by Kass, but created by me—and found myself making lists of new-to-me scholars in the field, creatively responding to her Work Alongs like vision boarding, doing mini-inquiries into Folk Schools, interrogating both my individual and our community goals *(do they really bend toward belonging and justice?)*, reflecting hard on the teacher agency scale, and truly revising my own approaches to learning design guided by all the historical and cultural models Kass generously offers us. My educator efficacy soared reading this book, at a time when it is so needed.

To be an educator is to understand that, universally, education has always been and always will be the most powerful reciprocal tool individuals, gatherings, and communities can both receive and contribute to society. It is critical to breaking cycles of crises: illiteracy, poverty, hunger, violence in all forms, armed conflict, and large-scale environmental and human tragedy. It is both the foundation and pillar of human sustainability. Educators also painfully understand that level of progress is not universally welcomed. I've had the good fortune of being in a community with educators around the country and around the world. This positionality only raises my awareness of patterns of systemic inequities that play out on the backs of kids and caregivers everywhere. With this lens, I am certain *Teaching Fiercely* is a book that can be used around the world, because personhood and joy are carefully held at the center. I applaud Kass Minor for modeling the level of learning in public we all must do in our collective commitment to disrupting these cycles on our pathway to justice.

Welcome to the world, *Teaching Fiercely*. We are better with you here.

Sara K. Ahmed
Educator and author of *Being the Change: Lessons and Strategies to Teach Social Comprehension*

Introduction

Early 2000s

When I began teaching in the early 2000s, "social justice," "equity," "ABAR,"[1] and "CR-SE"[2] were not buzzwords floating around in public rhetoric, and most certainly were not featured on television or other media channels. Conversations about the "science of reading" had not yet hit public airwaves. The heat behind schools' choices for literacy curriculum took place mostly within academic circles working at universities, not so much between those who worked at schools, with children. If you saw something on TV about reading, or about how children should act, at least in my fledgling teacher world, you were most likely catching a rerun of Levar Burton's *Reading Rainbow*[3]

---

1. ABAR (Anti-Bias, Anti-Racist) is a popular acronym to describe the framework used for cultivating an ABAR stance within school communities.
2. CR-SE (Culturally Responsive-Sustaining Education) is an iteration of Dr. Gloria Ladson Billing's Culturally Responsive Pedagogy framework, coined by Dr. Django Paris.
3. Popular children's show featuring children's books that aired from 1983–2009 on PBS.

or maybe listening to Prince Tuesday from *Mr. Rogers Neighborhood*[4] say a thing or two about how children should behave.

In the early 2000s, MySpace was still a thing, Facebook had just opened up to the community at large, and Twitter and Instagram didn't yet exist. In short, spreading information about what was really going on in schools—i.e., what kids were experiencing, how teachers were teaching, what parents and caregivers were saying—was much harder to access. As classroom teachers who remembered the strange undercurrent of both fear and jubilation during Y2K,[5] my colleagues and I were teaching our hearts out—and, honestly, there weren't a lot of people around us who had "boo" to say about it, let alone comment on what books were in our classroom libraries.

My partner, Cornelius, and I joke about how in those first few years of teaching life we were *feral* teachers, teachers who were given so much freedom in the name of kids' best interests that putting parameters around our work would have inhibited our ability to activate our instinctual knowing, our innate calling, that is, *to teach*. I'm talking about the kind of teaching that has limited support these days: the kind of teaching that is raw and gritty yet playful and effective. The kind of teaching that is labored, almost subconsciously, by a teacher's work with the kids and families and colleagues that surround her, through trial and error, love and rejection.

Sigh.

People often give the word "feral" a bad rap, a negative connotation. But I think there's a really beautiful association with it. For example, at the Brooklyn Public Library down the street from where I live, a perhaps feral cat has built a home, or at least, has insisted upon its housing. It (he? she? they? not sure of the gender) can be seen in the front garden of the library, nestled in a cinder block with a scrap of wood over it, surrounded by three bowls of food that are *always* full. I imagine it comes and goes as it pleases. When we see it, its needs are met, belly full, with access to the world, unfettered. Our children have named it Mr. Books. Every time I visit the library with my daughters, books in hand, my heart skips a beat when we near the entrance. I worry Mr.

---

4   Popular children's show featuring "The Neighborhood of Make Believe," supporting children's social literacy that aired on PBS from 1968–2001 in the United States.

5   Y2K alludes to the global fear that spread about what would happen to people's livelihoods when 1999 turned to the year 2000. Computers were not originally programmed for the year 2000 and there was public paranoia that chaos would break out at the turn of the century.

Teaching Fiercely: Spreading Joy and Justice in Our Schools

Books will be gone, that his scruffy self will be absent amongst the flowers. And yet, we haven't missed him yet. He continues to survive.

I often think about who I would be had I begun my career in the climate educators currently experience, a climate that is defined by relevant truths, ahistoricism, and a new, post-2020 reality. How would I be *me*? Would I still be as curious or loving or connected?

During those early days in my teacherhood, I felt a great sense of freedom. In retrospect, I also realize that maybe to be free requires us to be somewhat feral. But to be free also means to struggle to survive—and as much as I felt that freedom, I felt that struggle, too. I felt it then, and I feel it now, albeit differently. Lots of things have happened to me, to you, to all of us working in schools, in education, within the past 20 years. As a profession, as a people, we're all over the place. Who are we? What is it that we do? Where are we going? Where have we . . . been?

In the beginning of my career as a new teacher, like Mr. Books, I was cared for by others, particularly, by the immediate community of teachers surrounding me on a daily basis—and also the progressive school reforms that had been implemented within my school. We were included in the Coalition of Essential Schools (CES), an endeavor built by contemporary progressives like Ted Sizer and Debbie Meier to reinforce John Dewey's foundational concept of Democracy in Education: fundamentally, that kids learn best by *doing, interacting,* and *experiencing.* They believed schools should foster those elements within their curriculum and for their students. Many of my colleagues shared that belief, and so did I.

We were also part of the New York State Performance Standards Consortium, lovingly dubbed the Consortium by those who were a part of it, a group of secondary schools that replaced high stakes testing with performance assessments for graduation requirements, teacher-led and state-approved. Most CES schools in New York City were part of the Consortium. In short, during those first few years of my teaching, my colleagues and I were blessed with a freedom and flexibility that many teachers were not then, and most certainly are not now: project-based learning was the norm, and standardized tests were the exception. We were lovingly engaged in a world of curriculum that *we* innovated, created, and adapted.

With students, we teachers created project-based learning that was directly connected to the students' personhood and their place-based experiences. Teachers worked hard to design project-based learning with the *rigor* they were implored to demonstrate, building deep literacy and numerical reasoning with the students in their classroom communities. I took my first (of what would soon be many) walking trips to explore Times Square in Manhattan with students and their ELA (English-language arts) teachers. Students captured comparisons of the real-life media feeds displayed on 42nd Street to the media displayed in dystopian novels *Feed* by M. T. Anderson and *A Clockwork Orange* by Anthony Burgess.

> *Rigor* was one of the hottest edu-buzzwords of the early 2000s, and over time it's been grossly inflated. It's often associated with academically advanced material, or super-challenging instructional experiences. But rigor simply means to operate closely within a child's zone of proximal development so as to improve the likelihood that learning will stick and their ideas about new information will grow.

Another time, within the history department, we worked to capture the impact of a newly built IKEA in nearby Red Hook, Brooklyn. Students interviewed passersby, and created photo essays with shots fastidiously snapped from their Sidekicks—the popular cell phone of the time, pre-smartphone. They were able to demonstrate longitudinal shifts on their blocks; visual reflections regarding the impact of rapidly gentrifying Brooklyn on their families.

We even had students research one of the most polluted waterways in the world, the famed Gowanus Canal, a Superfund site[6] (epa.gov), to find out exactly which contaminants surrounded some of their homes.

One of my first independently designed projects was called America Speaks, an exploration of the history of school in the United States, exposing students to the Civil Rights Movement, the ACLU (American Civil Liberties Union), and the very relevant question on whether or not racial school integration made a difference for Black and Brown students. Out of the approximately 500 students who attended our school, fewer than 1% identified as white. Decentering my teacher self as the knower in the room, students and I grappled with questions like: *If America could speak, what would she say? Has integration "worked"? What are different ways people make change? What do we want our society to be like?*

---

6   Superfund sites are areas of land or water that have been heavily contaminated by humans. Highly toxic areas are identified, and monies are directed from responsible parties, as well as other funding sources, to the Environmental Protection Agency for cleanup.

I was deeply invested in all of it. My students, the teachers I cotaught and created with. The families who patiently waited for me to do better, to get better at teaching their children. Student government, the curriculum, the basketball games, the skateboarders, Brooklyn, I loved them. I loved all of it. It was a beautiful time for me; I felt like I had figured out what I had been put on this Earth to do.

But there was an ugliness to all the deliciousness in that work. David Chang, renowned chef and restaurant mogul, has a beautiful food docuseries on Netflix called *Ugly Delicious*, an homage to the food your grandmother might make, heap on your plate, and insist that you eat at least two servings of. It tastes absolutely divine, and you and your family agree on the delightful exchange between your tastebuds and said food. But for others, those who don't know the recipe, who weren't part of cooking it, rather than looking divine, the food looks *questionable. Unappetizing. Different*.

Chang says this kind of food is the "ugly deliciousness" that restaurateurs enjoy eating at home, or that chefs and line cooks and waitstaff enjoy eating before their dining rooms open. No matter how delicious, for diners in restaurants, those dishes are really hard to appreciate. Maybe they don't know what they're eating, maybe it's something they've not seen before . . . whatever the case may be, chefs have a hard time selling the food that comes from the deepest parts of their hearts.

This was the case of my school and our work: we were ugly delicious. As much as our students were learning, as seen as they may have felt, and as hard as we were working, the people who evaluated schools didn't have a metric to gauge what we were doing. They could not see the value of our work; even though it was from the deepest parts of our hearts. They didn't have the recipes for the projects, the alternate assessments, the anachronistic schedules, the communal cross-grade advisories we built: those ideas and programs didn't come from their kitchen.

I've condensed the 500-page story that paused our freedom into just a few sentences:

- We were categorized as a "failing school" by New York City's Mayoral Office.

- The visionary principal who led the school abruptly took leave, and later quit.

- A new principal took their place, and the city went through another iteration of school reform underneath former Chancellor Joel Klein and former Mayor Michael Bloomberg's leadership.

- The school withdrew from the Coalition of Essential Schools and the Consortium.

- It later turned into something entirely different, so I left and began working at an elementary school in a different part of Brooklyn.

For me, and many of my colleagues, "failing" wasn't something we thought a lot about. We were deep in the struggle. We were too busy figuring out how to teach, trying to understand what our students needed, and working to develop connections between the projects we were designing to the new Common Core State Standards[7] that had just been introduced. Most of all, we were doing our best to stay in community with our students' families. I'll speak for myself here: I felt like I was doing *the Work,* capital *W.* Many of us, including myself, identified our teaching work as *social justice.*

We were partnering with the immediate communities surrounding us, centering our students, and using what we knew about how learning works to bridge more opportunities within their lived experience. Most of all, we operated through a lens of honesty.

While there were certainly a great many things my school could have improved on, that *I* could have improved on (the school's uniform policy and restrictive rubrics are among the top practices that, to this day, make me cringe), I know a lot of what was happening there was special, unique, just— joyful. However, those positioned to oversee the best interests of students and their families in school communities weren't able to see what I saw. Instead of growth, innovation, and opportunity, they saw failure, the need for new curriculum, students who needed to be *fixed,* and teachers who needed to be *replaced.*

It pained me then, much like it pains me now, to witness such limited vision.

---

7   Common Core State Standards officially rolled out on a federal level in the United States in 2009, but schools were encouraged to begin utilizing the standards in beta form several years prior.

It pains me to see school closures touted as school reform.

It pains me to see teachers' methodologies boxed into categories like *highly effective* or in need of *development*[8] based on tiny experiences parsed from enormous years.

It pains me to see the same cycle of data sets in the same geographical spaces show the same outcomes for the same group of people decade after decade after decade.

It pains me to see robust inquiry-based learning replaced with a prescription for learning as a remedy for low test scores, reading levels, or graduation rates.

And you want to know what's most painful? When I see educators, especially teachers, leaving their schools, or sometimes this profession forever, because the "why" behind their teaching is no longer reflected in the job they've been assigned, or the rules they're told to follow.

More than anything, the continued witnessing of impaired vision warrants a thoughtful quest to introduce not just new equipment or resources to manage the work of creating the rich, full, learning experiences in school that few of us have experienced ourselves, but rather, a thoughtful exploration of who we are—who we want to be, and to develop, build, and *enact*; something different, something better, *something from our grandmother's kitchens*.

Those early experiences in my teaching life were a collection of tensions that marked the shape of my work as an educator for years to come. The undercurrent of heartbreak in the realm of joy: former students who've died while the others got married, built companies, or had babies. The kids who love you the most, from the families who rejected you the hardest. The curriculum that fostered the deepest engagement from the otherwise disenchanted child deemed inappropriate, unnecessary, and/or irrelevant by a concerned parent and spineless school board.

These days, when I'm working in schools and partnering with teachers to develop justice-oriented learning spaces, things feel very different. *Most teachers I know live somewhere between the space of restriction, negotiation,*

---

8   In the mid-2000s in New York City, a value-added model was put in place to rate teachers; the base evaluation was adapted from Charlotte Danielson's framework, often heard in edu-circles as "the Danielson."

and a careful restoration of self. Any one decision a teacher makes about their curriculum can initiate an email thread from a concerned parent so long, so potent, that an entire summer's worth of planning can be thrown in the garbage, and a month's worth of sleep is lost from everybody involved.

And things don't just feel different, they are different: at the time of this writing, half of the states within the United States are working to pass legislation that inhibit the teaching of whole truths, and have already moved to ban books that have previously been chosen to be read by entire school communities. The National Book Award–winning memoir *Brown Girl Dreaming*, by MacArthur Genius Grantee Jaqueline Woodson, has recently been banned in some school districts. *I Dissent,* a picture book written by Debbie Levy, demonstrating the life and impact of the late Supreme Court Justice Ruth Bader Ginsburg, has also been banned in some school districts. Books that document the lives of persons who have impacted our society in important ways are now seen as radical, controversial, and inappropriate by some communities.

Almost every day, I look into the eyes of teachers and educators and children and their caregivers, and I search for the antidote to build the kinds of learning that feel joyous—not necessarily comfortable, but joyous. The kind of learning that is driven by reverence for one's community, a deep connection to the people who surround us. The kind of learning that is fueled by deep conviction and stance, a belief so central to one's teaching that any given mandate or new politicized element of school rolls off an educator's shoulders and yields no traction within a classroom.

A kind of learning that, like Mr. Books, is unfettered; and maybe not necessarily feral, but free.

What This Book Is About

Teaching Fiercely: Spreading Joy and Justice in Our Schools offers educators important, practical antidotes to remedy injustices experienced by kids, teachers, and families in schools everywhere, every day, all the time. It also offers a treatment plan immersed in care and community, and poses that connectedness as a sustainable way to move forward. While many bodies of thought exist on social justice curriculum, culturally responsive and sustaining education, and diversity, equity, and inclusion, few resources offer a place for educators to carefully reflect on their past experiences with school; to thoughtfully analyze and train their eyes to *see* rampant injustices in the everyday practice of school. Few spaces are held for teachers to reflect, to consider how they matter . . . to, essentially, be heard. Here, educators will find space to plan, apply, and *activate* justice-oriented learning through reflection, radical listening, collaboration, instructional practice, and community-based school experiences.

This book focuses on *the how* more than *the what*. While content-oriented justice is important—that is, teaching diversity and inclusivity beyond a multicultural potluck or holiday—there are incredible resources for that work already, which I'll reference throughout this book.

This book is multifaceted. It calls upon educators to ask, to study, and to develop a practice in response to essential questions I've sought to answer, name, and apply throughout my entire career in education:

What is the *pedagogy* of justice? How is *joy* implicated in that pursuit? What does it mean to teach with our whole selves, *fiercely*?

One thing I know for sure—the pedagogy of justice is expansive. We use the term "pedagogy" to describe all the acts, experiences, philosophies, curricular choices, instructional moves, communication styles, classroom environments, project plans, and community collaborations that serve our purpose for teaching the humans in front of us. This book acknowledges that expansiveness, acknowledges that teaching through the lens of justice is more than a read aloud, a diversity workshop, or a social studies unit. It also acknowledges that working toward justice is not sustainable if we don't experience joy within that pursuit.

Driven by the possibility of building *more just and joyful learning* in schools for youth, teachers, and families everywhere, teachers will journey through this book by starting with a generalized understanding of justice, and then work toward building a more specific sense of justice in schools through their own pedagogy. Readers will relive their own experiences along with my own, and various partners along their personal journey in school, as well as connections in their outer communities. They will reflect on multiple relationships and roles within a school community—some of which they've held in the past or currently experience as student, teacher, teacher-educator, parent/caregiver, administrator, and, most of all, learner.

> More than anything, teaching through the lens of justice requires our whole self; it is a lifelong commitment, and it is a consideration of all that we are and everything we do within the ecosystem of school.

Like I said, it's expansive! How, then, do we commit without becoming overwhelmed? How do we reflect without walking away? How do we shift beyond just surviving? How do we transform in ways that are more than doable—that are just and joyful for kids and their families, for yourself, and your colleagues? How is any of this even possible in a time when the very idea of *justice* is riddled with tension, anxiety, and harm? How do we teach not just with our hearts and minds, but our instincts, too? How do we teach *fiercely*?

While we search for definitive answers to those questions, our work will inevitably serve us nebulous answers. It is up to us to conjure meaning, and make learning joyful and just for the communities we serve. This work doesn't have to be done alone, nor should it be! Together, we uplift teacher agency to make this work doable. This book honors both the urgency and fullness of teaching through justice in an applied sense by activating instructional practice through the lens of justice and joy. *This book is also more than doing; it is a treatment plan for unjust practices.*

This book acknowledges:

- The importance of reflective practice.

- Historically and culturally responsive teaching.

- Theoretical foundations of teaching and learning.

- Examination of the self in connection to community to cultivate real and sustainable transformative teaching practices that center humanity, particularly for the learners we teach.

As I write, I am surrounded by (I just counted) 18 books, all of which I am reading, none of which I have *read*. What I mean by that is that rarely do educators who work daily in classrooms sit down and read books about teaching from front to back—or, honestly, even chapter by chapter. It *can* be a wonderful experience when a book's author unpacks ideas for the reader's consumption, especially if a nagging question gets answered, or an inspired solution to a tricky situation presents itself, providing fodder for trying something new. But a book of *only* that could also feel like a 75-minute lecture that's a struggle to get through.

So I offer what I'm calling *work alongs*: spots to provide an impetus, a little motor for cultivating *your* thinking, capturing *your* experiences, developing *your* agency—perhaps now, perhaps later, or not. So, in between my ideas and experiences, and the research-backed practices and frameworks, throughout there will also be many opportunities for you to reflect, generate, and document the pieces of you that make your teaching unique. There isn't necessarily an expectation to *finish* this book; one's personal development of teaching can never *really* be complete. In fact, that's what makes this work-along experience so beautiful: it's an authentic representation of how personal growth works. It's cyclical, iterative, and—usually—done in small bites.

Read a little bit, reflect and write, try out some new things with your peers and/or partners, and *definitely* experiment some instructional strategies with the kids in your classroom. Interacting with this book is meant to catalyze our ferocity and activate our best selves in the learning spaces we occupy.

By reviewing the experience of school and the relationships we have to it, I hope that you as readers will learn to train your eyes to see everyday injustices. With that more clear-eyed vision we will also take frequent, deep dives to learn more about the historical, institutional underpinnings of unjust practices in schools. Most importantly, you'll be able to cultivate your own pedagogy of justice by bridging history, personal reflection, and instructional practice.

Together, we cultivate our fierceness in the classroom. We root ourselves in justice, and we experience joy along the way.

How This Book Is Different

There are many powerful books out there about equity literacy and social justice and ABAR (Anti-Bias, Anti-Racist) teaching. While there is a place for many of those books in our pursuit toward justice, this one is a little different.

This book works to recognize a teacher's reality; the ideas and experiences documented here have been created and told by witnessing teachers who, on a daily basis, are working within a school ecosystem. Within this text, we grapple with multiple truths. Particularly, these two:

> **Truth 1:** Now, more than ever, teachers have limited bandwidth to engage with the idea of re-existing in the world—soaking their pedagogy in justice while working in schools that have been, by design,

oppressive, insular, and exclusive for both the teaching profession and the student body.

Truth 2: Now, more than ever, changing the school experience for kids who are learning within that institution requires labor, instincts, and collaborative, creative, critical thinking from those who are most proximate to their experience. This means those same teachers who are working in oppressive systems—who are working incredibly hard, who are probably the *most* tired—must reengage or continue on as change agents for sustainable, child-centered shifts rooted in justice to take hold.

The acknowledgement of these truths requires us to grow in both intentional and strategic ways. In this text, I'll introduce frameworks that allow us to recognize both personal and systemic multitudes, while cultivating a sense of joy and justice in our work as educators.

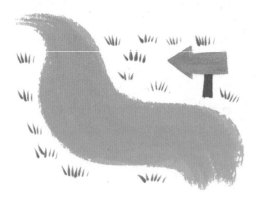

Reading path.

How to Traverse This Book

The landscape of this book is designed to support your individual needs as well as the collective needs of your community. I encourage you to journey through the text as you see fit. Alluding to those aforementioned teacher truths, we all know that time is precious. That said, it isn't necessary to read this book from start to finish.

However, I will say there are some ideas that start in Chapter 1 that grow throughout the text, tethering some of the concepts woven throughout the book. Specifically, Chapters 1 and 2 set the tone for activating social justice education in a way that underscores shared understanding around important terminology like "justice," "joy," and "pedagogy." The Structured

Generator of Hope is foundational to this text, shaping several ideas and activities throughout. As you read, it can serve as a point of reference for envisioning how the pieces of social justice work together.

If you're planning a workshop for your school community, consider using some of the work alongs provided to grapple with justice and how it operates in your community.

At the end of Chapter 1 you'll find the beginning of a recurring section called Historical Underpinnings, which explores the roots of the U.S. public school system to both help readers unpack the legacy of injustice in schools and also expose brighter moments of education that have been built outside dominant culture. (That journey continues online at https://www.kassandcorn.com/teachingfiercely/.)

Chapter 2 situates perspective as a key component for treating social injustice, and helps to surface and identify rampant injustices in schools through a series of anecdotes and activities. These are places in the text that will land differently depending on readers' identity markers. For example, there is an aside that discusses anti-Black racism. If this is a term you've never thought about before, consider discussing it with others who *also* haven't thought about it before. I say this because it can take some time to fully comprehend how this racism operates—so we can show additional respect to the Black folx who experience anti-Black racism by striving to understand it *before* discussing the concept with them to learn what their experience has been.

If you are reading as an individual, note spaces that may require more energy for you to unpack. For example, if you are someone who experienced high levels of trauma within your schooling, the reflective components woven throughout the text may be something you choose to do when you have time and space to process on your own before you reflect and share with others.

If you are reading with a partner or group at school, take notice of the various identity markers and experiences of the participants. In addition to considering your own challenges, anticipate what others may find challenging. Consider the different kinds of experiences people have had in their teaching lives; some folx might be brand-new teachers, while others may have taught for over a decade. Some material in Chapter 4—like Understanding by Design, Universal Design for Learning, and Culturally Relevant and Sustaining Pedagogies—might be very new for some teachers regardless of how many years they've been teaching, while those concepts might be a complete review for others.

Teacher agency is also another really big idea present throughout the text, but especially in Chapters 4 and 5. Chapter 4 denotes the curriculum-making journey underscored in teacher agency, while Chapter 5 demonstrates the meaningfulness of centering students in curriculum making. There is a special emphasis on joyful learning in Chapter 6, and a teacher I partnered with features her work. Real-life artifacts are shown. Note the curricular examples are from a kindergarten classroom, but the foundational ideas could be applied to upper grades.

If you are reading sections in Chapter 3, you'll be introduced to the Collaborate-Build-Nurture-Reflect Framework that highlights the potentiality for embedding care and community within the structure of school. Later on, in Chapters 7 and 8, you'll read about "negotiating the curriculum." Both ideas are quite different than what exists in many current educational paradigms. Some people might be immediately on board; for others, it will take some time to process and shift. To that end, be mindful of people's zone of proximal development if you are reading in community.

Also, consider priorities that feel engaging and exciting to focus on. Maybe you are excited to start building curriculum right away—head on over to Chapter 4! Want to embark upon a more personal, reflective journey—spend some time digging into Chapters 1 through 3, paired with dedicated writing time. Are you planning a workshop for your grade team? Chapter 5 lends itself to deep conversations on teacher agency, and Chapter 8 includes possibilities for justice-oriented learning designs. Is it a whole school workshop? Unpack justice with everyone in Chapter 1. Maybe you're planning out a few conversations with families; if so, begin with Chapter 6 or 7 to center kids. In any case, there's a little something for everyone.

Social Justice Work Illuminated: The Work Is Multifaceted

Social justice work in schools, generally speaking, has ignored the multifacetedness of listening to and honoring the communities educators serve, and has a tendency to skirt the surface of literacy practices that are nuanced enough to reach myriad learners. It is usually pawned off as a curriculum in and of itself, as opposed to a stance, or a way of being. Anti-Bias, Anti-Racist (ABAR) work, which is in fact an *infusion of the soul*, is often treated as "sit and get" professional development by school districts.

Equity Professional Development (PD), federally funded, has caused a race to the RFPs[9] and complete 360s from testing corporations and curricular juggernauts that have formerly only ever produced literacy assessments or word study PD. After both attending and teaching at research universities, I understand the headiness, the esoteric visions of *just* schools that academia professes to be true, but rarely lives within their own teaching experience.

For many, many people working toward justice in schools, the urgency is there, the fidelity is not.

So, what does that mean for us?

It means we have a lot of work to do. Important note: the *work* is not a special march or singular protest—it is the seconds we live and the air we breathe with the students we teach that creates pathways to joyful, just, and humane schools.

Like many of you, for my whole career, with numerous communities, I've worked to build, restore, and *teach* the kind of justices I'm talking about in this book. Just about every single school day, I meet with teachers, students, principals, superintendents, and/or caregivers and participate in the sojourn for more just schools. I live it, I breathe it. It is me. It is my life.

This book is an attempt to surface all the unjust practices in schools that I witness on a daily basis and that others communicate to me regularly. Moreover, it is written to help more people develop their lenses in which they, too, are able to see, name, and undo injustice by working toward—and, ultimately, activating—justice.

I do not have all the answers. I am only but one person, with a specific set of identity markers and unique personhood. But I have community, I have partners, and I have a very deep conviction that we can figure this out if we do it together.

So, let's highlight potential antidotes, and give *all* the people access to tools, resources, and community for a different kind of pedagogy; to help more folx see that justice work is not only an everyday practice, it is a *joyful* pursuit. This, readers, is what it means to teach *fiercely*.

---

9   Request for Proposals (RFPs) are solicitations from school districts and other groups that seek specific work; for example, Diversity, Equity, and Inclusion (DEI) workshops, workshops to develop adolescent literacy, etc.

Acknowledgments

Thank you . . .

to the foremothers, the matriarchs, the women in my family and outside of it, who have led their lives through an ethic of care before concepts like "ethics of care" were said out loud in educational and/or academic spaces.

to those who were with me from the very beginning: Mom, Dad, Kyle, and Shaun, you were the first to nourish my inquisitive spirit, and helped me shape it into one that remains joyful and curious. Mom and Dad, thank you for having me last; the independence you've gifted me from "being the youngest" initiated an effervescent pursuit toward justice that has never left me.

to the other side of my beating heart: Cornelius. The one who always holds my hand, keeps me centered, and stands beside me as I journey the longer distances from my head back to my heart.

to Soleil, your spirited inquiry and present love has been one of my best teachers.

to Indira, your strength and search toward goodness sustains my belief in better futures.

to Hawa, Cornelius I, Zoe, and Tino: the communal love you have shown me helps me negotiate this world through a clarified sense of family, and I continue to be in awe of your gifts.

to my 6th Street Family: Melissa, Robin, Simone, Jeff, Annie, Michael, and Laura, your presence in my life helped me build upon the idea that joy can be found even in the smallest moments.

to those communities and individuals who permeate/d my life in schools, vacillating on both sides of the personal and professional: The Neighborhood Schools Program, where I was first exposed to the impact of policy-making and instructional stance on classroom life; The Brooklyn School for Global Studies, where I began my teacherhood and learned to activate love in schools; PS 503, where my teacher agency fully blossomed because of community values placed on educator intellect; the Teachers College Inclusive Classrooms Project, one of the most powerful intellectual homes for me, where I learned to explore the nuances of relationship in schools and inclusivity and the impact of inquiry as stance (Celia, Britt, Kara, Erika, and Anne—I'll always be your fangirl). To all those schools and people I've partnered with through The Minor Collective—thank you for continuing to invite me into your spaces in the quest to find and build future goodness. To Breaths Together for a Change, I'm still developing words to describe the felt knowledge this community of people facilitated!

to Phil Bildner, Arlène Casimir, Sara K. Ahmed, LeUyen Pham, Amy Fandrei, and Kirsten Janene-Nelson, all of whom meaningfully connected with me throughout the development of this book.

to Brooklyn, the city I call home, to NYC educators, for providing the foundational community I've always sought.

to teachers everywhere. I am in awe of you. I see you, I appreciate you, and most of all, I believe in you.

Prologue:
Anthem for a Teacher

We often ask what makes a good teacher. We study those who are deemed effective, and do our best to replicate what we see and memorialize it so we can do it again on Day 3 Lesson 5 Syllabus X.

Most educators explain a defining moment in their careers that helped them crossover the imaginary but perfunctory line of "I don't know what the heck I'm doing/The kids are eating me alive" to . . . "I got this." It can be sudden, powerful, decisive.

I argue that a teacher's defining moment is the one where they not only find themselves in their classrooms, see themselves in their classrooms—but *they* are in their classrooms. The entirety of the imperfect, bodacious, let-me-learn-it-and-I-will-teach-it whole self finally, finally is *present*, and it works. Your kids are finally listening and learning from you, and you can feel it.

Because you're not hiding those bits of your authentic self that are stolen away from the regime of Extreme Standardized Testing, the paper version of *American Ninja Warrior*. Your whole self has surfaced, it has reemerged, and it's here to stay. It happened because maybe you're older, maybe you've fallen more in love with your students, maybe you've just said "F%*$ it!" to yourself, or even out loud, and you just want your students to learn and walk away from school equipped with a moral complexity that will allow them to deal with the world.

There is no metric for this feeling, and once you feel the ferocity of *I got this* you're no longer waiting for anyone's permission on how to be or what to teach in your classroom.

To teach fiercely is to be in community with your students and yourself; it's stepping outside yourself and looking into your soul. And not just your teaching soul, but your *soul* soul, because those two things aren't separate.

Chapter 1:
Building the Foundation:
A Structured Generator
of Hope for More Joyful
and Just Schools

A Structured Generator of Hope

We begin with building a structure that allows us to create more joyful
and just communities that we belong to, that we are in partnership with—
whether they be young people or adults. This is our *radical hope* work. *How
can hope be radical?* Let me explain what I mean.

Recently, I was invited to participate in a year-long excavation and reflection for white people to develop racial reckoning with their ancestral past and present, specifically the harm in which their ancestors spread amongst Black, Indigenous, and other persons of color; and also, to create open awareness for moving forward in the field of social justice and decolonizing practices in many different realms, not just education. The group was rooted in Indigenous knowledge and was created by an organization called Breaths Together for Change, codeveloped by author, documentary filmmaker, and traditional beadworker Cinnamon Kills First; founder of Good Medicine Woman LLC and integrative researcher Aminah Ghaffar; and diversity dean, meditation teacher, and Healing the Future by Design mentor Tommy Woon.

During one of our first meetings, I was in the "fire" group. (Each group was named after one of the traditional elements in Native healing.) We were asked to share with our small group members why we chose to participate in the project, which was described to us as an experience that would require a great amount of internal excavation and awareness, reflecting on darker parts of history, even parsing out our personal implications in those histories alongside building a deepening practice in somatic literacy (more on that soon).

One of my new peers, a wise, white woman 10 to 15 years my senior named Patricia, volunteered to go first. She worked as an editor and had grown up on two Native American Reservations, and had a profound way with words. She spoke, and the stories she told filled our ears with grace. I don't remember exactly what she said during that first fire circle, but it was something like this:

> I joined this group because I needed something different.
> I need something that will help me remain hopeful when everything feels dark or impossible. Something like a structured generator of hope, so to speak.

As I listened to Patricia, her words struck a chord. While remaining hopeful in times of darkness is not really a sensational concept, the idea of creating some type of structure like a generator with a bit of an engine behind it, built communally, packed with rituals, nourishment, and dreams that can be made real, to keep us going in our pursuit toward justice—a "structured generator of hope"—is *absolutely* sensational. And with communal development, it's also conceivably possible.

So, as we build these structures to generate hope within our school communities, we are building a specific type of hope, and that is *radical hope*—one of my favorite ways to work forward, in a protected space of reflection and creativity. It's also one of my favorite phrases[1] to describe the work that I build with people.

Jonathan Lear, a philosopher whose work focuses on the ethics of how humans interact with one another and themselves, describes the term "radical hope" as follows:

> The thing about radical hope is that it is directed towards a future goodness that transcends the current ability to understand what is . . . Radical Hope is our best weapon against despair, even when despair seems justifiable. It makes the survival of the end of your world as you know it possible (Lear 2008, p. 103).

It is no surprise to me that Lear arrives at the idea of radical hope after extensive research on Native American life, and a thorough analysis of the Native American Crow warrior Plenty Coups. Even after Plenty Coups's community experiences hundreds of years of cultural devastation, Plenty Coups' people continue to exist. Their life carries on, even though conceptually and experientially they do not have schema for finding a way forward, *but they do so anyway!* The Crow, along with many other Native American tribes, historically and *presently,* work through this space, the space of radical hope.

There is a lot to learn from Native American lifeways, and this is one of the many notes of Indigenous wisdom for us to consider as we work toward building something better, even when, perhaps *especially* when, we're having a really hard time imagining what "better" looks like.

Perhaps Lear's take on radical hope feels a little intense, but nonetheless, it is a powerful way to describe the pursuit toward building justice, joy, and teacher agency within schools. Essentially, we *do* want to end the way schools operate as we know it! It *is* hard to leave a culture of teaching and learning that we've been living our whole lives, even if the culture of schooling is unhealthy, even when we've been directly or indirectly harmed because of it.

The part of radical hope that is essential for us to focus on is what the "future goodness" of our practice in teaching and learning within our communities can look like. In this future goodness, we move past the ways in which dominant culture expects us to operate and/or perform in school. Instead, we soak ourselves in alternatives, adopting humane, holistic, and kid-centric (student-centered) practices to incorporate within our pedagogy.

The treatment plan toward justice includes routines and rituals that allow us to both reflect and reimagine school and practice, instructionally and creatively. These routines and rituals we build are parsed throughout the daily teaching and learning the world of school is immersed within. Through these acts, we work to build a *structured generator of hope*—something to help us remain hopeful when everything feels dark or impossible.

During the time we spend together, reader, it is *my* radical hope that your teacher spirit will be rekindled to experience the joy required to do build justice in school communities.

Generators don't actually *produce* energy. Rather, they are used to translate energy from one form into another to create power that is useful for keeping rooms lit, freezers cold, and homes warm, especially when the traditional power grid is unreliable and inconsistent for providing power for basic human needs (for more see generatorsource.com).

The cool thing about generators is that they are a flexible and affordable option for many people around the world who do not have access to traditional means of electricity, like the electric outlets that many people from advantaged places do. Sometimes, when people do have access to electric outlets, the power grid from which the electricity comes doesn't work properly and consistently goes out.

Many people who live within those contexts who have enough resources use generators as backup to ensure they are able to meet they and their family's needs. In essence, they've created an alternate operating system for themselves that is more reliable than the systems that have been provided for them that enable them to lead healthier lives.

We seek to do the same, but within the context of school. I've created an image to help visualize what this transformation looks like.

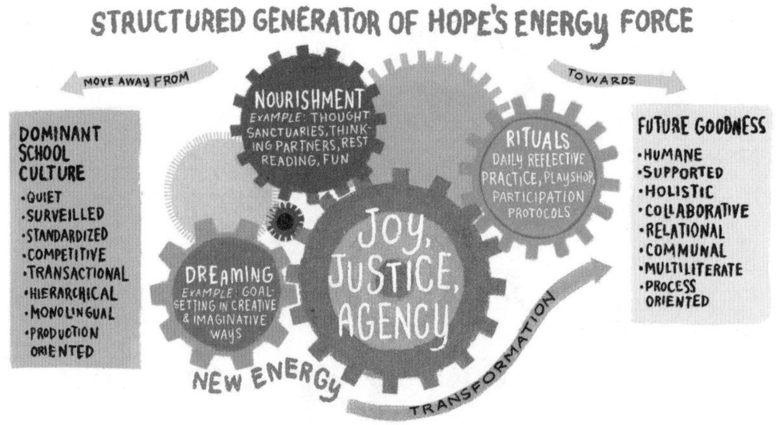

FIGURE 1.1 Structured generator of hope.

Figure 1.1 is a visual representation of the structured generator of hope, unpacked. The "Dominant School Culture" box lists systemic constraints that have been shaped throughout the history of public schooling, which we will periodically dive into as we work toward justice in schools. Part of our work is to recognize and understand how those components of school operate unjustly within our own contexts, especially for our students, and then to develop the ability to move away from those practices. We'll practice developing our vision—not just for dreaming, creating goals, and moving forward, but also to ensure our daily vision provides us with the clarity to see, name, and change parts of the daily practice of school that are harmful for youth and grown-ups alike.

The Pedagogy of Justice

Earlier we talked about how expansive the term "pedagogy" is, *especially* when we tack a word like "justice" on to it! For any group to experience a sense of positive community and connectedness, it's important to create shared understanding around the terms and ideas that matter most. The goal is to build each individual's pedagogy of justice. With that, I am working to ensure each reader, and all the people they learn from and with, have an opportunity to experience joy as they journey toward that goal.

Let's start with exploring the term "pedagogy." What feelings or memories do you associate with that term? Does it make you think of graduate school?

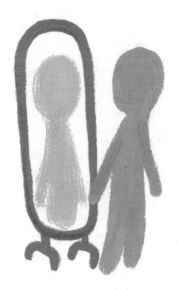

Reflection.

> Take a moment to note your initial sensations when you hear the term "pedagogy."
>
>
> Then, sketch out your ideas about the term "pedagogy" in response to the questions above.

Paulo Freire?[1] I wonder, does it overwhelm you, or incite a sense of trepidation or feeling blocked? Or do you experience more positive feelings?

I ask these questions because, in so many teaching spaces, teachers are told what to think, how to act, what to say, when to move, how far to go. Instructional methodologies and curriculum often circulate most frequently when people offer teacher support. While curriculum and instruction are powerful

---

1   Paulo Freire, the renowned Brazilian educator, literacy activist, and forefather of critical pedagogy, wrote *Pedagogy of the Oppressed*. Over 1 million copies have been sold since it debuted in 1970, and it is the third most cited book in the social sciences of all time.

FIGURE 1.2 Pedagogy unpacked.

components of our teaching lives, our *pedagogy,* holistically, is what we'll be talking about moving forward.

Figure 1.2, readers, is pedagogy unpacked.

Since it's important we create a shared understanding of the terms we unpack, I certainly don't want to limit your ideation of pedagogy. I invite you to join the Work Along to follow.

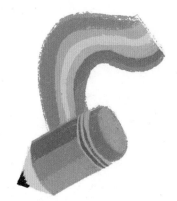

Work along.

> **Reflection: Unpacking the Term "Pedagogy"**
>
> What might you add to our word web? What examples might you include to describe your own pedagogy? Do any of the components feel strange to you? Would you have omitted any?

What Is Justice?

All right, so now that we have a growing understanding of *pedagogy,* we'll grapple with the larger question at play—the one I've been with my whole career and, now that I think about it, my whole life: *What is justice?*

I'm sure many of you have been asking the same thing. Or perhaps, felt like you had arrived at an understanding and have already begun to implement social justice in terms of what you, your school community, or a curriculum have named *just.*

Real talk: finding justice is far from a destination; it's a journey. Who we are, where we've been, where we live, and what we're told determines how we develop our understandings about what justice means—and, moreover, how it lives within a school community.

The work of changing paradigms requires our whole selves including building our imaginative capacities, our abilities to be fully present in school spaces, and also reifying our stance and purpose with the highly politicized components of justice, joy, and teacher agency. This paradigm shift is underscored with developed agency in our own literacies as well, including literacies oriented in justice such as racial literacy, social literacy, media literacy, and somatic literacy. Broadly speaking, these various literacies are encompassed through the term "multiliteracies."

The International Literacy Association defines *multiliteracies* as "an instructional framework that supports an awareness of how new communications media are shaping the way we use language in a highly diverse and globally connected world." The concept of multiliteracies includes four parts: "(1) learning that takes place in the same context in which it is to be applied; (2) interactive teaching and learning that involves both instructors and students; (3) questioning what counts as 'truth' for whom under what conditions, and with what consequences; and (4) transformed practice, which equates to applying what was learned in the three previous components" (ILA, n.d.).

Social literacy is the way in which humans interpret interactions between one another. For example, oftentimes people refer to the ability to "read the room." This figure of speech is used to describe one's social literacy—that is, their ability to determine when to say what, with whom to speak, and what the general affect of the communal space might be. For example, many teachers and students rely on one another's social literacy to engage in classroom dialogue in ways that feel affirming and supportive as opposed to out of context or alienating.

Media literacy is "the ability to (*) Decode media messages (including the systems in which they exist); (*) Assess the influence of those messages on thoughts, feelings, and behaviors; and (*) Create media thoughtfully and conscientiously." For example, educators and students work together to interrogate means of communication, especially mass communication, such as books, newspapers, magazines, radio, television, motion pictures, internet, audio/video recordings, and recordings (Media Literacy Now n.d.).

Racial literacy is "the knowledge, skills, and awareness that are needed to talk thoughtfully about race and racism. This includes having a rich vocabulary, including terms such as race, racism, prejudice, ally, upstander, and so on. Racial literacy is also the ability to identify racism when it happens, having strategies to counter or cope with racism, and understanding the role racism plays in society" (Sesame Street in Communities, n.d.). For example, if a teacher notices a child patting down their' peer's Afro, racial literacy is important for the teacher to know that that act carries racist, historical weight, and must be called out in the moment, not to shame the child patting the other child's Afro, but rather, to prevent further harm, and support the development of racial literacy within children, especially those from a dominant culture.

To develop more agency in these justice-oriented literacies, let's work on a few exercises that begin with reading visuals and build upon our schema of what we already know. If possible, I recommend completing these activities in groups of two or more, since multiple perspectives contribute to complex meaning-making.

Work Along: What Do We Mean When We Say "Justice"?

Note: This work along was originally designed for adult educators. To adapt it for youth, see the next classroom activity.

ONE: With a partner, or in small groups, analyze the figure. To more carefully view the photo, refer to "Visual Grid" instructional strategy in the following classroom activity. Write down a list of everything you see in this figure. Just what you see. *No interpretations yet, please! For now, this is a low-inference activity.*

TWO: Now, interpret the intention behind the inclusion of each element you included on your list. For example, you might discuss with your partner/s:

- Why is she holding a balance—what does that represent?

(You may wish to discuss other elements instead, such as the book, serpent, blindfold, etc.)

THREE: Now, before you discuss step four, think on your own for a few minutes:

- How are the symbols and your understanding of their relation to justice connected to the *world* that surrounds us?

FOUR: Now, with your partners:

- Discuss a similar point: How are the symbols and your understanding of their relation to justice connected to *schools in general*?

- Or, if you really want to dig deep: How are they connected to *your* school community?

Lady of Justice. (Deval Kulshreshtha via Wikimedia Commons) This is one of the most universally recognized symbolizations of justice. This is a statue called the Lady of Justice. She is a rendering of Justitia, the Roman goddess of Justice.

Lady Justitia: Perspective Shapes Our Ways of Knowing

Spoiler Alert! This page will offer interpretations of Lady Justitia's symbols. If you're not done parsing out your thoughts about the symbolism within this rendering of Lady Justitia, do not read on!

IMPARTIALITY

TOGA: garment that shows a philosophical attitude that embodies justice

Weighing of evidence; lack a foundation to show that evidence should stand on its own

Good and evil, poison and medicine, death and rebirth

Authority; Justice can be swift and final

Lady of Justice symbols.

Take a few more minutes with your group, or individually, to be sure you have thoughtfully expressed your ideas behind these symbols. I urge this because activating justice calls for developing agency—and clarifying your own thinking *first* will leave on you a deeper imprint and more expansive understanding of justice than if you simply read my version.

While Lady Justitia is a common frame of reference for justice around the world, she is, predominantly, a Western reference, the dominant culture's view of justice. *What is just* and *what is right* is a powerful beam in life that we all work to balance from. *And* . . . it's also important for us to consider the multiple iterations of justice that permeate our communities. Consider this: Lady Justitia was preceded by powerful representations of justice from other cultures.

Classroom Activity: Use Visual Grids to Support Learners

In the classroom, use this visual grid shown in Figure 1.3 to support learners with discovering details, nuances, and multiple layers of perspective within a visual text. For this activity, a visual text is defined as a photo, drawing, artwork, or other visual where a story, message, or experience is shared with little to no alphabetic print. Photographs, cartoons, advertisements, Instagram posts, and/or paintings are all considered visual texts.

FIGURE 1.3 Visual grid example. (K. Minor 2022)

The visual grid is essentially a paper tool (although it could be adapted into digital form) divided into quadrants, with one quadrant omitted. The remaining three quadrants cover up the rest of this visual, while learners focus on the portion of the visual text that is uncovered. By focusing on one portion of the visual text at a time, learners can focus more attentively because their cognitive load is decreased.

When using the visual grid, support your learners with guiding questions, and model the use of the resource before they engage in pairs or independently. With time, the visual grid can be a go-to literacy strategy for your learners, and less demonstration will be required.

Questions that pair the visual grid with the examination of a visual text:

- What do you notice?

  - Label the nouns, or persons, places, and things you see in the picture.

  - What colors, shapes, or shades do you see?

- Describe what you think is happening.

  - What verbs would you use to describe what you see?

  - What does this make you wonder? Question?

- What connections or disconnections can you make between yourself and/or your community to this text?

You may wish to invite students to share after each domain, for a collective representation of thinking.

Alternately, you may wish for the students to move at their own pace, using the visual grid as a tool to increase attentiveness and decrease cognitive load at each interval. For example, after five minutes, you can invite your community of learners to move on to the next domain.

If you are using visual texts like photos that you want to reuse, consider putting the text in a plastic sleeve, and giving students dry erase markers to write their noticings directly on the domain they've been assigned.

You can also instruct students to cut the text into four sections, label them sections 1 through 4, and glue them on a larger paper.

TABLE 1.1 Lady Justice's symbols.

Symbol	Interpretation: What does this symbolize through the lens of justice?
Blindfold	The blindfold is meant to symbolize impartiality. You might recall the saying "Justice is Blind." Essentially, this means justice should be applied universally, to all humans, no matter their identity markers, positionality, or relationship to institutions.
Toga	A classic saying comes from Ancient Rome: *Cedant arma togae,* which translates to "let arms yield to the toga: let military power give way to civil power" (Merriam-Webster n.d.). In short, one interpretation of Lady Justice's toga is that the toga is an homage to Ancient Roman Culture, that wearing a toga represented the power of "civilized" society. Think about how people nowadays might put on joggers and a hoodie on their way to the gym . . . these clothes show they are probably going for a workout, or some kind of athletic activity. If you were in Ancient Rome, wearing the toga showed you were a civilized member of society, perhaps even ready for philosophical discussions.
Sword	The sword is meant to convey the ideal of justice as sort of a be-all-end-all in forming decisions about the law. Justice was thought to reign supreme in all that happened in a court.
Scales	The scales show that evidence should be weighed with equal consideration, with balance, to determine whether or not someone is guilty or innocent.
Snake	Serpents throughout time have shown up in multiple texts as an important motif. While in some Asian and Indigenous cultures serpents symbolize transformation and rebirth, this particular snake sitting atop the book at Lady Justice's feet symbolizes the danger of deceit and lies finding their way into the narrative of what's right or just.
Book	The book represents the written law: the words and sentences that guide justice.

TABLE 1.2 Iterations of Justice: imagery and explanations.

Explanations	Imagery

Maat: The first recorded personification of Justice hails from Africa. As early as 2680 BCE, records show that Egyptians looked to the Goddess Maat for guidance toward justice. She represented the moral spirit of the law, underscoring the important elements like truth and harmony through fair social interactions as representations of justice. Rather than books, togas, snakes, scales, and swords, different objects were used to show this ideal.

The *ankh* serves as a symbol of truth.

The scepter serves as a symbol of authority. There was also a feather—this you may have heard of. Maat's *feather of truth* was used as a metric alongside a person's heart upon their passing to determine their fate in the afterlife (Mark 2022). If the heart was heavier than the feather, their afterlife was condemned to a nonexistence. Conversely, if the feather was lighter than the heart, they were gifted with a virtuous afterlife.

What's more is that Maat had a multilayered presence amongst Egyptians—she was more than a representation of justice. In addition to showing up in regards to justice, truth, and morality, she was also credited with guidance for wisdom, cosmic presence, harmony, seasons, and order.

Maat.

Themis was a Titan, a goddess of Ancient Greece representing *divine* order and justice. Married to Zeus, she was often referred to as the "lady of good counsel." The rendering on the right occurs long after the depiction of Maat, and was developed in 300 BCE.

Like Justitia, Themis also carries a sword; however, in the context of Ancient Greece, the sword is more representative of Themis' final say, as opposed to what may have been most fair or equitable. Like Maat and Justitia, Themis is often seen with scales representing balance as well.

Also . . . take note! The rendition of Justice through the lens of Themis share the stance of Ancient Egyptian wisdom-women, who were often positioned in both cultures as wise thought leaders!

Themis.

Explanations	Imagery

And Justice for All Album Art, Metallica:

Ancient renditions of justice are held powerfully all over the world, and are uplifted through modern day art and culture. I invite you to search Google Images for "Metallica Justice For All." There, you'll see album art by Metallica, a heavy metal band most popular during the 1990s and early 2000s. The album cover reveals a wobbly Lady Justitia, toppling over, scales spilling, being pulled apart through tense bondage. Like any other rendition of justice through art—through religion, law, or personal creeds—what this cover reveals in context to current happenings in our society is up to your interpretation. What *does* this art mean for *you*?

Google
"Justice for All album art by Metallica"

These renditions of justice personified have been used as a strong lens to determine what's right and what's wrong, or who is guilty and who is not throughout time. To this day, all around the world, these statues still hold symbolic weight when decisions are made for social justice within various institutions. However, as we look across the various renditions of justice and meaningful symbols, it's clear justice means something different depending on who is naming it and where it comes from.

Scales (Figure 1.4) are all part of Themis', Justitia's, and Maat's stories . . . but did those scales, when balancing evidence and truth, operate in the same ways given the difference in culture, perspective, and time period? Themis represented justice through a social order that was ruled by Titans; Justitia

FIGURE 1.4 Scales of justice.

represented justice through various Roman emperor's say-so; and the Goddess Maat represented justice in multitudes . . . most notably within a tomb in Ancient Egypt where a woman's presence was held in the highest regard. The environment, attitudes, and beliefs of the people would have all contributed to the shape justice took, even if the scales, empirically, read the same.

The same is true for us, as we work to define and name what justice looks like in the spaces we teach, where learners look to us for guidance to figure out what tools they need to determine what is right, what is just, what may be wrong. As we are naming and surfacing and creating vision for what social justice looks like in our schools, it's important for us to consider the multiple ways people show up to the idea of justice.

Sonya Douglass Horsford considers how this difference in perspective and experience manifests in schools. In her *Education Week* article "Whose Vision Will Guide Racial Equity in Schools," she cites educational theorist Beverly Gordon:

> Whose vision of the role of African Americans, other people of color, and the disenfranchised will prevail? For what purposes might people of color be educated? How might education assist people of color in challenging the societal structures that maintain and reproduce inequality? (Gordon 1990)

I share Douglass Horsford's review on Gordon's work from 1990, because more than 30 years later, they are still relevant. When justice and equity are defined and envisioned within school communities, oftentimes white people are at the helm. Nearly 80% of educators within the United States are white (Taie and Goldring 2020, p. 7). Compared with the United States' general student population, which is 46% white, 15% Black, 28% Latinx, 6% Asian, and less than 1% Indigenous, we have a decision-making body that doesn't mirror its constituents. That means tradition, culture, and customs shared amongst white people and other folx who subscribe to whiteness are disproportionately represented when it comes to painting a school's worldview on justice.

That disproportionate worldview is referred to as *dominant culture*. According to researchers Rodriguez and Swalwell (2021), *dominant culture* in the United States is the centering of heterosexuality, cisgender identities, maleness, Christianity, whiteness, able-bodiedness, middle- and upper-class positions, documented status, English language, the Global North, settlement, and colonialism.

Earlier, I talked about the *structured generator of hope*, and how it is integral for us to move away from dominant culture to achieve any sort of justice, or future goodness, within schools. One of the first acts in this movement is to be able to name how this dominance manifests (1) within ourselves, (2) within our classrooms, and (3) within the schools we work.

Certainly, those groups of white people who are in decision-making bodies may not hold every single identity marker that falls within the realm of dominant culture. Additionally, there are persons within communities of Black, Indigenous, and other Persons of Color (BIPOC) who identify with many parts of dominant culture. In conversations about diversity, equity, inclusion, and social justice, oftentimes there is a perfunctory line drawn between these two groups . . . white people and BIPOC folx. But we must introduce nuance into this conversation: although there has been a definitive binary between these two groups, there are considerable differences within groups of people who share BIPOC as an identity marker. The same is true for white people.

I won't speak from perspectives that I cannot fully understand: I can only speak from my white, woman, cisgender, heterosexual, Christian, mother, daughter, wife, working-class Midwestern upbringing, artist, designer, educator, researcher, creative, New Yorker identities. But what I can do is name events and happenings I've witnessed and directly experienced in schools that have helped me identify nuance in the conversation of justice iterations amongst different groups in the realm of school. Here are a few examples that I've witnessed within the past few years that complicate applied justice pending on culture, place, time, and identity markers.

Classroom Activity: Design a Read Aloud to Explore Justice

As you parse through various iterations of justice with your peers, consider designing a parallel lesson for the student you teach. Preet Bharara's picture book *Justice Is . . .* is an excellent text to provide context for building perspective on justice, and how it lives in your school community.

Justice for Whom? (In the Realm of School Integration)

While this is a story of New York City, it's also a fractal that reflects similar patterns and happenings in schools all across the United States—and, to some extent, across the globe—where schools are attended by students from different races, ethnicities, and social classes.

In 2018, New York City's Mayor Bill de Blasio appointed Richard Carranza as chancellor of the New York City Department of Education, where he governed the city's 1,800 public schools. Carranza, the city's first Mexican American chancellor, led through a campaign called Equity and Excellence, where former anti-bullying programs like Respect for All were taken more seriously through the lens of racial justice, and professional learning around implicit bias and culturally responsive teaching were normed around the city's public schools.

Disparate outcomes amongst racial groups were examined, and clear plans of action were pursued. The flavor of teaching, learning, and school culture was on the precipice of change. People were both uncomfortable and comfortable at the same time, but the intentional shift toward equity was omnipresent.

One of Carranza and De Blasio's most notable initiatives, school integration, was popular at first, and was met with surface-level-yet-widespread support from people representing varying racial and ethnic groups. However, when it came time to activate school integration, especially amongst the city's top-five specialized high schools, support splintered amongst various racial groups, especially amongst Asian families of Chinese descent (Xiaoqing 2021).

To qualify for one of New York City's most coveted public high schools, referred to as "specialized high schools," the admissions process requires students to take competitive entrance exams to be considered for enrollment. In 2019, Asian students represented 62% of the seats available in these specialized high schools. The racial imbalance of the schools was stark: 70% of New York City's student population overall was Black and/or Hispanic, while 11% of students in the top-five specialized high schools were Black and/or Hispanic (New York City Independent Budget Office Schools Brief 2019).

To achieve a more equitable playing field, city policy makers moved to reserve more seats for Black and Hispanic students, while decreasing the number of seats available for Asian students. Many folx lauded the policy move; it was seen as an equitable move toward racial justice that took shape in the form of creating more opportunities for Black and Hispanic students to attend (what are viewed by some as) the best public high schools in New York City. However, many Asian families, primarily of Chinese descent, were not pleased (New York City Independent Budget Office Schools Brief 2019).

And this is what's really important to underscore within the context of nuance and perspective when we think about binaries and racial groups in the context of this big question: *What is racial justice in the context of school?*

Rong Xiaoqing (2021) reports multiple perspectives within the New York Chinese community, and not all of them align; tension within the Asian community on the matter of abolishing school entrance exams presents itself. There are some Chinese families who are advocates of meritocracy, the belief that if you work hard enough, you will succeed. In their belief system, an iteration of the American Dream is present in their way of life. For many Chinese families in New York City, specialized high schools are a way to access better education—a cultural tradition. For example, one parent activist from this community stated:

> I am not against admission reforms, but it has to be for improving students' academic performance rather than reaching a racial balance. . . . Even when I was in China, I was enchanted by Dr. Martin Luther King Jr.'s vision of a nation where people are not "judged by the color of their skin but by the content of their character." But now what they are doing is the opposite (Xiaoqing 2021).

Xiaoqing's series of interviews shows that abolishing the entrance exam and, especially, taking away seats from the East Asian community, triggers intense memories of Maoist policies that disempowered many Chinese people, and some Chinese families who advocate for testing experienced this firsthand. Others feel remnants of the Chinese Exclusion Act, legislation passed in 1882 that prohibited Chinese immigrants coming to the United States legally for the subsequent 10 years (History.com n.d.). For example, when Chinese workers' general productivity and proficiency showed up all over the West coast, white male lawmakers thought jobs would be threatened for white men, and simply made it illegal for more Chinese immigrants to come to the United States legally in response.

And then there are other East Asian families, most of whom are second or third-generation immigrants, who have a different understanding of American history, white supremacy, and the implications of post-Jim Crow South for Black and Hispanic people.

Here, an Asian policy maker who advocates for abolishing entrance exams states:

> We cannot allow the system to sometimes use Asian Americans as a model, and other times vilify us. When you say the kids who get into these schools, they test fine, they work hard, and they deserve it, it perpetuates the inequity for all sides. It erases the struggle so many families face and makes them think, "it must be my fault," when the system is set against them in a lot of ways (Xiaoqing 2021).

New York State Senator John Liu offers nuanced perspective; naming the gray matter, the lack of cultural recognition that the heavy-handedness of this policy communication failed to address:

> Equity is about fairness, and excellence requires some human measurement which, in this country, has often been discriminatory against Blacks. For many Asian immigrant families, they have no part of that perspective. The perspective they have is a cultural one where people prepare their entire life to take exams (Xiaoqing 2021).

Senator Liu touches upon a crucial point, often ignored or tabled as moot in this debate: he names the specific oppression Black people have faced and continue to experience. The human measurement he speaks of surfaces all over the school paradigm, particularly in the form of assessment, grades, tests, school admissions . . . and it stems back to an ugly history, namely the Jim Crow era. Liu understands this deep, important penetration of injustice within U.S. history, and he understands it enough to know that justice requires it to be surfaced and grappled with, especially when only 10 Black students are admitted to a specialized high school in the year of 2019.

You might be wondering where the voices of Black, Indigenous, and other persons of color are in this conversation of abolishing high school entrance exams. Just as justice is omnipresent in the work of equity development, so are the voices of BIPOC folx. Perhaps you will not find them as frequently in the spaces of dominant culture, or in highly publicized news media, but BIPOC voices are everywhere and they are not one and the same. What's more, you will only hear them if you actively listen. In this case, BIPOC voices were active directly in the advocacy of two of the city's recent chancellors: Richard Carranza, who is Mexican American, and Misha Porter, who is Black.

Additionally, BIPOC voices are indirectly present in the public omission of their commentary. I've researched and experienced this specific school-integration debate around abolishing specialized high school entrance exams, and I've found that most of the reporting is about East Asians, reported by East Asian or white people. And one might assume that creating more space in specialized high schools for Black and Hispanic students would garner agreement, or maybe even just interest, from their families. But, remember the question Sonya Douglass Horsford asked? *Whose vision will guide racial equity for schools?*

It's important to recognize that the interests of people *within* racial groups vary. The argument that people from one racial group are monolithic, that they will want, or even need the same thing, doesn't always hold in conversations about "what's best." When Mayor De Blasio's policy change was posed to the city, there was an assumption that eliminating specialized high school entrance exams would be favorable for Black and Hispanic students and their families, and treating those communities as a monolith commenced. There were many families and other stakeholders representing needs and perspectives who were not heard. Without intentional and strategic inclusion of local community members, the voices we hear reported are typically political leaders, those with university-based positions, and/or, ultimately, people with the most power.

Aside from media clips of prominent Black leaders like Al Sharpton evading the topic, few local Black and Hispanic people were included in media reports covering former Mayor De Blasio's omission of specialized high school entrance exams. When reports included the voices of Black folx, the focus was on their "rifts" as opposed to their stated wants and needs: Madina Touré reports in *Politico* an article entitled "Fight Over Specialized School Reveals Rifts Among Black Leaders" (2019). Noted in the article are a variety of perspectives from Black leaders, such as Al Sharpton, Assemblyman Charles Barron, Political Science Professor Christina Greer, Public Advocate Jumaane Williams, amongst others, all of whom named different opinions on what was best for the Black community. Nowhere in the article were the intersections or interests of the Latinx community mentioned, nor were other perspectives within the spectrum of BIPOC people such as South Asians and Indigenous folx.

As we think about Douglas Horsford's question: *Whose vision will guide equity in schools?* We are called to reorient ourselves to justice—not just what it means for us, but especially, what it means to our community, and to those who have been harmed both presently and historically. When we work to develop equity through the lens of justice, it's important to remember that with the omnipresence of equity and justice development, so, too, should come the omnipresence of the voices of the people who are supposed to benefit from said equity and justice development.

As these debates take place within and across various communities, I am both a witness and an active participant. School integration plans are pursued across New York City, the most segregated school district within the United States, and I am a direct participant in working to activate integration as I work with three of the five districts that have been awarded grants earmarked to plan for integration. In partnership with surrounding communities, I develop equity and justice with numerous players who carry various identities and experiences. I often feel like I am working within the field of alchemy with other teachers and kids and families.

And what's more, even as a white woman educator who has spent my whole career with BIPOC students, teachers, families, and school leaders, I don't get a pass; I don't magically know what I'm doing simply because I am *near*. I still have to intentionally learn new ideas, dive into uncomfortable experiences over and over and over again, read and reread and listen and listen more. And I also have to unlearn parts of my worldview that are incongruous to BIPOC folx' worldview.

The dominant culture permeates almost every part of a school's ecosystem. Kids experience both injustice and justice on a granular level, especially as it operates within the walls of classrooms, and between subtle exchanges in the hallways, the lunch line, and the school yard. Suspension rates, student surveys, and educator retention data show that this disproportionate worldview is not working out for many, many folx, most of whom have few identity markers that fall within the realm of dominant culture.

Historically and presently, this paradigm hurts the educational experience for many, many people; most potently, students, families, and teachers who are

Black, Indigenous, Latinx, Asian, queer, dis/abled, speak a first language that is not English, and/or also . . . girls.

At the National Convention for Teachers of English in 2021, former First Lady Michelle Obama reminded educators: *Teachers can make or break the soul of any child*. It's true . . . as teachers, within our sphere of influence, the power we yield on students' well-being is tremendous.

Because of the widespread presence of white decision makers in schools, it is *paramount* that all community members, from various positions and identities, are included intentionally in the creation of social justice vision in schools.

Let's work toward figuring out what this means in the context of school.

Work Along: Whose Vision Will Guide Racial Justice in Schools?

Using Douglas Horsford's ideas offered in "Whose Vision Will Guide Justice in Schools?," statistics on school demographics, and the anecdote regarding school demographics, choose a few symbols portrayed in the images of Lady Justitia, Themis, or Maat. *R*econsider your previous interpretations, and in the same working groups you were in before, talk about what implications those symbols have for justice in your school.

Everyday Implications: Interpreting Symbols of Justice in Schools

	Blindfold	Toga	Sword or ankh	Scales	Snake	Book	Feather of truth
Grading/expectations							
Discipline policies							
Curriculum							
Instruction							
Community traditions							
Family-school relationships							
Adult-student relationships							
Routines/ schedules							

Where Is Joy Located in the Pursuit Toward Justice?

Joy is nebulous and that's the most beautiful part about it. There is the type of joy that resonates from a birthday party, or choosing the flavors for a shave ice on a hot day. There is the joy of wedding celebrations and friendship banter. But if you're trying to find that kind of joy in schools, you might be searching for a really long time.

I'll admit: in recent years, joy has been more difficult to come by in school spaces. I've had to search harder. But when I do find time to pause and dust off the orifices of school spaces, I've been able to find it more consistently. And we have to find it, because without it, none of this justice work is possible.

But what is it? What is joy? If it doesn't manifest in its traditional form in schools, how are we supposed to find it? One time I made a "recipe for joy" for teachers; I am not sure it worked so well. Because just like the way we feel, see, or experience justice and injustice differently, so too, do we feel, see, and experience joy differently.

Joy harnesses our energy. I find it in lots of spaces, but in school I am only able to find it so consistently because I have become adept at appreciating it in multiple forms. I recently administered a "feelings circle" to a group of first graders in an outdoor class. It was sweet: kids learned new feelings words, matched them to paper cartoon expression faces, and named the feelings that applied to their current state of being. As people who deeply understand childhood development, we know that giving kids language tempers their unrest. The same is true for adults.

Do you know about Gloria Anzaldúa? She can help us understand where we might find joy within ourselves, and in our schools. Anzaldúa gifted the world by making the concept of *nepantla* more prolific. *Nepantla* is a Nahuatl word that translates in English to "the middle." It is most widely known through its conceptualization by foremother, writer, queer theorist, and Chicanx leader Gloria E. Anzaldúa (Anzaldúa 2012). Using her language, she describes *nepantla*:

> Removed from that culture's center you glimpse the sea in which you've been immersed but to which you were oblivious, no longer seeing the world the way you were enculturated to see it (p. 549).

In Western scholarship, this is sometimes referred to as the third space.

The state of *nepantla* is the in-between space, the place tucked within the hyphens. *Nepantla* literacies are practices from the margins, the cognitive, emotional "borderlands" (Anzaldúa 2012). It's a space where deep confusion, anxiety, and uncertainty often live. It's also the space where openness exists, where possibilities come into fruition, and where ideation is birthed from both familiar and new entities. Few definitive factors exist within a *nepantla* space, except for (a) they offer us a space for transformation and (b) they are often unclear.

For me, I find joy mostly within the third space, the in-between parts of schools: the hallways, morning drop-off, impromptu lunch meetings, the bodega across the street with the man who will crush Doritos on my tuna sandwich at no extra charge (it was his recipe). For me, joy also lies within the borderlands of the mainstream parts of schools: classrooms, offices, the speech teacher's room, the gym.

Sometimes, I long for the first pattering of students arriving to school, the ones who bumble into my classroom, tell me "all the things," request their favorite Michael Jackson song, and then proceed to display all their Poké-mon cards on their desk before the day has even started. Or the alliances I would make with the specials teachers (gym, drama, art) where we'd engage in student advocacy in unexpected ways. I remember an elaborate plan the gym teacher (shout out to Safa!) and I created for a student who became emotionally taxed while he was learning to read, learning Brooklyn culture, and learning to speak English. We worked to prevent and/or alleviate his frustration by creating a unique position for him: assistant kindergarten gym teacher (he was a fourth grader). This student was athletic, brilliant on the basketball court and soccer field, and he was able to practice his oral, social, and emotional literacy in ways that didn't create a ball of anxiety. Joy, for us, was establishing a third space for our teaching, and joy for our student hap-pened because he was very much functioning in the third space of school. He recalibrated his sense of self by capitalizing on his strengths. His deep-ened sportsmanship impacted the well-being of our classroom community tremendously.

You'll read later in this book, too, about the joy I find in the tiny, yet consistent spaces in school. Like teacher lunch time. It was, and perhaps still is, one of the most transformative spaces for the development of my pedagogy.

It is true, classrooms spaces full of children, throughout my career, have most certainly knocked me down. There is no way I can tell you that all the moments with kids in schools have been joyful. But I can say, I love love love helping kids search their minds for the questions they really want to ask, but perhaps haven't quite figured out how to say. I'm in love with illuminating their curiosities in different places with their peers, and I'm in love with the mental and experiential trek it takes to figure out how to explore their inquiries in relevant and meaningful ways. I am in love with documenting kids' growth. I am in love with literacy, and I love teaching kids of all ages about literacy, I love helping them build their literacy.

I'm about to write the long story of my joy, but in short: I am obsessed with teaching and learning in ways that support kids feeling like their whole human selves in the place we call school. That is the undercurrent that has enabled me to function in school, grow its third spaces, as well as find joy that has been tucked along and hidden away in the corners of schools I've worked in.

Dreams, Nourishment, Rituals: Toward Future Goodness

It's one thing to name "dominant school culture" and the parts of it that are unjust; it's a whole 'nother thing to move away from it! To change it! To aspire toward something better and different! That's why we must create a different operating force; we cannot rely on traditional practices to fuel our imaginations toward that future goodness. Those bubbles in the middle of our structured generator of hope—*dreaming*, *nourishment*, and *rituals*—are packed with a newer kind of energy force that I believe—alongside other educators, students, families, and research based-practices—is the energy we need to manifest to transform our schools toward future goodness:

- When we **dream**, we can develop goals in creative and imaginative ways.

- When we **nourish** ourselves and our communities through the development of *thought sanctuaries*—including thought partners, rest, and engagement in multiliteracies for pleasure—we experience more positive human connection within our daily teaching and learning lives.

- When we participate in **rituals** like daily reflective practices, body check-ins, participation protocols, community circles, and educator, caregiver, and student play shops.

On play shop . . . I chuckle as I write "play shop." I chuckle because the essence of learning is within play—even though nowadays including something like play within a school day is seen as a radical act. Play shop is simply providing time and space for people to interact with each other and materials in ways that are open and released of specific expectations. For example, play shops are most common in kindergarten and first grade classrooms. There might be a corner of the room equipped with a "play kitchen" and pretend food. Kids will be invited to "play" in small groups, with the only expectation being that they use their imaginations and work together to experience something that everybody in the group enjoys. This can also happen in middle school, high school, and even staff meetings. At the secondary-school level, play shop could include a bin of materials (not unlike what you might see in a maker space) and students could be tasked with creating an invention of their choosing by "playing" with the materials. In a school staff meeting, teachers could have a meeting in someone's classroom where they are tasked to "play" with classroom environment materials like new school furniture, rugs, and manipulatives to create an ideal learning space. The most important ingredients of play shop are released expectation, encouraged imagination, and elements of cooperation that support a joyous experience for all contributing group members. The group members get to decide the guidelines for what that joy might be.

These energies work together to fuel our ability to find joy, work toward justice, and teach with agency, instinct, and ferocity. And this, reader, is where the transformation toward future goodness happens—the transformation of school as we know it changes into something many of us haven't yet experienced, something we're working to imagine and name. Something that will come into fruition when we develop this new platform for energy, like a structured generator of hope.

Work Along: Vision Boarding Toward Future Goodness

Okay, so we've read, we've journaled, and we've discussed; now it's time to exercise a little art-making as part of our thought process! Here, I'll introduce the concept of vision boarding to support our work in dreaming. As I said before, dreaming allows us to develop goals in creative and imaginative ways. When we engage in using our hands to support our thinking, we're building something visually that shows what *future goodness* in school could look like.

Vision boarding is a versatile strategy. I've used it in the classroom context with early learners, adolescents, and adults. For example, during Spring 2021, when kids, teachers, and caregivers were transitioning to summer and an unknown Fall due to COVID-19, I developed transition activities supported by vision boarding for kids to reflect on the year they were finishing so they could get a little more control over their feelings about their near-futures.

We talked about the discomfort in not knowing what the Fall would bring us, the anticipation of renewed summer fun after the first round of COVID-19 vaccines had been dished out (summer camps were just reopening), and the celebration of accomplishing a really weird, tough, and somewhat unimaginable school year. Figures 1.5, 1.6, and 1.7 show some examples of their work!

Figure 1.5 is an example of a vision board created by a third grader in Spring 2021. This is what she created in response to the prompt: "What are you proud of? What do you hope for this summer? What do you imagine for 4th grade?"

The vision board in Figure 1.6 was created for a similar envisioning activity, but adapted for a first grader. This is what she created in response to the prompt: "What do you hope for this summer?"

Figure 1.7 is a demonstration vision board I created to model with a group of fifth graders in anticipation of their transition to middle school. It was called "The Arch of Transition." We focused more on imagery as opposed to description to encourage their visualization. On the left, you see a picture of a library, showing the intense reading taking place at the end of fifth

FIGURE 1.5 Upper elementary student vision board example.

(Continued)

FIGURE 1.6 Lower elementary school student vision board example.

FIGURE 1.7 Teacher demonstration vision board.

grade, paired with a few rides from Coney Island Amusement Park in Brooklyn. The images show the juxtaposition of fifth grade rigor with newfound, more independent outdoor fun. Several parks and gardens were opening up for the first time after the beginning of COVID-19 during the summer of 2021, so I included images showing the incredible artistic and cultural experiences New York City had to offer, like the New York Botanical Garden Kusama exhibit, and even an I ♥ NYC T-shirt! The pending 2021 Fall bore anxiety for so many people—all the players in a school, so the dreams for Fall were pretty simple: they included being in closer proximity with friends, hence the hugging and dancing cartoons. Finally, I summed up the image in the right-hand corner, with the unfinished phrase, "The Revolution Must Be . . ." because although I, we, didn't know exactly what the revolution must be, we knew it needed to be something.

No matter the age or developmental stage of human, I like to use vision boarding to spark the neural pathway that moves away from meta-work toward instinctual imagination, the kind that runs through the mind to the heart to the stomach and manifests by creating with the hands. As a former design student myself, and a fledgling jewelry maker, I create vision boards to establish new iterations of style, influencing my next creations (Head over to Pinterest at https://www.pinterest.com/mskassminor/new-mood-april-2021/new-york-spring/ for an example of a vision board I created named "New York Spring" that inspired a line of earrings I created called "Petals and Trash.") Vision boarding is nothing new. Design thinkers who hail from all over the art world, such as interior designers or landscape architects, often partner with their clients to create vision boards that demonstrate their style, including various objects, colorways, and/or images that help to surface their personal aesthetic, or even a newer iteration of what they *desire* their aesthetic to be. Couldn't we educators do the same for schools?

Dr. Jamila Lyiscott (2019) writes extensively on supporting communities to build justice within and outside the walls of schools, and she has multiple predecessors and contemporaries who share similar thinking when it comes to building justice, although those people are not always rooted within the realm of education. Lyiscott named the concept of "vision driven justice," saying that to be driven by a palpable vision of the world we want to see is an entirely different energy than being perpetually driven by the world that we do not want to see (p. 18). The idea of envisioning justice is yet another one of those really old ideas that has finally found its way in the thruways of popular culture. Brilliant writers and thinkers have been doing this work for a long time, but their ideas haven't always made their way to mainstream culture.

Audre Lorde and Octavia Butler, Adrienne Rich and Gloria Anzaldúa; they all published great works in the realm of both fiction and nonfiction that provoke the public imagination to enable life to be different, to be . . . better, more just. Various iterations of Lyiscott's term, *vision driven justice*, are continuing to pop up everywhere, because it is so essential for joy and justice to coexist in school. adrienne maree brown, Dr. Bettina Love, and Lana and Lilly Wachowski have written and created various works and other forms of media that walk toward iterations of justice in multiple forms, all of which require dreaming, reimagining, and looking beyond *and* within the current paradigm.

Nonfiction Reads, Literature, and Film for Provoking the Imagination Toward Justice and Joy

Essay Collections

Sister Outsider by Audre Lorde

On Lies, Secrets, and Silence: Selected Prose, 1966–1978 by Adrienne Rich

Blogs:

"We Need to Keep Dreaming, Even When It Feels Impossible. Here's Why" by Luvvie Ayaji Jones

"Justice, Community, and Adrienne Rich" by Jordan Namerow

Books/Film (Science Fiction)

Parable of the Sower by Octavia Butler

The Matrix film series by the Wachowski Sisters

"Lana Wachowski Describes What It's Like Returning to The Matrix" via Youtube

Nonfiction Books

Black Appetite, White Food: Issues of Race, Voice, and Justice Within and Beyond the Classroom by Jamila Lysicott

We Want to Do More Than Survive: Abolitionist Teaching and the Pursuit of Educational Freedom by Bettina L. Love

Emergent Strategy by adrienne maree brown

Borderlands/La Frontera: The New Mestiza by Gloria Anzaldúa

Picture Books

Remember to Dream Ebere by Cynthia Erivo

What if by Samantha Berger, illustrated by Mike Curato

Vision boarding is a cathartic endeavor. It is simple, creative, and fun, but it requires presence, reflection, and risk. Essentially, with thoughtful intention, you are plotting, pasting, mapping out possibilities that you may not have said out loud before, to yourself, and especially not to your colleagues or your community! Although this strategy may look like a vapid crafting escape, the act of vision boarding *in response to the call for dreaming* up a visual take on what the future goodness in schools looks like, how justice and joy manifest, from *your* purview in *your* community *without* writing paragraphs upon paragraphs . . . is an incredibly powerful act.

So here we go, let's put those two things together: vision boarding + imagining joy and justice. On your own, take a moment to unpack that box. What might those components of a future goodness look like in your context? In what ways might you have experienced them already?

Historical Underpinnings: Exploring the Roots of Schooling

Digging.

My paternal grandmother is a voracious weeder. She plucks every dandelion and creeper ivy way down to the umbilical cord that connects it to the earth, tossing it aside with both diligence and respect.

I think about her now, in her late 80s, weeding, and how it's the physical manifestation of a radical act. The word "radical" comes from the Latin *radix* for root. Angela Davis (1990) tells us that to radicalize something means we grasp it by the root (p. 13). We shake it, attack the meaning, dig and dig until we find mutual truth. Still, we continue to question. Eventually, we come closer to finding something that resembles an answer.

Dandelion seeds.

Here I sit, writing this book, recognizing that I'm approaching this inquiry into schooling in the same radicalized way my grandmother approaches her garden bed. As Cornelius floats his first memory of meeting my grandmother, where she sat indoors in the cool air conditioning, holding a worn copy of Alex Haley's *Roots* in her lap, I realize we are all grasping at truth and definition, albeit in different ways.

The challenge is to find convergence in our truth lines, and part of this requires us to act as thoughtful, brave historians who prime ourselves to honor our communities by exploring the roots of the spaces we all operate from when we gather in the place called school. Just as we must know ourselves if we are to truly transform into a better version of who we want to be, we must know the institution we work in.

There are named pockets of history we expose our students to, developed within various common core and state standards, woven throughout curriculums across the country. In school, learners study U.S. history, global history, and concepts like community workers and geography, too. Sometimes, they will dabble into a few social movements like the Civil Rights era in the 1960s working toward a big study on the Cold War. If students move through curriculum quickly, they may be exposed to the Vietnam War, and if they are very lucky, they may even learn about the Black Lives Matter movements in 2013, continuing on presently.

However, in very few school spaces is the role of school and education, and its evolution within American society discussed with kids in depth or with any sort of detail. School is one of the few institutions almost every single person in the United States has had some degree of experience with, yet the depths of what it has done unto us as a people has yet to be fully understood by the masses.

Sure, the Progressive Era is widely known, written into various social studies curricula, as well as surface programming on integration and *Brown v. Board of Education*, but how much does the average teacher preparation program, or K–12 program, focus on the iterations of public school in America with the general public throughout time? The conversations between Horace Mann and John Dewey, the tensions between Booker T. Washington and W.E.B Dubois, Teddy Roosevelt's commentary on what he named "The Indian Problem"? The promise of *Brown v. Board of Education*, and its subsequent failures? The richness of Historically Black Colleges and Universities? The origins of "Patriotic Education"?

Many of us live in places where school is the connector of a community. Through the lens of student experience, or our own teacher experience, we witness hundreds of thousands of decisions made for us or by us, and for better or for worse, those decisions are a prism reflected by an evolving educational trajectory that holds unmet promises, and incongruously meets its mission to serve, as Horace Mann once said, "as the great equalizer."

As teachers, just as we must know ourselves to truly transform into a better version of who we want to be, we must know the institution we work in, school, just as well. All of it, the good, the bad, and the better and *the worst*.

In both graduate and undergraduate programs in college, the historical evolution of school is usually an elective. At one point in time, I thought it was my first exposure to the competing interests of various thinkers and members of society. As I dig and dig, I know my exposure to those competing interests began much, much earlier, all the way back in kindergarten. Now, as a former student and public school teacher, current teacher-educator and caregiver of young people in a public elementary school, my awareness of how school is operationalized in favor of some over others is crystal clear and razor-sharp.

Again, throughout the journey of this book are several "learning corners," so to speak, the *historical underpinnings* waiting for you online. At various junctures in this text, I'll identify spots where we can go back and forth between the layers of our personhood, our teacherhood, to consider how the historical imprint of education within the United States has shaped who we are in those realms. It's important for us to consider the layers of our personhood and our teacherhood to that history because it is through this connected excavation that we can set a strong foundation for exploring possibilities for enabling who we are and what we believe into our praxis within the school communities we work in.

I want to note that history doesn't always shape us in a linear way; more often than not we are shaped by themes—typically, themes that are common in talk around education, and themes that have only become "themes" because they have happened repeatedly throughout history. For example, equality, opportunity, and access have a Newton's law–type relationship to their evil stepsister-ish themes of inequality, oppression, and barriers.

If we are to build justice from within school communities in the various roles we play and through the identities we carry, we must understand the injustices that are inherent within the foundation of the U.S. public school system. To move forward, *we must look back*. To change a thing, one must first understand it deeply—so let's do that.

Along with our inward-bound journey, we'll take a trip through a sequential timeline to help unpack and explore this idea of school and what it's for, especially as it coincides with children's (and teachers', too!) well-being and development. Eventually, we'll deeply understand what's happen*ed* in connection to what's happen*ing,* all of which will guide our pursuit toward justice as an everyday practice.

On that note, we'll hop around the past 250 years of school in the United States, between 1779 and 2022, approaching the history of schooling like my grandmother approached her garden bed: at the root. The first installment of this timeline includes a series of events that explain significant markers within U.S. history that have improved the present-day circumstances[2] of groups of people who have historically been left out of the consideration of the "best practices" within education. As you read, I hope you will reflect on which groups you identify with, are a part of, or feel outside of. Take notes on what you read that you already know, as well as what information is new to you.

Let me share a quick note about my historical research. Each one of the short bursts on the timeline is the product of hours of research from multiple sources. There is so much to say about each component, but I am also wary of going too in depth, since I'm trying to mind both your time and your energy. Although one might consider this level of delving somewhat of a luxury, it remains true that to move forward we must look back.

Also, now that I have excavated both lightness and the darkness from the United States' multi-century experiment with education, I feel I am more equipped to undo the dark parts because I understand them more clearly. I share them because I hope you can, too.

I also find great solace in the lighter pieces—the elements of care and ethical learning that some folx initiated, held on to, and created beautiful experiences with, despite the narrative and realities that others had created to shape who public education was for.

As we work to teach and learn in a public education system that is constantly in flux at the hands of lawmakers and other public officials, we can learn from our predecessors, who faced similar hardships. For the first installment, please visit https://www.kassandcorn.com/teachingfiercely/.

---

2   This timeline encompasses groups of people, but certainly *not all* groups of people, who have been underserved consistently across time within and throughout the inception of democratic education within the United States.

Chapter 2:
Seeing and Feeling the Pressure of Injustice: Perspective Changes Everything

My whole life, my eyesight has been terrible. Nearsighted with astigmatism, I've worn glasses as long as I can remember. As a child, I lost my glasses several times. As I waited for a new pair of glasses to be shipped, life was different while <u>everything</u> was underscored by a state of blurriness. Trying to decode the pale chalk lines on the worn out green chalkboards in school was absolutely exhausting. Figuring out who was at the other side of the cafeteria? Impossible. Identifying my school bus number? Wasn't happening.

At seven and eight years old, I got pretty good at finding creative ways to hide what I couldn't see in the classroom, looking and listening for other clues in the world to help me know where to go, or which bus to hop on. Nobody really suspected I had any issues re: access because I could be compliant, I could be quiet, and I could tell a good story. It wasn't that I didn't make an effort; I tried to figure out what was being written in the front of the classroom, but it was exhausting. Most of the time, I was checked out, deep in my internal world building a very strong set of daydreaming skills! Besides, there weren't many grown-ups probing my vision situation, so flying under the radar became my specialty.

There are many people who are doing the work of teaching and learning, in schools, in a similar state: they are truly working hard, trying their best to decipher various social situations, cultural components of learning, and/or numerous lifeways in literacy. However, like me and my nearsightedness and astigmatism, it's really, really hard to see without the proper tools and equip-ment. *And*, if they've never been diagnosed with having a vision problem, the state of blurriness in which they move throughout the school commu-nity feels normal.

Honestly, the thing that brought me to clear sight wasn't my bad vision, it was my sister: six years older than me, in high school while I was in elemen-tary school, there wasn't anything she did that I didn't try to emulate, and she just so happened to wear glasses. Because I wanted to be more like her, I asked my mom to take me to an eye doctor. My mom obliged, taking me to the optometrist located at the Base Exchange (BX) on the air force base we currently lived on, and then it became an annual thing. With every visit, my eyesight got worse, my prescription grew stronger, and I got to choose a new pair of glasses, totally in sync with the trajectory of my sister's eyewear! Those new glasses were such a treat! In addition to being one step closer to my sister's style, the relief I felt from my new and improved vision when I put on those new frames . . . whew! It was ah-maz-ing.

I would put on those new glasses and move through the world in absolute awe; it was almost incredulous that this is what the world looked like when you could actually *see*. The lines in people's faces were distinct, trees had collections of single leaves, and the name of the street I was crossing was no longer a mystery. To this day, after the blur and haze of the journey from my bed to the bathroom, I relish the clarity in vision I feel every morning when I put on my glasses or contacts.

If you are not someone with impaired vision, then you may not know about the afflictions that come with new glasses or lenses: the ache you feel in your temples, or distorted perception of space that splices your eyesight. At first, the glasses feel great—you can see everything, and you feel like you're queen of the world! And then the strangeness creeps in with the stronger prescription, and there's a great amount of temptation to just take the new lenses off, put the old ones back on, and even sometimes, *just go without anything to help your vision because it feels better.*

My metaphor is getting more obvious! Our motivations to understand what's happening in school, that is, *What is unjust?*, *What is just?*, and *What are we supposed to do about it?,* come from different places, from different people in different ways. However, in my experience, I have found that no matter where the motivation comes from, once people are truly engaged in identifying injustice and justice, powerful outcomes in school communities occur.

With proper tools, equipment, and practice, you will begin to see how something as simple as the tone in a teacher's voice displays a sense of injustice, how the parameters for family engagement time excludes specific demographics of people from attending school events, or even how recess policies are in favor of one gender over another. Beginning to see how school, as a system, is underscored with injustices, absolutely takes some adjusting to— especially if you've been operating within the status quo for most of the time you've been in school, first as a student and then as a teacher.

It will take time. Adjustment is necessary to get used to clarity in vision. Powerfully, with every injustice you're able to identify, you'll have an opportunity to create justice for children, colleagues, and families you're connected to within your school community. *But those opportunities are absent from teaching and learning life if you're not able to see what's not working in the first place.*

There will be time for rest and recuperation, but the clarity in your vision doesn't disappear. Once you see what you are able to see, it cannot be unseen. At times, this weight, sometimes referred to as *emotional labor*, might be categorized as a burden, and it can be frustratingly exhausting to walk with and wear this knowledge.

But I think it's important to note—we are working toward building our ability to move through a just lens, not only *some* of the time, not only through a few lesson plans here or there, but all the time, everywhere. There is a specific beauty to this work, this clarity in vision. And as tiring as the emotional weight can feel of seeing and understanding everyday injustices in school, joy beckons as we create opportunities and uncover robust and student-centered learning across the minutes and days and years kids, and teachers, spend in school.

> **Classroom Activity: Plan a Read Aloud to Build Perspective with Students**
>
> It's exciting to think about the trajectory of your own personal growth, and it can be just as exciting to think about building a similar skill set—that is, clarity in vision—with the students you teach as well. Here, I invite you to consider planning a read-aloud experience for your community of learners using texts like *Sight: glimmer, glow, SPARK, FLASH!* by Romana Romanyshyn and Andriy Lesiv and/or *They All Saw a Cat* by Brendan Wenzel to instill a sense of perspective-taking with your students.

Dominant Culture: Perspective Changes Everything

Glasses.

There are all kinds of things that surround us in school that, to the naked eye, are harmless. Take, for example, the school chair. The ubiquitous navy-blue chair, made with hard seats, chrome legs, and memories from its tiny squeaks created from every transition passed on from year to year to year. Maybe you, like me, also sat on this chair for most of your elementary, adolescent, and adult school life. Most of the time, as student or educator, you think nothing of it. Until one day, it's the *only* thing you think about!

As I belabor this point, I invite you to find a blue school chair to sit in for full effect!

A singular, common perspective of the school chair is that its purpose is to serve as a place for students to sit as they are learning in classrooms. Seems simple, but it's far more complicated.

Let's grow that perspective from multiple vantage points:

The antsy student: *"The blue school chair dictates how I can position my body to learn!"*

When the perspective of an antsy child or grown-up is considered during a lesson or independent work period in any kind of learning environment, sitting in the blue chair might feel like a constraint, uncomfortable. Having a sore bottom is one of the first things my own antsy child (and self) talks about after a long day at school! Meanwhile, at home, those same "antsy" people might be reading, computing numbers, making posters, and/or engaging in the most organic of conversations with their entire bodies sprawled out on the floor.

Let's think about a few other players' perspectives, such as school leaders and school business managers, those who are responsible for equipping the school with furniture.

School leaders and/or business managers: "The federal government dictates when I can buy chairs, how many chairs I can afford, and what chairs I am allowed to buy!"

Those responsible for buying school furniture usually are not sitting in kids' chairs. Consequently, the way their bodies are positioned to learn within their workspace isn't necessarily similar to what students are thinking. Rather, they are tasked with budgeting for all kinds of operating expenses and priority school items like books, curricular materials, supplies, and, yes, desks and tables and chairs. Here's the thing that's tricky: budgets are finicky, incumbent on many different factors, such as Title 1 Funds, PTA bank accounts, and the number of kids and teachers in the school demographic.

What's more, when spending government money, it is really difficult to use funding outside of companies that are already enlisted as vendors and contractors with local and/or federal governments.

Maybe you're thinking "TMI Kass!" Maybe you're right.

But here's the thing, all these details help us build perspective. The hard blue school chairs the school leader had to order from one of the three Blue School Chair companies contracted with the government were probably a great bargain. That great bargain might have allowed for a whole 'nother teacher or teaching assistant to be hired for the following school year. The thing that is super uncomfortable for a whole bunch of kids is *also* the same thing that allowed a teaching assistant in their classroom, enabling oodles of comfort to be provided in different ways throughout the school year.

Teacher: "The blue school chair limits how I can organize my classroom environment to optimize learning!"

Earlier, we addressed the "comfort" component from the learners' perspective, but let's work to get closer to omniscient perspective as we unpack what a teacher might be thinking in terms of comfort and communal learning at the behest of the blue chair. One of the resounding memories in my teacherhood is that *screeeechh* that hit the ears between every period when the bell sounded, as students leave their desks to head to their next class. (If you close your eyes, you can probably hear it, too. If you are an active teacher, this sound is no stranger to you!) While chairs are the most common option for positioning how kids learn in a classroom, they limit a teacher's ability to create a calm, comfortable, communal space. *Calm* is often the first thing derailed by chairs.

Developing a *community* of learners within a classroom space is an important force when building social justice. As a child of the 1980s, I did not feel a deep sense of communal learning in elementary school. When I became a teacher, aligning desks in rows and handing students responsibility for their chairs was a practice I carried with me from my own school history, and I took solace in the quietness that rows and cold chairs promoted.

This classroom setup was part of the culture of dominant schooling I brought with me from my childhood—sitting in blue chairs in desks lined up in rows was normal for me, throughout all my school experiences (in college, too!). Hefting chairs on top of desks as a child with my tiny kid muscles was part of my classroom routine. The "chairs and rows" classroom environment was in my blood.

However, I learned very quickly that classroom quietness was not synonymous with classroom engagement. Rather, I learned that silence was an indicator of kids' boredom; the loudest sounds were the sighs of relief attached to the teacher carrying all the intellectual labor. By sitting in their blue chairs quietly, students' learning engagement was optional and checking out was easy.

The only time period in my teaching career that my classroom was decked out in rows was that first few months of my high school teaching life. That year, I was in grad school. I remember talking about the importance of group work and its impact on student engagement in classroom communities. Because group work made noise and sparked paranoia about pending chaos, I avoided group work at all costs. Even when I learned that students learn more powerfully from each other than they do from teachers, I still planned my workshop model as individualistically as possible because it felt safe . . . it felt *quiet*.

Soon, group work became unavoidable. Not because my school mandated it, but because one of my grad school classes required "implementing group work" as part of my official New York State teaching certification. I found myself with an assignment that required me to design a lesson for groups, where students worked together and learned from one another. I was pressed for time, working extra hours to afford New York City rent, full-time teaching and full-time grad schooling, so I was not about to waste planning time on something that I wasn't going to use.

I took a deep breath, and chose a group work structure to plan carefully. I decided to implement a simple Jigsaw activity for a text on a topic we were reading about in our biology unit—fetal alcohol syndrome—and committed to the Jigsaw Protocol the very next day. After I taught the mini-lesson on "babies in utero," I instructed the kids to move into groups [resounding *screeeechhh* from blue chairs] and to sit where they like. [Slight panic on my part: *Would my class explode into mayhem? Would kids start the dance for "Chicken Noodle Soup"*[1] *as they headed to a different area of the classroom? Would they actually engage with the text?* Note: Since I was a novice, transitions were not smooth in my class, hence my rows and chairs and mostly independent activities.]

---

1   "Chicken Noodle Soup," a song produced by Da Drizzle, featured on the hip hop group's Webstar album: *Webstar: Caught in the Web*. Rapped by Young B and the Voice of Harlem, this song had a dance associated with it. The dance was originally choreographed by Allie Bernard, and was incredibly popular with youth culture the year it came out, 2006, which also happened to be my first year of teaching!

It was loud. Some of my panic had merit: kids *did* start dancing to "Chicken Noodle Soup." Their bodies were folded, flat, standing, sprawled in all sorts of ways. And they were talking *a lot*.

And yet . . . they did the activity! They proceeded to read their sections, identify the topic, create a poster, and did a little "teach out." It was nothing like my own school experiences. It was communal, and kids were learning.

No blue school chairs were involved.

That first Jigsaw experience, for me, was a turning point. It allowed me to witness kids interacting in the classroom space in ways that were loud, yet full of learning; slightly chaotic, yet vibrant.

While a quiet, somewhat motionless learning environment made *me* comfortable, I realized it was making the students I was working with *un*comfortable. *I* may have been super engaged with the content, "teaching" science with flowery vocabulary for 20 to 30 minutes a time, but that time was clearly for me. You know those old sayings, "Sage on the stage" and "The one who does the most talking does the most learning"? That was me, 100%!

Inadvertently, I was developing nap-like notes of disengagement for students, and while they may have appreciated the comfort that comes with rest, they deserved better.

From that chairless, semichaotic, yet super-engaged pursuit toward group work, I learned that oftentimes my students' comfort required my discomfort.

I chuckle as I look back because, honestly, the *discomfort* of creating engaging teaching and learning spaces has never left me. I often joke that I'm like the Incredible Hulk, not because I'm green and angry, but because I've taken a page from his playbook when it comes to managing my presence in learning communities. There's a scene in one of Marvel's *Avenger* movies where Black Widow asks Hulk how he learned to stay in his human form, rather than transforming to a green angry monster due to negative emotional charges. His secret? He stays angry.

Like the Hulk, I've chosen how to be in spaces: not angry, but slightly uncomfortable. Because I've made that choice, more often than not I'm able to responsively adapt to people's learning needs, especially when it comes to their communal environments.

Work Along: Designing Group Work in Your Lesson Plan

Jigsaw Activity Protocol

Try it out! In my first group work exercise, I used the Jigsaw Protocol, a learning structure that allows people to work closely with another both simply and powerfully.

Effective for the youngest learners to the oldest adults, the gist of Jigsaw is fairly simple:

- Assign sections of a text to teams of students.
- Each team becomes an "expert" on the topic.
- A "share" or more sophisticated "teach out" is facilitated by each group to the rest of the class about their assigned topic.

Essentially, when students are working in a Jigsaw group model, they each take responsibility for certain sections of a text and share their understanding of that text within a small group. The group documents their learning, working toward a level of expertise in the given topic.

Groups share their learning with the rest of the community. The share can be done in a variety of ways. For example, if students are reading a text for the first time and are sharing the same day, the share can be a simple surfacing of the main idea or a few interesting facts they learned.

If the text is longer or requires more time to gain a more sophisticated understanding, a more formal teach out can be facilitated. In the more formal teach out, learners work in their Jigsaw team, taking responsibility for their section of the text. This time, they create a substantial teaching artifact like a chart or set of slides to teach their section of the topic to the rest of the community.

Consider using the Jigsaw model in connection to a chapter in this book to learn within a professional learning community! Below, find guidelines for using the Jigsaw structure with the most recent section of text, "Dominant Culture: Perspective Changes Everything."

Jigsaw Structure Guidelines for "Dominant Culture: Perspective Changes Everything"

1. Divide one large group into teams of two or three people
2. Assign each group one of the following sections:
   a. The antsy student
   b. School leaders and/or business managers
   c. Teachers

(*Continued*)

3. Each group is responsible for reading the section of the text to learn more about the perspective assigned to them. Since the sections are short, reading time shouldn't take more than five to seven minutes. However, to create a more textured understanding of assigned perspectives, consider allowing more time for teams to research their assigned perspective.

4. Each group can now informally share the "gist" of their assigned perspective *or* they can spend 10 minutes creating a teaching artifact to demonstrate their learning to the rest of the community.

5. Pay special attention to the share or "teach out" component. While folks are spending time reading, becoming familiar with, and/or unpacking their assigned perspective, in this particular sharing, often times, there will be tensions as new paradigms are opened or old problems are surfaced.

Alternate Jigsaw Mix

Rather than having small groups take on the same assigned topic, each individual within the small group can take on a different perspective. The same Jigsaw process occurs, but rather than sharing out to the larger group, the share is done within the small group. This allows for more intimate conversations. However, it is important to create support and protection during conversations that have the potential to create deep conflict. If your community is newer to one another, ensure you have a facilitator in close proximity to small groups, and consider waiting for relational trust to develop before you engage in contentious conversations.

For more information on using the Jigsaw Grouping Structure, visit *School Reform Initiative* at schoolreformini-tiative.org. In addition to Jigsaw Grouping, there are bountiful protocols and grouping structure for all types of learner and learning spaces!

Catalyst for Change: Knowing How to See and Feel the Pressure of Injustice

To build our capacity for envisioning justice, we have to create multiple lenses in which we can not only *see and understand* various perspectives, but also, *feel* the pressure to change the injustices so many people in our schools experience daily. This well of empathy equips us with the ability to *identify and prevent* potential harm.

Too often, educators and families view school through rose-colored glasses: believing the false reality that it's all good so long as there's no overt, loud, and/or super-visible trouble happening. The pink tint of nicety only operates when school life is seen through one lens, one way, and in one particular shade. Mono-perspectives often go hand in hand with the concept of neutrality, this idea that "rocking the boat" is bad because once you name something as being problematic or racist or inequitable, you may get in trouble, create more work for people, and/or life becomes harder in some ways.

This is when people start insisting they have no power to change a thing, or that it doesn't matter what we think about issue X, because it's outside our role or job jurisdiction in the realm of school. But here's the thing: viewing a problem from one lens, claiming neutrality, always meeting in the middle, sacrificing your power in the name of "keeping the peace" is equivalent to maintaining the status quo—the underlying source of injustice in schools.

It's true. Deepening perspective and identifying problems does challenge people's workloads; it does make life harder in some ways. Because of this, many people who *are* able to see injustice with clarity feel as though they don't have the time or bandwidth or even permission to name it, and their jobs and livelihood are quite literally in jeopardy. Nonetheless, those same folks, disproportionately BIPOC and disproportionately Queer, have been naming injustices in schools since the inception of public schooling.

Oftentimes, the general public situates the unjust nature of schooling in the past. When people think about equity or equal rights, the Civil Rights Movement, Thurgood Marshall, and the Little Rock Nine come to mind. Those who have spent time studying education or who have children with IEPs (Individualized Education Programs) might even think about the Individuals with Disabilities Education Act (IDEA) that passed in 1975 and was later revised in the 1990s, granting access "for a free and appropriate education," special education, and other related services for any children who qualified. Or perhaps those familiar with gender discrimination laws or who were in secondary school in the 1970s might think about Title IX, an educational amendment passed in 1972 banning sex discrimination of any kind in educational spaces (most widely known for allowing girls to play school-sponsored sports).

> Interested in further reading about laws that made a difference in education? Read Robert Kim's book *Elevating Equity and Justice: Ten U.S. Supreme Court Cases Every Teacher Should Know.*

Those were all major victories and powerful shifts for equity in American schooling. However, the ubiquitous, quiet, everyday injustices that haven't necessarily made their way to the Supreme Court are also powerful—powerful enough to produce the same inequitable schooling outcomes for socially and economically disadvantaged students for the past *70* years. Since public schooling was revamped in 1938 toward the end of the Great Depression, policy and legislative changes, even when designed in favor of marginalized groups, still haven't changed the experiences for those students powerfully enough (Rothstein and Jacobsen 2007). Graduation rates, attendance, suspension rates, and family participation all show data that leans in favor of kids from well-resourced families and the dominant culture.

Although injustice is often historicized, we must understand that it is very much part of our here and now. We are all implicated, *and* we are all empowered to choose change.

There is Strength in Numbers in Choosing Change

I remember listening to one of my favorite teachers, Jess Liftshitz, describe her fifth grade classroom inquiry project during a panel presentation at an educator conference in Chicago. She spoke about a multifaceted, exciting curriculum she created to improve kids' criticality, to support them in learning argumentative writing using research skills and text-based evidence, all important parts of fifth grade standards in every state within the United States.

Having recently taught the unit, Jess featured her students' work and shared powerful anecdotes regarding their learning during the presentation. However, she had a difficult time celebrating the curriculum and her students' learning because she experienced frequent pushback and skepticism from her students' parents: some of the texts her students examined within the unit featured Queer characters.

Her school was in the Midwest in an affluent, mostly white suburb. Even at the time of this conference, she was a veteran teacher, experienced lots of success within her student-family relationships, and students were excited to see her name when they received their class assignment in the Fall. *And* she is also a Queer, white woman who had a classroom library that was well-balanced and representative of the human demographic.

It's important to note that well-balanced libraries that are representative of the human demographic are *rare*.[2] Other teachers in her school had classroom libraries closer to dominant culture, including books by predominantly white authors with predominately white, heteronormative characters. Her

---

2   The Coalition of Educational Justice (2020) reports that for every one book written by a BIPOC author, there are five books written by white authors represented in classroom libraries (p. 5). The problem of accurate human representation continues to grow as book bans have become political agents in various legislative agendas.

simple act of including books that more accurately represented the human demographic became radical for two reasons: (1) she was one of the few teachers in her community expanding her classroom library in a way that represented humans in the world, and (2) because she is Queer.

When people who are not part of the dominant culture read books or provide books to children that are also not part of the dominant culture, fear has a tendency to pop up amongst folks who have been living comfortably within their "normative" lifestyles. In this case, heteronormative parents and caregivers were fearful of their children reading books that featured Queer characters. Their fear grew when they learned their kids' teacher was also Queer. Fear of what, exactly, is hard to name. At the time of this writing, this fear has catalyzed catastrophic anti-Queer legislative movements such as the "Don't Say Gay" laws for schools in Florida, as well as similar laws in Ohio and Kentucky. But the general sentiment that *difference* was introduced into their schema for how people *should* live their lives was enough to make this Queer educator's teaching life harder and more uncomfortable.

Merriam-Webster tells us that heteronormative means "of, relating to, or based on the attitude that heterosexuality is the only normal and natural expression of sexuality." Heteronormativity is more than just someone identifying as "straight"—it's the assumption that the only way people should be attracted to one another is girls and boys, women and men. It rejects the idea that being gay or gender nonconforming are appropriate ways to live.

As Jess created more critical-thinking opportunities and identity-affirming spaces for her students, teaching life became harder and more uncomfortable for her. Emails from parents and caregivers demanded the removal of the books featuring Queer characters, and their body language and tone of their voices became abrasive when they communicated with her. What is evidenced from many bodies of research as supporting joyful curiosity, growing inquisitive minds, and affirming positive school experiences became a radical act.

When working to ensure an accurate representation of humanity was provided to children in her classroom rather than a simple part of teaching, families and colleagues challenged her work. To enact justice, if more people from the dominant culture *also worked* to represent humanity just as hard as this teacher in their classrooms, the outcomes from this experience could have been different.

During the panel presentation, Jess spoke about the frustration that often works in tandem with enacting social justice in the classroom. Her primary frustration: working through the lens of justice was lonely. She was one of the few teachers in her school community who was committed to providing a robust and socially just curriculum to students. An audience member, a person who represents almost 80% of teachers in the United States, asked, "As a straight white woman, what can I do to support you? To make social justice work more comfortable for people in my school community who live outside dominant culture?"

Jess replied:

> Feature texts and people in your curriculum outside of your comfort zone. Work with people in your community who are already committed, listen to them, and practice opening up possibilities for more just spaces in your community. Make planning and exploring texts part of your department meeting agendas. And then make it a regular part of your teaching practice so I don't have to be the only one affirming the existence of Queer people and BIPOC people in the classroom space. As a Queer woman working in a heteronormative space, it's a lot of water to carry.

Her testimony was powerful, and I wasn't the only person in the audience taking it in. When we fail to look outside our own perspectives, when we just embrace the fairytale of neutrality, we leave students, colleagues, and families in the shadows—unseen, dehumanized, and erased.

We become agents of change when we choose to unlearn neutral habits and dare ourselves to feel, on a deep level, the injustices experienced by others on a daily basis. This empathy—paired with recognition, thoughtfulness, and action—is the catalyst for change that moves communities toward justice. Individuals make up those communities, and those communities drive change.

In short, communities are groups of individuals who have the ability to create joy and justice, and there is great power in that momentum.

Teaching Fiercely: Spreading Joy and Justice in Our Schools

Identifying Layers of Perspective

Identifying layers of perspective requires us to engage with one another through sharing, digesting, and actively listening to one another's stories. Not just reading research papers or articles on "best practices," but listening to *stories*. I'm going to begin this storytelling with a walk back in time, offering a snapshot of my first year of classroom teaching under the magnifying glass that was instrumental for building my own lenses. This allowed me to start unpacking layers of perspective and injustice from a very early point in my career.

Earlier, I talked about the blue school chair, and how it is symbolic of varying points of view. Let's dig deeper and consider how competing points of view on something like a chair represent deeper problems within a school community.

Storytime

There are times in a classroom where if you spend a moment too long thinking about what to do next, kids get hurt. This is a story about one of those times.

My spry self entered the teaching force at the tender age of 23. As a transplant in New York City, my experience in urban life equated to two years previously spent working in Chicago. While my energy and resilience was strong, my "knowing how to teach" was not. I was a New York City Teaching Fellow hired as a special educator to teach in a "high-need" secondary school[3] near downtown Brooklyn.

My teaching assignment included working with multiple integrated co-teaching classes[4] in ninth and tenth grade, as well as teaching science to all four grades in the high school's self-contained special education classes. At 19 and 20 years old, some of the students I taught were nearly the same age as me. It was an interesting year in my classroom teaching life; in tandem with deep self-learning began the continuous discovery on how school is designed powerfully for some—and as an afterthought for others.

---

3   Secondary schools in New York City often refer to schools comprised of grades 6 through 12.

4   Integrated Co-Teaching is a service model for students with IEPs that is comprised of two teachers working in collaboration to provide accessible teaching and learning experiencing within a variety of co-teaching models and smaller groups of learners within a shared classroom space.

A note on "high-need" schools: "high need" is nomenclature often paired with schools that are segregated, located in proximity to low-income housing, and comprised of primarily BIPOC students. I put the term in quotation marks because, while schools identified as "high need" are usually in need of a great amount of resources, there are also many schools—often well resourced, more affluent, and more white—that are also "high need." Albeit the latter's needs are different: those school communities are usually in high need of social justice development and shifting community mindsets toward more equitable belief systems.

Sometime in the late Fall of that school year, November I think, I witnessed an event in my classroom that illuminated my perspective on school systems even further. In that learning, my understanding about the perception of the community surrounding school regarding mental health services, students with named disabilities, and special education deepened.

Here's a five-minute snapshot of that experience.

Circa Fall 2006

It's my lunch hour and I am debriefing with the Field Experience Supervisor from Brooklyn College, an older, seasoned teacher in his 60s: white, male, and dually licensed for special and general education. As he affirms my lesson objective and schedules his next visit, two students from my eleventh and twelfth grade self-contained science class charge into the classroom I share with the math teacher.

The lunch period is just ending, and students begin to reclaim the quietness of the tranquil hallway atmosphere. While elements of chaos post-lunch are typical within high school spaces, this chaos was different. The two students who appeared before us—Delia and Tremaine[5]—having escaped the cafeteria early, were doused with ketchup and other condiments. Their audible presence and ripe notes of McDonald's permeated the space, while the echoes of their peers wafted from the far ends of the hallways.

My bones tingle; I spring out of my blue chair—something was off, something was wrong, something was about to go down, fast. All my body alarms initiate as

---

5   Pseudonyms to protect privacy.

Teaching Fiercely: Spreading Joy and Justice in Our Schools

Delia, one of the oldest students in the class, wearing her freshly stained ketchup shirt, screams at her classmate, Tremaine, who had just transitioned to the class from a different school. She screams an expletive, Tremaine shouts back, tears in his eyes. Seasoned Field Experience Mentor gets up and removes himself from the main space of the classroom, grabs his bag, and stands frozen to the wall, hugging his clipboard.

It's easy to say that altercations function in binaries—that there is perpetrator and there is victim. But this experience is different: both kids are in turmoil.

Internally, Delia is in her biological fight mode. Tremaine is in biological fight mode. Both are visibly shaking, yelling, and audibly breathing.

Erstwhile, in the backdrop of this moment: if you've ever been in a hallway of a high school during passing period, you'll know that each teacher is doing their best at ushering kids into their classrooms, and risk mayhem in their own spaces if they leave their posts. And you also know that anytime you feel tension or hear tension between two different parties, it's an absolute magnet for masses of kids to come and watch the pending fight.

It's my instinct and my teacher peers' experience that are able to protect the young people in these moments. At a mere eight weeks into the profession, I know enough to not let other students enter this classroom. I shut the door. I know enough, in this moment, that protecting Delia and Tremaine from harm is the most important thing in my life. And I know enough that what I'm witnessing from Delia, by the look in her eyes, the pulsing in her words, the heaviness in her breath, is her body announcing a loss of control, and a fight for her survival.

About 30 to 45 seconds after Delia and Tremaine entered the room with just me and Field Supervisor present, Delia flips over a table, Delia throws a blue chair. The table hits the floor, *THUDD!* The chair screams louder against the wall, *screeASHHH!* No one is hit or hurt, physically. I keep moving, reacting, solving.

Through the masses of students congregating in the hall right outside the door, I'm able to usher Tremaine out of the room without any physical harm. He's shaking, and luckily Maria,[6] the paraprofessional across the hall, receives

---

6   Pseudonym to protect privacy.

him in her arms. Demetria,[7] the teacher across the hall who is Delia's closest connection in the school, enters the classroom. Now it's me, Demetria, Field Supervisor, and Delia breathing in the potent air of what will happen next. Demetria signals for me and Field Supervisor to exit, and we do.

Field Supervisor tells me I didn't follow protocol, that I should have called the police. That it is my obligation to call the police when students demonstrate this kind of physical violence. That my school needs to file a report, and that I need to improve my de-escalation strategies. I nod, turn on my heel, and move quickly. Within the next minute, advisory starts. I shepherd the mass of my students into the classroom across the hall and start attempting to teach some semblance of advisory.

My heart leaves the lesson, my left eye focuses on the door; I viscerally feel Delia's pain.

Field Supervisor exits.

Somehow, someway, Demetria is able to calm Delia. Delia leaves school early.

And . . . scene.

Tools for Perspective Analysis: More than a Decade Later

When I reflect upon those moments in time, it isn't the seismic activity of the chair being tossed, or even the students' responses to the incident that are most salient to me. Rather, what is most memorable for me is the ocean of pain I saw in Delia's eyes as the chair got tossed, and the terror in Tremaine's eyes as he witnessed his peer lose control. And my Field Supervisor's response: that I should have called the police.

Here, I'll introduce an analysis tool to uncover the layers of perspective, why they matter, and *what the heck* the chair has to do with our perceived realities.

In teacher preparation programs, there is always a course or two on childhood development, and a psychology course is a prerequisite for all college degrees. However, no matter the books you have read or the analyses you've

---

7   Pseudonym to protect privacy.

written, there isn't a whole lot of print-based literacy that will prepare you for witnessing the kind of pain students experience when they throw classroom furniture.

When I witnessed classroom furniture being thrown, I was working under a "Transitional B Teaching License," which allows teacher candidates to teach kids *while* they are still learning how to teach in a grad school program. Symptomatically, those programs produce many teachers who are ill-equipped to de-escalate behavior or to support kids and their specific dis/abilities. At the time, I was one of those teachers. However, what I lacked in experience I made up for with instinct, with empathy, and, most of all—with practice and commitment.

Reader, to follow are some pertinent details I left out.

First, both Tremaine and Delia were Black, Afro-Caribbean teenagers who had varying degrees of humor in their personalities. Delia loved to shop with her friends. She'd break out into "Chicken Noodle Soup" dance at random intervals throughout the school day. She had deep affinity for a few teach-ers, and was generally participative during class conversations. Tremaine had jokes of all kinds, and wrote long stories featuring various fantastical char-acters. He was new to the school, and didn't have many classmates who he called his friends.

Also: in Brooklyn's public schools, both Tremaine and Delia had been par-ticipating in special classes (one of the most restrictive special education environments in community schools) from the time of their elementary school lives. Both had classified disabilities, and very thick Individual Edu-cation Plans (IEPs). At a young age, Delia had been diagnosed with bipolar disorder, and Tremaine had been diagnosed with autism. They each lived in nearby public housing projects. Some days, Delia slept for hours with her head on her desk. Other days, she would come into class shouting at no one in particular. Her oral literacy skills were strong, her print-based literacy weaker. At times, her working memory challenged her. Tremaine spoke in the same loud, high-pitched tone for all forms of interactions. He often was not aware of his body in concert with his surroundings, and bumped into people, furniture, and walls easily. His stamina for literacy was strong—however, his ideas and focus often meandered.

This, readers, is where perspective comes in. If I were to extract the story of Delia and Tremaine and place it in a news report or social media feed outside the context of this chapter, the perception of what happened—and, more importantly, *why* it happened—would differ.

Let's think about various ways this story could surface and be told:

- Local media news report: "Underfunded School Fuels Classroom Brawl"

- National news report: "Urban Schools' Special Education Programs Disaster"

- Social media EduTwitter: "What is this WYTE Teacher Doing?!"

- School yard banter between students: "Delia was Lit!" "Yeah, but what about that other kid?" "Who?!" "I don't know his name, but he was crying like a b**CH!"

- Text exchange between parents: "Did you hear what happened in that new teacher's class? I hope my child never gets her!"

Moreover, if I were to attach to the story a *picture* of Delia and Tremaine and the post-furniture-flipped classroom, the story of perpetrator and victim gets louder. The perception of Black youth; new, white teachers; urban schools; and their relationship to one another is underscored by whatever stereotypes different groups of people have about those players. At first glance, nobody knows about the state of anyone's mental health or experiences. People create stories not about truth but about perceived reality based on their own experiences and exposure to the players in the event.

This is an opportune time to note that posting pictures of students and their classroom environments is a violation of students' rights according to FERPA, the Family Education Rights and Protection Act. (Unless they have signed media consent from legal guardians . . . and even still . . . media consent usually has a clause that would forbid the posting of an incident like this.) Typically, newspapers and magazines have less access to the inside of classroom walls, but the proliferation of technology and phones as documentation tools has surfaced lots of classroom happenings, especially on personal social media feeds. Conversely, the use of documented events in classrooms from the student perspective have also been used to film teachers to capture both harmful events and banal happenings. While adults also are entitled to privacy in learning spaces, the need for students to protect themselves from curricular violence warrants the use of documentation, even if their privacy is infringed upon.

There are so many different factors that impact perspective around high-tension events like the one I described. And oftentimes in school, space for reflection and careful attention to not just safety, but health and well-being, are overlooked.

Careful consideration of various perspectives is often the thing that makes the most difference for how people, especially youth, experience school. The imprint of people's pasts impacts their reactions during these kinds of "in the moment" events—as do the more intentional choices educators make when they *do* have longer periods of time to consider how to be and act in school. Building our perspective by viewing events through multiple lenses equips us to more powerfully parcel out truth and justice.

Work Along: The Choosing Change Tool

Analyzing perspective requires us to spend some time thinking about each *player* in this event. Players don't necessarily have to be people or active participants. Players are any persons, artifacts, roles, or institutions that are present during events and experiences.

Players can be obvious or hidden. No matter how players are presented, it's important for us to exercise our sight over time with lots of practice. This builds muscles that help along peoples' ability to identify and unpack multiple perspectives, working toward justice more closely.

After analyzing multiple perspectives, the choices you make for change will be more informed and strategic, allowing for positive outcomes to coalesce sustainably.

Here, we'll practice doing this work with the Choosing Change Tool. Below, I've used the event described earlier as an example to pair with steps in the process of using the tool.

Part I: Identifying Multiple Players in the Event

1. Identify the human players.

   Who are the people directly and/or indirectly involved? Begin by naming people who were present.

(Continued)

In the story I shared, the present humans included are:

Students	Teachers/School Staff
Tremaine	Ms. Kass
Delia	Ms. Demetria
Kids in hallway	Field supervisor
	Ms. Maria

Naming present people is the most simplistic component of this perspective analysis. The more nuanced parts include naming what can't necessarily be seen, including people who weren't physically present but who still impacted the in-the-moment perceived reality.

Hidden people:

Families, including:
- Tremaine's
- Delia's
- Their peers'

School leaders:
- Principal
- Dean
- Assistant principal

2. Identify environmental players.

Environmental players, such as classroom spaces, hallways, furniture, school yards, etc., don't necessarily have a perspective of their own as they are not living things. However, where the event happens and in what circumstances it happens impacts the perspectives of human players. For example, if physical aggression happens at a school yard in an outdoor environment, one perspective of human players is that kids are naturally more inclined to be physical during recess. A classroom teacher is less likely to be impacted, or "at fault," because they were probably on their lunch. And yet, though teachers usually aren't considered responsible for academic learning at recess, there are deep judgments around teachers who are not able to prevent physical aggression in their classrooms. Where the event happens and in what circumstances it happens impacts the perspectives of human players.

Environmental players:

- Classroom furniture

- Hallway energy

- Cafeteria energy

- School lunch food

3. Identify systemic players.

Systemic players are institutions, stigmas, and cultural aspects that impact the perspective of human players. This part is harder, and often impacts perspective most deeply. It's difficult because these entities are more like particles in the air you breathe at a school; omnipresent and unavoidable.

Systemic players:

- Housing segregation
- Disproportionate special education referrals.
- Mental health services.
- Teacher preparation program.
- Behavior codes and referral systems for youth in public schools.
- Anti-Black racism
- Tax laws and school funding.

It can be overwhelming to notice and identify all of the different players at work in events like chairs being thrown in classrooms. However, it's important to understand that events live within systems, and that we have power—both individually and collectively—to change those systems. Especially the way in which those systems impact the youth we serve.

After you've done your best to name the multiple players at work in the event or ongoing problem, it's time to unpack their perspective. This process of writing down the perspectives of each entity or person isn't meant to be cumbersome or riddled with paperwork. Rather, it's meant to be a thought-provoking exercise that ensures folx are doing their best to build empathy for students, their families, and each other. It's meant to complicate situations that are otherwise painted along either/or binaries, such as why the event or problem occurred or how each party is feeling.

It's understandable that some might feel overwhelmed about a situation after all the different players are named and once all the different systems at work have been surfaced. However, there is also clarity in identifying all the complexity. Abby Covert, professional Information Architect, helps people and organizations make sense out of "messes" such as the ones that may surface by a group of people engaging in perspective analysis. To move from a space of shared understanding, she suggests, quite literally, for people to create pictures of what's going on in their heads. From there, people compare their pictures with one another, and then the group creates an image that conveys shared understanding of the situation. It's important to note that the artistic quality of these pictures is not important. Covert says, "These pictures are not pretty pictures to be presented or sold to others. The intention of these pictures is to change, so don't be protective of them. These pictures are not of solutions or interfaces. They are pictures of problems and complexities to sort out." Ultimately, developing pictures helps along the process of perspective taking because ideas that formerly lived inside people's heads are now common knowledge.[8]

(Continued)

---

8   Note that sharing mental models visually can be used in many different teaching and learning contexts, especially with young learners in classroom spaces.

We're able to initiate change when we can develop a specific focus on a particular event or an ongoing problem, and Abby Covert's visualization process of individual and group mental models helps this process. Before we move on to the second part of the perspective analysis, identify two to three players within an event or ongoing problem that make the most sense for *you* to prioritize.

For me, it made the most sense to focus on myself, Delia, classroom furniture, Tremaine's and Delia's families, and anti-Black racism.

As I chose which players to focus on, I considered the following: *Which players have the greatest impact on the overall well-being of the classroom space?*

Delia's energy was profound. When she had a tough day, it was really hard to help her and the rest of the students in my class. Tremaine was more independent and he was able to generally participate without major shifts in his behavior. I knew by concentrating on Delia's mental health and environmental needs, I would be able to improve both her and her classmates' experiences.

I also chose to focus on myself. Similar to the adult putting on an oxygen mask on an airplane before assisting others, as a novice teacher it was absolutely necessary I consider the energy, knowledge, and skills—especially in terms of de-escalation strategies—I had available to change the course of the students' experiences.

Next, I asked myself: *What environmental players are within my sphere of influence to create change?*

The first time I did this analysis, I chose "cafeteria energy." I knew that what happens during the outside spaces of a classroom affect what happens inside the classroom space on a very deep level. Chaotic hallway energy, cafeteria energy, schoolyard energy, morning-walk-to-school energy—all are deeply infectious. However, as a newer teacher who was still learning the ropes of my curriculum, I didn't have the energy or social capital to develop new systems for hallway order or cafeteria communication. So, I chose to focus on what I could control, what I would encounter for the most minutes of every day—and that was what was in my classroom space: the furniture. Given my energy and social capital, eliminating unnecessary chairs, creating more spacious walkways and alternate, soft, and separate areas for students to hang out in was absolutely something I could create within my sphere of influence.

Other, more experienced teachers or those with different roles could choose to focus on a different environmental player. Maybe "lunch duty" is part of a person's teaching schedule. If that's the case, cafeteria energy *does* makes sense to focus on.

My next consideration: *Which systemic players are most directly implicated in the ongoing problem or specific event?*

This is a tough question to consider. For starters, *all* those systems are major contributors to ongoing problems connected to youth in crisis at schools. And so, it's necessary to view the situation through an intersectional lens. Audre Lorde once said, "There is no such thing as a single-issue struggle because we do not live single-issue lives" (1982). Housing segregation, mental health services, and anti-Black racism matter a lot in many instances in school, including ones where students throw furniture in a classroom while screaming at one another. I am not letting go of the larger issues at play when I choose which systemic player to focus on, but I *am* considering the most *strategic players* given my sphere of influence and my role.

Both Tremaine and Delia are Black students who, as I described earlier, are recipients of systems (school, healthcare, housing, taxation) that have neither worked nor been designed in their best interests. From mental health services to special education services, from housing availability and tax laws, anti-Black racism has been a present force in their lives. I know that I alone cannot solve anti-Black racism, but I do know that this is what all those systemic players share. For that reason, anti-Black racism is the systemic player I chose to focus on.

What is anti-Black racism? How is it different than plain old racism?

It's important to understand the difference between *racism* and *anti-Black racism*.

The term *racism* refers to the belief that race is the most important factor in determining human traits and characteristics, and that some races produce traits and characteristics that are superior to others (Merriam-Webster). The construct of race and racism was birthed from the field of eugenics in the late 1900s in response to white Europeans' and white Americans' perceived threat of immigrants and African Americans who were moving from the countryside to more industrialized urban centers to seek economic opportunity. Essentially, competition for jobs increased for white people, and they sought to blame "society's ills" on "the other" (Facing History and Ourselves n.d.).

Facing History and Ourselves describes lead eugenicist of the times, Frances Galton, below:

> Francis Galton, an English mathematician and Charles Darwin's cousin, offered an attractive solution to those who believed that these groups posed a threat. Galton decided that natural selection does not work in human societies the way it does in nature, because people interfere with the process. As a result, the fittest do not always survive. So he set out to consciously "improve the race." He coined the word eugenics to describe efforts at "race betterment" [or "the cultivation of race"] (Galton 1883, p. 17).

It's important to note that racist ideology existed long before the eugenicists started defining and naming racist constructs through their "scientific" lens. Racist ideology precedes the shared understanding and

(*Continued*)

common use of the term *racism*. Enslavement, sorting people by skin tone, and justifying maltreatment of people who were not white through religious texts happened long before the term was coined.

Galton and other Eugenicists played a major role in promoting racist constructs, especially white superiority, through the written word, publishing harmful "science reports" about "white superiority" in renowned journals such as *Nature*. There is far more to unpack regarding the construct of race and racism, the legacy of white supremacy, and the ugliness its roots have spread throughout time. We'll certainly continue this discussion, but for now, to discover more at this juncture, visit the Resource Library on the Facing History and Ourselves website. Specifically, the "Race and Membership in American History: The Eugenics Movement" curriculum.

To sum up, the term "racism" is used to describe ideologies, events, circumstances, experiences, artifacts, texts, policies, etc., that position the white race and aspects of whiteness as superior, and other races and aspects of other races as inferior.

Now comes the distinction between racism and anti-Black racism. In the words of Professor Tyrone C. Howard:

> Anti-Black racism challenges the idea that there is a one-size-fits-all approach to tackling racism. Yes, racism affects all people of color in a multitude of ways, and Black people are part of that vociferous and untangled web. But anti-Black racism speaks to the specific ways in which Black people are seen, targeted, dehumanized, and often killed in a manner that is unlike any other group of people in the United States (2020, p. 1).

The primary difference between racism and anti-Black racism is that instead of "other races" and "aspects of other races" being seen as inferior, anti-Black racism recognizes, with precision, that Black people and Blackness are treated with inferiority to not just white people and whiteness, but to other racial groups as well.

If we prioritize everything, we prioritize nothing.
—Cornelius Minor

It will be hard to choose which players to focus on when trying to analyze perspective and figure out where our sphere of influence lives within change-making. As educators, there is a great desire to make all the things better, all at once. While it may feel incomplete to prioritize one area of focus over another, it is essential we move with strategy and intention.

Part II: Choosing Change

The next part of our work is to thoughtfully and intentionally unpack our individual and collective roles. Then, we strategically place ourselves in close proximity to places within systems where our sphere of influence is most powerful in both preventing harm and promoting healing for young people.

1. **Describe your role, and the responsibility that comes along with it.** The role of educator is ever-evolving. Teachers, principals, paraprofessionals, guidance counselors, and countless other school staff all play an important part in kids' lives as they experience school. But who are you in that role, and what are you there for?

   There is power in naming your role and responsibilities and redefining them through the lens of justice. The imprecision in self-described roles makes changing outcomes for kids murky—i.e., people aren't sure what they're supposed to do or if *x, y,* or *z* is within their "job description," so they don't act. However, if they don't act, positive outcomes are limited. Instead, systems will continue to produce the same results they always have.

   Here's an example of me describing my role and responsibilities as the teacher, one of the players in the event.

   Present Player: Ms. Kass, Teacher

   Role: Provide a safe, engaging, and developmentally appropriate learning environment for students that is supportive in both their personal and academic growth.

   Responsibilities:

   - Assess students' personal and academic needs.
   - Create a learning environment conducive to the variety of students' social, emotional, and academic needs in multiple classes.
   - Develop and/or revise curriculum and instruction within students' zone of proximal development with multiple entry points.
   - Communicate regularly with students' families to discuss growth, potential areas for home-to-school partnering, challenges, and successes.

   Regularly collaborate with different parts of the school ecosystem—including colleagues, school leaders, and other school staff—to ensure the well-being of the student body.

2. **Place Self**

   The next part of the Perspective Analysis is to place yourself as an individual within the context of the various players. Essentially, you're trying to figure out where to best place yourself within the institution of school to prevent harm from happening to the students you teach.

(Continued)

I'm not suggesting you turn this analysis into a dissertation or a thesis for grad school. Understanding how each one of these players functions in the event of two kids, a teacher, and a hurled chair is an intensive endeavor, requiring deep self-excavation, cross-cultural listening, and multilayered research. However, it's imperative that folx involved in educating youth at the very least *consider* how these players' perspectives have the power to change outcomes for youth involved, and that those outcomes are, at worst, woefully tragic—we're talking prison pipeline, substance abuse, death. But, at best, restoration is possible—the road toward well-being, bolstered with emotional and academic confidence in tandem.

When schools talk and think about events like the thrown chair, oftentimes the communal conversations will be couched in the details that are most quantifiable from a socially scientific perspective. Meaning, what can be categorized and what can be official are the things that get talked about: race, disability, medical condition, reading levels. Official behavior codes to name when documenting the event. Subsequent consequences pending on determined behavior codes.

What often gets lost are the most important considerations: the well-being of individuals, how to partner with kids' at-home support systems, and perhaps, most urgently: how to prevent and/or reduce harm from happening to the greatest extent possible.

Timeline Pedagogy: To Move Forward, We Must Look Back

Hourglass.

To find and create the future goodness of school, we're going to have to revisit *school* in both past and present iterations and, especially, your relationship to it. This journey requires reflecting upon *your* experiences in school along the way . . . as well as the ancestors' experiences (whether they be your ancestors or someone else's). Together, we'll navigate historical narratives about public school within the United States, starting with its inception. Essentially, we are traversing the *stories of us*.

Whether or not your engagement is done individually or communally, the goal is to surface both convergence and interference across historical, ancestral, and personal timelines in order to develop a more sophisticated, nuanced perspective on how teaching, learning, school, and education manifests in present circumstances.

This part is integral for developing deeper conviction around one's teaching philosophy. While I'm talking about how my own teaching philosophy developed through both personal experience and historical reflection, you, reader, will have an opportunity to create a parallel trajectory that supports your understanding of how your own philosophies show up by developing a more robust shaping and naming of your learning and teaching identities.

Timeline Pedagogy

Timeline, as a pedagogy, differs from how it is typically conceptualized in school. In the context of school, timelines are most widely utilized as an instructional strategy to chart events across time. For example, in a social studies classroom, a teacher and her students might include a timeline of events that led up to the American Revolution. As the teacher and her class continue to delve into different areas of American History, the timeline continues, and different events are added. Usually, the timeline is displayed for the class to see in a prominent spot within the learning space, and learners refer to the timeline as they discuss social studies to make sense of concepts like cause and effect; beginning, middle, and end; and/or to develop a stronger sense of time passing (How long is a decade? How significant is one hundred years? etc.). Strategically, it makes sense to use timelines as a learning tool in those ways.

Timeline pedagogy refers to charting our shared experiences in school, both personally and publicly, along the backdrop of time. As part of our pursuit toward justice, the exploration of the past and present seeks truth—and with finding truth comes joy. As self-discovery and truth are surfaced throughout the landscape of time, people, especially teachers, develop more agency.

Personal Reflections on Early Schooling: Why Reflecting on the Past Is So Important

When I reflect upon the years I spent as a classroom teacher, I hear the forever-old refrains "In the real world . . ." or "When you get to college . . ." echoing from my lips, echoing way too often with a sense of urgency that failed to honor the present, and the fumes of history's aftermath. For me, and for many people I've worked with in school communities, the past has been separated from ourselves. In school, the focus lies within students' and teachers' *nows* and *futures,* only paying slight homage to our pasts, and especially *the* past. We are often hyperbolically aware of our young people's *futures* when we curate their educations in the various roles we play, whether it be principal or teacher or caregiver.

In schools, the past is distributed in sprinkles, usually in the shape of a social studies or history class. In fact, many people are taught *not* to "dwell on the past." This makes the "now" a confusing, *ahistoric*[9] space. Forgetting about the past and whatever role you and your ancestors played works in the same way: without digging into it, acknowledging what happened, and how we are connected to those happenings, how will it ever be possible to grow a better version of our present?

When I use the term *ahistoric* I'm talking about the ways in which people and/or institutions are positioned without considering how history, that is, the *factual* past, impacts various facets of life. For example, when one applies a more historical perspective when considering the progress of students with special needs in community schools, it's important to think about the implementation of the Individuals with Disabilities Education Act (IDEA) in 1975, essentially, the United States' "special education law."

It wasn't until the 1970s that students with developmental disabilities, autism, and other special needs were provided with a free and appropriate education from public schools. For an entire century, they were excluded from public schooling, categorized as "other," and segregated from their peers in different locations that were usually scant in programming and underfunded (Lee, n.d.).

Perhaps you are thinking this is an extreme example . . . maybe you are saying to yourself, *Kass, why did you go there*? I went there because since I have been working in the field of public education, I have witnessed parents and caregivers insist that their child be placed in "any class but the ICT class," and I have heard educators insist that kids with varying disability classifications on their IEPs "belong in a different setting."

This is the same line of thinking that was present pre-1970s, this idea that people with neurodivergence should be separated from other children, and learn in a different location. Even when over 30 years of research shows that everyone benefits from inclusion models,

---

9   A space with no history.

many people still back away from learning spaces that challenge their traditional notions of academic opportunity. Moreover, those same people who insist their child be sorted into a gifted and talented space, or learning space that doesn't have children with IEPs, are running diversity and inclusion book clubs in their school communities.

To demand what one thinks is fair without considering history, in this case, histories of exclusion and othering in the field of special education and the dis/ability community, is a prime example of how ahistoricism impacts the types of educational experiences children have access to.

To plough forward in time with such a sharp focus on the future denies both students and teachers rich allowances for a more humanizing education. We have to walk away from this idea that meritocracy works in schools, and that it's all right to move about on the paths we walk in school *ahistorically.*

The past is our teacher, and too often, she is ignored. Rather than neglecting her impact, we will instead treat the past as we would treat any teacher who holds important stories for us to learn from: with respect, with deep listening, with active participation, and with acknowledgement.

To understand where we are going as teachers, we must thoroughly understand where the school systems we work in have been, and how our roles as teacher and learner have evolved. There's a branch of this understanding that comes from personal excavation, digging into our ancestral past through our individual histories. Yolanda Sealy-Ruiz names this Archaeology of the Self. Sealy-Ruiz describes this process as "an action-oriented process requiring love, humility, reflection, an understanding of history, and a commitment to working against racial injustice."

While the excavation Sealy-Ruiz describes is multifaceted and requires a broad span of awareness, in the Historical Underpinnings portions of this book (available online), we primarily focus our work through the lens of histories, especially those that are oriented in education.

School is one of the few institutions that most people have experienced in one way or another as *students,* and for many reading this book, as *student* and *teacher*. Some folx also experience school through the additional layer of *caregiver.* In this section we ask: What happens when we connect our individual school histories to the larger collective we all work in?

Before we start our historical exploration of school as a stand-alone entity, let's first dabble in our personal histories to explore the types of relationships we've had in our own schooling—with ourselves, and with others.

Reflection: Your Early Years in School

Dictate, journal, sketch, or convey a few memories from your early years in school, perhaps guided by the following prompts. (Try to include something regarding your friends' experiences.)

- Where was your school geographically located?

- Are your memories of early schooling mostly positive or negative?

- In your classroom community did you feel mostly included or excluded?

- What do you recall about some of your friends' experiences who shared similar identity markers to yours? What about your friends' and/or peers who didn't share many of your identity markers, or who were a part of different racial and/or ethnic groups than yours?

- Have you witnessed similar happenings in the school communities you are currently connected to?

Here's mine.

Kass's Early Years in School Reflection

1987.

I'm at Randall Elementary school, near Scott Air Force Base in Belleville, Illinois, a suburb of St. Louis, Missouri. I'm one of the few kids who attends the school whose family is in the military. Since we live off base, I don't go to the school located on base, where all the other military brats go. In the morning, I wait at the end of the driveway with my big brother, Shaun, for the bus to come. My mom waves goodbye to us. My dad is already at work. My teacher has short dark hair and her last name begins with a Y.

Like me, many of my classmates are white, with peachy, Play-Doh-like skin. We haven't quite begun to sort ourselves according to phenotype. I sit next to Tiana,[10] one of the few Black children in our kindergarten cohort. From her, I learn about Jheri curl hairstyles.

---

10   Pseudonym to protect privacy.

One day I put Vaseline in my hair and my sister looks at me sideways. My teacher holds a drawing contest in our class—she announces she is getting married, and would like for us to submit a picture for her wedding program! Only one drawing would be picked. I painstakingly capture my best version of "man and wife" with a thick black crayon, submit it earnestly, and am surprised and proud when it is announced that I, Kassie Crockett, am the winner!

For me, kindergarten peaks at that moment. The other moments I remember about kindergarten are pretty banal: The minty paste that came with the little white plastic stick that my friend Oliver and I secretly tasted and compared notes on, when my teacher quizzed me on my phone number and I failed, not because I didn't know my phone number, but because she had the incorrect one. This boy Ryan who used to chase me on the playground and yell "I'm going to kiss you on the back of your sweater!" The horror I felt when he called me at home (I had given my phone number that day in recess in exchange for an agreement not to chase me), that same horror reflected on my mother's face.

What strikes me most as I remember my kindergarten year is how ambivalent I feel toward most of it. Nothing incredibly remarkable happened, and it is precisely this ambivalence my mind and body feels that is presently alarming. The absence of body alarms,[11] in this reflection of my first year of school, is common place for many white people who grow up in working or middle class America who share my identity markers: white, able-bodied, cisgender, working class, English-speaking, two-parent hetero-married family.

School, quite literally, was written and created for people like me.

Unpacking Memory: What Our Reflections Reveal About School and Its Impact on People

Did you answer that last question about your friends' experiences in school? I included that because it's important to realize that others may have had entirely different experiences because of their *identity markers*, that is, their cultural, physical, and/or family representation.

As I unpack my memory from the lens of my more experienced, adult, educator self, I realize how much young children outside dominant culture endure, even in the early 2000s, of their existence in school. When I witness similar happenings in schools I've worked in over the years as a classroom

---

11   Tommy Woon describes the phenomenon as the body's autonomic-involuntary nervous system—a protective response as warning system to perceived threats.

teacher, and more recently as a coach and community organizer, my empathy deepens as I attempt to name and understand what my peers' early years in schools might have been like—and even consider what their lives might be like now.

For example, how did my friend Tiana experience that same kindergarten class? Unfortunately, research has shown that Black children's experiences in predominantly white schools is not positive. From the time Black children enter school, they are disproportionately represented in discipline, punishment, and special education referrals. Monique Morris's seminal text *Pushout*[12] reveals some jarring statistics:

Black girls represent 16% of girls in schools, and also represent 42% of girls receiving corporal punishment, 42% of girls expelled with or without educational services, 45% of girls with at least one out-of-school suspension, 31% of girls referred to law enforcement, and 34% of girls arrested in schools.

Based on those statistics, there is great probability that Tiana would have experienced high levels of stress and lateral trauma, even in her early years of schooling.

I also wonder what Oliver,[13] my paste-eating accomplice, whose family were first-generation Japanese immigrants, would say about his first year in American public school. Was he cool with the culture of English-only in our classroom space? Would he and his family have preferred a translanguaging experience, where he got to show us all the beautiful parts of his home language too?

Legislation from the 1980s shows that Oscar's family had little choice in the matter. A few short weeks after Ronald Reagan became president of the United States, he was asked about his thoughts on bilingual education policy. In response he stated: "It is absolutely wrong and against American concepts to have a bilingual-education program that is now openly, admittedly

---

12   *Pushout: The Criminalization of Black Girls in Schools* by Monique Morris should be required reading, especially for those who have begun to work toward actualizing #BlackLivesMatter. In it, you'll find arresting statistics about Black girls, and the very real consequences of white supremacy upheld within disciplinary policies.

13   Pseudonym to protect privacy.

dedicated to preserving native language and never getting adequate in English."[14]

Even when policies like Title VII, The Bilingual Education Act, are created to benefit and promote bilingual education, when it's misunderstood by decision makers, children from bilingual families suffer. If a child's home language is never represented in their schooling, they become more accustomed to speaking English. While their children are exposed to and taught English, caregivers usually are not, resulting in communication gaps between children and their caregivers that live across generations.

Few opportunities to enroll in bilingual education programs existed during the Reagan era, and ESL programs frequently existed in name only, meaning that many schools labeled children in need of ESL[15] services, but did not administer appropriate instructional opportunities for their English language development, nor did they work to preserve students' first languages.

A few years into Reagan's presidency, his team encouraged the use of alternative methods of instruction in preference to bilingual education because his Educational Review team reviewed a body of research and determined "the case for the effectiveness of transitional bilingual education is weak." Debates about bilingual education and translingual education continue, fraught with arguments over the role of patriotism and Americanization in the classroom to this day. In Chapter 5, we'll explore how pairing quantitative data with qualitative data provides a more robust, holistic picture of how bilingual education policy and implementation has impacted kids, families, and teachers in schools today. Huge swaths of evidence show that when students' native language is honored, appreciated, and taught within school systems, *all* kids benefit.

And what about Ryan, the white boy in my class who chased me around the playground . . . did anybody ever check him for his behavior? Did he grow up feeling entitled to telling girls what to do with themselves, with their bodies? Did school offer a place for him to work out his white male privilege? When he showed his emotions, especially sad ones, was he quieted and told to "man up"?

---

14   President Ronald Reagan said this statement in response to his team's policy monitoring of Title VII, The Bilingual Education Act.

15   ESL is the acronym for English as a Second Language.

It's not so simple though, right? It's the subtleties of toxic masculinity that plague almost every orifice of the ground we walk on that Ryan probably has never thought to reckon with, because it's simply not talked about enough, if at all, within classroom spaces or even family dinner tables. As I write this, it is horrifying to think that at the young age of five, I experienced my first, among many, #MeToo[16] moment.

We also can draw many conclusions about what kind of instruction, social-emotional learning, and classroom community a kid like Ryan was exposed to based on the gender pay gap. When I was in kindergarten, that gap was stark: according to the Economic Policy Institute, in 1987 women were paid just $0.69 to a man's $1.00. Today, the ratio has increased from $0.69 to $0.89 (Gould, Schieder, and Geier 2016). Those figures compare wages for comparable work. How society views the value of men over women is reflected in how much employers choose to pay each group.

Also, I can't help but think about the child in my class who didn't see a reflection of their own family, or themselves, in the drawing contest, where marriage and love happened between a man and a woman. Collections of U.S. Census data indicate a high probability that kids from one-caregiver households were certainly present—records indicate that in the 1980s between 19 and 24% of children in the United States lived in single-caregiver households (U.S. Census Bureau 2022). Although there is no known raw data representing accurate counts of the number of children identifying as Queer in school, U.S. Census data does show that between 2 million and 3.7 million children are currently being raised by at least one Queer-identifying caregiver in their home (Family Equality Council 2017). Did any of the kids sitting in my kindergarten class already feel a sense of alienation, as their family representation was not shown to help shape our kindergarten schema regarding "what makes a family"?

So let's revisit these classmates looking through a different lens.

Tiana: History would simply have to scroll through social media hashtags or accounts like "#blacklivesmatter" or "@blackatprivateschool" to show the multitude of harrowing and traumatic experiences Tiana may have

---

16   #Metoo, a transformative social movement founded by Tarana J. Burke in 2006, originally sought to provide healing to survivors of sexual violence. In 2018, the hashtag #metoo went viral on social media, growing the movement to a worldwide endeavor where individuals share their experiences to surface the gross misuse of power and subordination impinged on those who have less power, primarily from men to women. Metoomvmt.org documents the trajectory and impact of the MeToo Movement's growth.

witnessed . . . a son's murder, a daughter's expulsion, an underpaid job, maltreatment at a hospital, stolen intellectual property,[17] are all common experiences disproportionately represented among Black women.

Oliver: If we looked to history as our teacher, she would show us that Oliver rarely, if ever, had an opportunity to speak Japanese in school, and that retaining his first language throughout life would have been challenging.

Ryan: History, impatient yet clear, would explain to us how Ryan's domineering behavior toward women has consistently been labeled "assertive" or "leader-like," pointing him to a job that almost certainly pays him more than a woman who does the same type of work.

Queer families: History, with many receipts, would illuminate how the child who may have identified as Queer or who had Queer parents and/or caregivers would have experienced consistent family erasure and/or erasure of self throughout time spent in school, growing a base of trauma that they will have to work through for the duration of their life.

As we continue to excavate, witness, and reflect on the histories we have lived through, we are charged with understanding the lesser explored versions of school that have both undermined education for some and exquisitely facilitated it for others.

We look back to our far away pasts and our near pasts, and we immerse ourselves in both personal and disconnected histories. Certainly, the strings of our hearts will be pulled. Depths of feelings we've never met will be felt. And to that, I say: embrace.

Working Toward Future Goodness

It's important to make space and time to process new or old information you're exposed to; bearing witness to the histories of our students and their families and ourselves and each other enables us to cultivate a more full and more humane version of *what it is* exactly we aim to do in the world of teaching and learning within a school in whatever role we may occupy.

---

17   Black women, intellectually prolific in the field of social justice education, are often left out of academic research, and scholars continue to steal their intellectual property without citation. Christen A. Smith founded #CiteBlackWomen in response to the erasure of Black women's intellect within the "canon," and to highlight, hold, and spread the valuable contributions they've made and continue to make in the body of knowledges we use today. www.citeblackwomencollective.org provides an excellent blueprint for acknowledging Black women in knowledge-making.

Reflection: Making Time and Space for Learning that Sticks

To create sustainable learning, learning that sticks, that shifts, *changes* people and their praxis, it is absolutely vital to make space and time for reflective opportunities. Reflection often is undervalued in the field of professional learning in schools, often seen as a time-wasting sentiment when more "productive" experiences could occur. "Sit and Get" professional development has become the norm, where teachers receive some kind of prescriptive thing and are told how to do the thing by an outsider or someone who has been named an "expert." But the work of marrying your mind and heart, and creating the alchemy of information into action is something quite different, it's collective learning, it's generative, it's felt knowledge, it's continuous.

It's important to name what's happening in your inner life here, in this work of understanding who we are and where we've been. As we cultivate ideas that grow into beliefs about who we are as teachers, there are no boxes to check. There are only more fully understood ideas about who we are in context to where we work, and in connection to who we work with. The more allowance we give ourselves and each other to process information, feelings, and outcomes, the richer our points of human connection within school communities.

So, after initiating this historical trek, it's a good time to beckon and surface more reflection. This can be done individually or in small affinity groups of three to four people. Chances are, you are likely working in a professional learning community where experiences are dotted throughout the spectrum of histories surfaced here or histories within your group. Affinity groups are sometimes necessary for authentic processing to occur. Monita K. Bell[18] says that when we make space to process stances in affinity groups around social action or hard truths, "Gathering in safe spaces around shared identity allows students to engage in conversations about how they can subvert the structures that push them to the margins." The same is true for adults.

Journal.

You may wish to journal first for a few minutes before sharing, and journaling can be done in lots of different multimodal ways, that is listing, drawing, sketchnoting, audio-recording, video blogging, etc.

---

18   Monita K. Bell is a managing editor at *Learning for Justice*, and this quote is cited from her article "Making Space." It is a resource I continue to refer to as I work to build transformational change within school communities. No matter what our experience may be, I find Bell's resource an excellent blueprint for navigating turbulent waters of social change, particularly when anticipating pushback from community members.

Reflection Questions:

- What feelings came up for you as you navigated your memory about your first years of schooling?

- What do you feel presently?

- What do you anticipate feeling as you are about to read through lesser explored versions of school for groups you share identity markers with? For groups in which you are mostly an outsider?

Chapter 3:
A Framework for Social Justice Work in Schools and Gentle Notes on Learning

In reading this book so far, we've already done so much! We've interrogated big ideas like radical hope, the pedagogy of justice and joy, and the history of school. We've begun to envision new ways forward to spread joy and justice, and have even parsed out a few ideas on where to begin that work. But I would be remiss if I went on composing chapters as if developing more just and joyful opportunities for teaching and learning in schools was as simple as following a manual and engaging in a few discussions.

For transformational change to occur in any part of life, whether it be personal, organizational, or institutional, it requires people to think differently. Within the realm of education, it's important for educators to build and revise their schema on what school is and how they operate within it for any kind of substantial justice and joy shifts in school to happen. This type of schema revision is in reference to our existing *mental models* (Senge et al. 1994) that tell us how school is *supposed* to go, or how we are *supposed* to teach, or even how kids and their families are *supposed* to learn.

Cognitive scientists refer to *mental models* as "the semi-permanent tacit 'maps' of the world which people hold in their long-term memory, and the short-term perceptions which people build up as part of their everyday reasoning processes" (Senge et al. 1994, p. 237). It is no easy task to press the restart button on a system that most educators have been a part of for much of their lives. Nonetheless, thinking differently is necessary for *acting* differently. It's a lot of work to build new mental models, but it's also a lot of fun! In this chapter, I introduce a framework for doing just this, building social justice that reorganizes our notions for "how to do school" in ways that energize the human spirit, inner knowing, and our ability to reflect with one another.

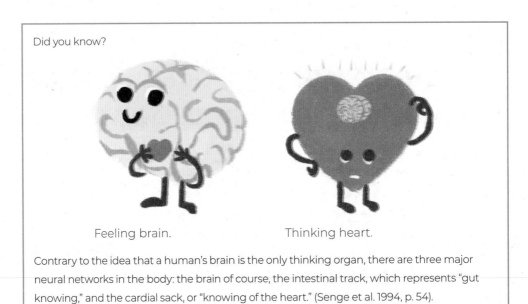

Did you know?

Feeling brain.   Thinking heart.

Contrary to the idea that a human's brain is the only thinking organ, there are three major neural networks in the body: the brain of course, the intestinal track, which represents "gut knowing," and the cardial sack, or "knowing of the heart." (Senge et al. 1994, p. 54).

Here, we'll work to *collaborate, build, nurture,* and *reflect*, on repeat. Below, find the foundational concepts behind this framework that allows the work of spreading joy and justice to become more sustainable.

Collaborate

Big idea: The answer lies in the room.

Educators need timely, practical, and powerful strategies that live within and come from school community spaces—not just in academia or in a packaged curriculum.

I learned this lesson a long time ago. In 2004, I was hired to work as a Tutoring Program Supervisor on the South Side of Chicago. As a 21-year-old white woman, I learned quickly that all the things the University that employed me told me to do and all the theory my brain held from my degree I had earned just a few months previously were mere suggestions for how school *could* go, and meant not a whole lot in terms of how school actually *went*. Upon my hiring, I had never been to an urban school in my whole life, had never lived in a city, and had rarely been the only white person in predominantly Black African American spaces. Suddenly, I was put in the position of *knower,* but what I knew in terms of what the school communities I was working with needed, was basically *nothing*.

That was nearly 20 years ago, in the babyhood of my teaching life. Every moment that has passed since has provided a powerful learning trajectory for me . . . one that has increased my capacity for deep collaboration with those I am connected with in school communities—whether they be grown-ups or children.

Now, in the realm of collaboration, I understand my position to be that of both learner and purveyor of knowledge, and that my connection (or lack thereof) to the community I work in dictates the experiences educators, students, and their families remember.

When I use the term "collaborate," this is what I mean:

- To engage in meaningful acts of listening.

- To position oneself *alongside* the humans you're learning with—not above or over.

- To put forth ideas, frameworks, and strategies as *offerings*, not nonnegotiables.

Reflection: Unpacking Collaboration Journaling

Let's dabble with a little journaling!

In the spaces below each component, think about your own experiences with each part of the framework. Document your thinking in whatever ways make the most sense to you.

Journaling questions can include:

Journaling.

- In terms of collaboration, do you generally resist collaboration, or are you drawn to it?

- What else would you add to the term collaborate? What does it mean to you?

- What collaborative experiences stand out to you in the realm of school? Were those experiences positive or negative? Why?

What component of collaboration mentioned above would you like to explore, or experience on a deeper level? What are next steps that might help you toward that goal?

Nurture

Big idea: Thought sanctuaries for teachers support joyful curiosity!

- Educators need thought sanctuaries in which to develop the kind of change that social justice movements in school require.

- This book attempts to create that protective space in partnership with its readers.

When I think of teachers, I think of full, human beings who execute tremendous tasks on a daily basis. However, from my experience, more often than not teachers are forced to execute those tasks and develop their practice in the soul-deafening landscape of scripted curriculum, top-down initiatives, and antiquated schooling norms. It's hard to hear yourself think in those conditions, let alone develop strategies and solutions and new learning paradigms for young people!

This is probably not a great surprise for those reading this . . . but humans (and most other mammals, too) only experience positive curiosity when they feel safe, secure, and a sense of belonging within their environment (Shah et al. 2018, p. 380). Prachi Shah and her colleagues describe this as "joyful curiosity." For teachers in school, this manifests in lots of ways. It's the project-based learning you create with your colleagues over lunch time after students ask questions about a shared experience. Or maybe it's experienced by a group of first graders who just learned that their teacher's dad is the mystery reader for class one morning. It's even the energy you receive after reading a really helpful article that makes you want to try something different or new in your classroom. However, in too many cases, that foundation of safety, security, and belonging has been crushed for teachers by those aforementioned soul-deafeners.

When that foundation is absent, joyful curiosity in inhibited. Humans still get curious, but not in a healthy way. This other kind of curiosity stems from survival instincts, and it is triggered by an adrenaline response that creates an anxious need to acclimate to new, sometimes threatening environments. It's a teacher's racing heartbeat when school leaders or guests come to observe their classroom. It's the panic-induction from a parent's or caregiver's accusatory email. It's the annual school-wide inquiry focused on students who are "high leverage" who have also been named "underperforming." The distinction between those two types of natural curiosity is clear. In this text, we work toward instilling joyful curiosity while moving away from survivalist curiosity by carving out thought sanctuaries in the physical spaces of school.

While the word "sanctuary" is often associated with holy, spiritual, and/or religious connotations, its meaning also extends to a space that provides safety and protectiveness from danger. In the context of creating a thought sanctuary for educators to gather and think safely, maybe even joyfully, there are a few different components to think about when building that space. First, it's important to consider the actual physical (or digital) space available for people to gather. This space should be adequate for people to gather, reflect, meditate, concentrate, and study. It should also be adequate for people to converse, move about, develop materials and artifacts, and be animated with one another. Finally, and perhaps most important, it's essential to develop thought sanctuaries in the context of protection, a space where people can gather without judgment, evaluations, or outside threats.

Thought sanctuaries are bountiful outside of school for teachers, and those spaces are important—whether they be in virtual affinity space with people who share identity markers that are most central to your life experience, at a weekly happy hour with people of your generation, or maybe even on Saturday morning walks with folx who enjoy exercising. Certainly, it's integral to our well-being to find space to connect and think and reflect.

When I was a classroom teacher, thought sanctuaries were not an actual separate physical space in the school. Rather, they were classrooms transformed by organic, teacher-created meet-ups. Every Thursday, in one of the other fourth grade classrooms down the hall, my grade team met. Not upon assignment or mandate, but upon invitation and affirmative welcomes by peers and colleagues, who later transformed into great friends.

It was in this space where I learned more about my students and their families, understood the nuances behind my colleagues' identities and instructional choices and teaching philosophies. Also, it was the space where I laughed and I cried and messed up, where I shared childbearing woes and teacher evaluation heartbreak.

No school leaders were present. Agendas were not created. It was a group of people who were in community, working together, striving to build something better through shared relationships. That space was a powerful thought sanctuary for me and my colleagues. This space is elaborated on in Chapter 4, including suggestions for building similar spaces in your own community.

So that we also may feel a sense of well-being while we're working in our classrooms or sitting in a professional development workshop, it's integral that we also carve these spaces within teachers' daily lived experiences at school. While safety and bravery cannot necessarily be guaranteed, it is a worthwhile effort to build these protective spaces.

In this text, the term "thought sanctuary" means:

- Spaces within or outside of school where your needs are met.

- Spaces where joyful curiosity is enabled.

- Spaces that underscore the value of flexible thinking and loose or absent agendas.

- Spaces that pair well-being with ideation and creativity.

Envisioning.

Build

Big idea: To build is to cultivate learning experiences through the lens of justice. This is what happens when joyful curiosity comes to life!

- All people connected to school; kids, teachers, school leaders, and families need opportunities to contribute materials to *the build* in the form of knowledge, culture, and resources that work toward shared values.

- To build, strategic collaboration between humans needs to take place within a thought sanctuary.

When I think about working with others to build justice and joy in schools, I lean on what I know about how learning works. Old friends from our educational studies like Jean Piaget, Lev Vygotsky, Maria Montessori, and John Dewey help us understand important ways to activate joyful learning. All of them played a major role in developing constructivism, that is, the central premise that all new learning is built upon previous experiences, or prior knowledge, referred to as schema (McLeod 2019).

And then, there's also this idea that it matters who participates, and *how* they participate in this construction of knowledge. While Piaget, Vygotsky,

Montessori, and Dewey spent lifetimes figuring out experiential learning in ways that led to brightness and fun for many teachers and children, considerations for cultural traditions, family literacies, and configurations of school environments were not fully recognized in their research (Meacham 1996, p. 301), and many children were not considered wholly in their work, notably those with dis/abilities, Black children, poor children, European immigrants, Latinx children, and Native American children, among others.

Here, I propose we construct knowledge in robust ways, honoring the agency of teachers and other educators, while also including students and their families along the way!

Lucky for us, there are many people who *have* spent lifetimes generating a platform that envelopes all types of family literacies, cultural traditions, and various types of schooling. When we build, a primary source of wisdom we'll draw from is the concept of *funds of knowledge,* the work of Norma González, Luis Moll, and Cathy Amanti. Funds of knowledge are skills, attributes, and literacies that people learn from their families and other home environments.

When we consider including the voices of all people in our build, we must think about what some people know, what some people don't, and how to bridge those knowledges when tensions within the community are heavy.[1] Most importantly, funds of knowledge are viewed from capacity orientations from González and others, encouraging teachers to incorporate and build upon those experiences in school (González 2005, p. 5). Working through the lens of justice requires us to work in tandem through the lens of capacity, too.

In short, to build strong foundations requires us to:

- Consider multiple perspectives.

- Deeply understand how learning is connected to the brain, heart, and instinct.

- Expect messiness, and to engage in trial and error.

- Share the value of risk-taking as a community.

---

1   We'll address the important work of navigating community tension throughout the text. This is the part where we begin to name "the what" and "the why." The "how" comes in the section called "Perspective Shapes Our Knowing."

Teaching Fiercely: Spreading Joy and Justice in Our Schools

To be strong, foundations don't have to look pretty; but they do have to be deeply rooted in the ground, they have to withstand pushback from all types of weather, and they have to outlast those who leave the building project.

Reflection: What Have You Built?

- What physical creations have you built recently?

- What skills did you need to build the object/creation?

- Was the process smooth? If not, what did you do when you experienced challenges?

- Have you ever built something that has fallen apart?

- How does the physical project relate to any community building you've engaged with in your school?

Reflect

Big idea: To move forward, we must look back.

- The personal histories of all people in school communities matter.

- Experiences and policies of the past have shaped the way school operates today.

Essentially, I assert that to move forward, we must look back. The work of joy and justice in teaching and learning supports the curation of strong, clear, and thoughtful teaching philosophies that insert an individual's personhood within the wider landscape of school.

We will work on developing a guided practice for connecting our personal histories to our teaching philosophies. One of the most important components of our journey together is to excavate our personal histories before we landed in our grown-up educator roles. These pieces of ourselves matter. They inform our personal convictions—the *why* behind our teaching.

For example, throughout our time together interacting in this book, I'll share how my experiences in schools, as student, teacher, mother, coach, and community organizer, have shaped my pedagogy, my stance, my curricular choices, my teaching journey. In those spaces, I've witnessed how the multiplicity of experience is a reflection of both connection and disconnection across all the persons within the ecosystem of school.

The more we all recognize how those connections and relationships manifest in our work, the more we enable ourselves and each other to develop a more sustainable, joyful, and just paradigm.

I hope you'll join me in culling the unique experience of your adolescence paired with your current school community, crafting a personal teaching statement that articulates your stance, and supporting choices that match your educational philosophy—all to help you along a path to a more healthy teaching journey.

We will also do a fair amount of work learning more about social and historical context of schooling, especially within the United States. In this book, Timeline Pedagogy will be a guiding force in our work toward justice, which we'll explore and unpack throughout the text, as we've already begun to do with the Historical Underpinnings work.

Connecting the Collaborate, Nurture, Build, and Reflect Framework

Naming North Stars.

It's easy to get caught up in reinventing the wheel and become overwhelmed by the enormity of barriers that find themselves in your way and stop the work—because you're exhausted and you feel *done* by the seeming impossibility of it all. Sometimes reinventing the wheel *is* necessary. It's necessary because we're trying to create a joyful and just learning paradigm in school—what so many of us have not experienced, as kids or as adults.

That said, as we reinvent and reimagine what school *can* be by operationalizing the Collaborate-Nurture-Build-Reflect Framework, it is useful to study models of learning, or "North Stars," in people-based institutions that have operated similarly toward the pursuit of human-centered care and social justice.

Using North Stars as Guidance for Our Work

The term "North Star" can be thought of in a couple of ways. First, you could think about the North Star in terms of its placement on Earth, directly to the North of the North Pole (aka "Polaris" in your science textbooks!). Or, you could think about the nativity story from the Christian Bible in the Gospel of Matthew, where "three wise kings from the East" are inspired to follow the North Star, or "Star of Bethlehem," to Jerusalem to find the revered Baby Jesus. The North Star is also mentioned in other religious and spiritual texts like the Quran, as well as the Torah. Hindu astronomers discuss "sacred alignment" in connection to the Vedas and Upanishads (Bhagwath 2020).

However you like to think about the term, the point is that the North Star serves as a point of guidance, giving us direction when we feel lost—spiritually and/or logistically. In our work toward finding joy and spreading justice in schools, it's integral for us to name, study, and hold metaphorical North Stars close to us in our work. Throughout this text, I'll name numerous North Stars I've found helpful, that communities I've partnered with have held tight, and that you may choose to study carefully as well.

Here, I invite you to contemplate your own North Stars! They can come in various shapes and sizes, including notable figures from both past and present, memorable events, people you know who have left an imprint on how you walk through life, or even documents that serve as powerful reminders for social justice work.

I'll start. As I'm writing this section, it happens to be International Women's Day,[2] and I'm thinking about all the women in the world who, 'round the clock, care for others. And they do so while solving problems, maintaining careers, and attempting to search and sustain their own dreams.

The first North Star of mine I'll share with you is not necessarily a singular person, but rather, a widely shared role, and that is The Matriarch; the grandmothers and mothers and aunties who serve as connectors and caregivers and intellectuals and makers and lovers, but have routinely been underrecognized, or unrecognized altogether. The term I use to describe the dynamism of these roles is *foremother*.

(Continued)

---

2   I think these thoughts on almost all the days, outside of days named for formally recognizing the significance of womanhood.

Foremothers who shine brightly as North Stars in my mental model for how to *be* in school spaces are situated in groups within the realm of matriarchy. These spaces are many, including classrooms while teaching children, school cafeterias running workshops with teachers, and even in museums while chaperoning school field trips.

I refer to these women as blueprints for working toward joy and justice in the various groups and positionalities I occupy in those different environments:

- I think about Georgia Gilmore[3] and the group of Black women she organized called the Club from Nowhere. These women sold pies to fund gas and cars during bus boycotts during the Civil Rights Movement in Montgomery, Alabama. Aside from Georgia Gilmore, the other women in the group remained anonymous. She was the only person who knew where the money came from when she distributed the funds to people who were leading the movement. The Club from Nowhere helped sustain the Civil Rights Movement, and did not step onto a single pedestal or proclaim their stance in public or in writing. Rather, they activated justice with careful planning, commitment, and clear actions in collaboration with one another.

- I think about my maternal grandmother, who divorced her husband in the late 1950s. Rejecting this social more at the time in smalltown northern Ohio, she marched through the trial of ending her marriage anyway for the sake of her and her children's happiness and livelihood. She managed to finagle a career while single-parenting my mother and my aunt, never losing her sense of humor or ability to find magic in life's otherwise mundane moments.

- I think about my own mother, her tenacity, and how she organized my brother, sister, and me all around the country as my dad's career in the military required regular moves across state lines. She created experiences for us kids that left powerful imprints on our ability to see ourselves in the world, as well as connect with other people—all the while managing full-time work, sometimes by herself as my dad embarked upon multiple tour of duties.

While some might say the work of these foremothers is just "regular life," I argue it is in the subtleties of their everyday actions that have created the significant changed outcomes for individuals and groups rather than mere shifts in people's circumstances. Their work did not come in the typical containers of leadership or go-to blueprint for "how to be in schools;" they didn't stand on a pedestal and make a speech, they didn't write a bunch of essays

---

3   Read more about Georgia Gilmore with students in the picture book *Pies from Nowhere: How Georgia Gilmore Sustained the Montgomery Bus Boycott* by Dee Romito and illustrated by Laura Freeman

declaring their intent or their accomplishments. Rather, they met people over a series of micromoments that over time impacted lives.

Think about it: the ability to bake pies, organize others to also bake pies, sell them for a profit, and put that profit into the hands of the right people will not be found in your *hypothetical* Activism 101 course. Walking away from your partner will also not be found in that hypothetical manual, and neither will a "creative child-rearing" chapter.

However, distinct purpose, clear bottom lines, reverence for humanity, the ability to act swiftly, and devotion to a specific cause or idea for the betterment of people's lives can be surfaced from all those foremothers' stories, and those are the components of their blueprint that work together to form the Matriarch-ness of my North Stars.

An "asterism" is a prominent pattern, or group, of stars. As you work across your community, you will need different guides, different blueprints for how to move forward. My grandmother, Georgia Gilmore, and my mom are not the only North Stars I can rely on, nor should I rely on only them as I work in community with so many others. This is why asterisms are important. (Such a great word, right?! I just learned it recently during a family trip to the planetarium.) So, if I think about an asterism, a cluster of North Stars as guidance, I am in much better shape for this school year journey. Add my coworkers' North Star, perhaps their grandmother, or Eglantyne Webb, to the mix? Already, we are in really great shape!

Imagine you are adding the North Stars of the people sitting next to you as guides on your journey. Keep this idea at the forefront of your mind as you plan on how far—or where—to go this year.

Applying the Collaborate-Build-Nurture-Reflect Framework Through a Case Study on Folk Schools

One thing I often think about is how freedom movements of the past are connected to the freedom movements of today, and, especially, how they can serve as blueprints to provide guidance for us (North Star guidance!) within school spaces—particularly classroom spaces.

Here, I'm introducing a brief case study for you to engage with on your own, or with a team of people at your school. The case study navigates an important North Star for joy and justice work, connecting the conceptual foundation of Folk Schools and real-life, mainstream[4] schools in the United States. I'll start with a brief historical overview on the inception of Folk Schools, and afterward, you'll read about Highlander Center, a space developed for collective learning that grew in both popularity and impact during the Civil Rights Movement. From there, I'll apply the foundational characteristics of those ideologies to school spaces I've worked in to name what has been possible for spreading joy and justice. Finally, we'll use the Collaborate-Nurture-Build-Reflect Framework to see how you can activate those components, or even imagine different variations on joy and justice in the spaces you teach and learn.

Folk Schools hold collective responsibility, community empowerment, and oral traditions in high regard. However, it's important to note these ideals existed across the globe within Indigenous communities and other collective societies[5] long before Folk Schools came to be. The Folk Schools you read about here are as close to the "institution" of school as we get in terms of moving toward human-centered education that promotes collective responsibility.

I want to take a moment to clarify the word "folk"—it's one of my favorites! In short, it simply means "knowledge of the people." Everyday people. Not necessarily teachers or professors or tutors, but people from everywhere who occupy all different walks of life. You also may have noted in the style guide that when I refer to folx in plural, I've been using an "x" instead of an "s." The x is meant to underscore the significance of gender expansiveness within a group of people, or folx.

The formalized concept of Folk Schools originated in nineteenth-century Denmark. In the quest to move from Greek- and Latin-centric studies to more democratic, humane experiences in education, Nikolai Frederik Severin Grundtvig developed the foundational philosophy that Folk Schools, to this

---

4   I define mainstream schools as the types of school that the majority of kids living in the United States attend, including private, independent, charter, and public schools. Although many children participate in schooling that isn't mainstream, that group is significantly smaller in the U.S. demographic. Examples of schools that are not considered mainstream in this context are Forest Schools, Folk Schools, Freedom Schools, home-based education, unschooling, and/or full-time private tutoring.

5   Later in this text, we'll unpack a few oral histories in those Indigenous communities to discover the saturation of care and intention between interpersonal relationships in the scope of life learning. See "Historical Underpinnings: We Might Know Our *Now*, but Do We Know Our Legacy?"

day, are borne from (Eiben 2015). First and foremost, Folk Schools evolved from the concept that "learning is based on an understanding of human identity that includes an individual identity, a cultural identity and a democratic identity," and that the individual cannot be separated from community (Eiben 2015).

The first Folk Schools in Denmark were created between the 1830s and 1850s. Christen Kold operationalized Grundtvig's philosophy within 50 schools, building those schools around the philosophical tenets that Grundtvig formed:

- Education must consider the nature of children and youth and their needs.

- Students must be given time to develop the capacity for feeling before learning facts, and appreciation before learning skills.

- The living word (oral culture) is central.

- The wholeness of the individual is experienced only in the context of community.

- The purpose of education was to respond to the needs and struggles of common people.

- Education should embrace heart, mind, and body. The main purpose of education is not to teach factual knowledge, but for "life's awakening." "The school should be for life, for the spiritual, and for that which is of the heart" (Grundtvig, in Borish 2005, p. 196).

- The school should be free of government control, and there should be no tests, grades, or certificates of competence given (Borish, in Eiben 2015).

Folk Schools made a lasting impression on many political progressives within the United States, and scholars/community organizers like Myles Horton, one of Paulo Freire's good friends and collaborators, studied them in depth. Horton later founded the prolific Highlander Folk School, a place where Rosa Parks, Martin Luther King Jr., Septima Clark, and Fannie Lou Hamer all studied.

> ### North Star: Myles Horton
>
> I work hard to emulate Myles Horton's work in creating lateral, participatory change through my positionality, as a learner, as a coach, as a parent, as a volunteer, and, *especially,* as a former teacher. Myles Horton was a tacit hero in the educational landscape in America's history. His last published work was a documented conversation called *We Make the Road by Walking* between himself and his friend and contemporary Paulo Freire.
>
> Many folks who've studied education or any of the social sciences in undergrad have met Freire's work in such-and-such 101 class. Few have been assigned Horton, for he was a person whose actions were so much louder than any word he wrote. Horton notably fueled his education principles and teaching practice *from* and *with* participants and learners in his community as opposed to delivering knowledge *to* the community members he worked with, who were mostly poor, rural workers who did not read.
>
> His participatory approach led to great trust alongside all sorts of marginalized folks, including the disenfranchised American South: He helped to found the Freedom Schools throughout Mississippi during the Civil Rights Movement, supporting many, many community members to learn to read, and then creating a base for those newly print-based literate folks to teach others to read as well, growing the African American voting base across the South. He also provided physical meeting spaces for SNCC, and moved out of the way to let young Black people steer the movement.
>
> I deeply identify with Horton's work as an on-the-ground local, community-based educator constantly searching and seeking ways to build capacity for all people in school communities to bear responsibility for kids' positive, inclusive, equitable schooling experiences. This isn't to say that teachers are the same as folks who couldn't read, but it is to say that teachers are marginalized because of the socially constructed narrative that American media has woven into their occupation. For this reason, folx who work with teachers to improve learning for kids should assume they need to build trust with those teachers, and that decisions for *how* to improve learning for kids should be done in co-creation.

Highlander became one of the few places within the United States during the Civil Rights Movement where people from different racial groups could gather safely to organize liberation movements for all people. Folx at Highlander worked together to build adult literacy, develop fair labor practices, offer safe haven for various freedom movements, and help people gain legal citizenship (Our History: Highlander Research and Education Center). To this day, Highlander serves as an instrumental force in organizing for racial and economic justice within the United States.

I could say a lot more about Folk Schools, but the gist is that these were places of teaching and learning that placed relationships, culture, and personal and community empowerment at the center of life. When those elements worked in concert together, they formed a school (Eiben 2015). The conceptual ethos of Folk Schools was centered in the belief that it was far more powerful to produce equitable relationships than capital and rote memorization.

Highlander Folk School has translated Grundtvig's aforementioned core Folk School Philosophies to serve their mission to "build more just, equitable, and sustainable systems and structures . . . and bring people together across issues, identity, and geography to share and build skills, knowledge, and strategies for transformative social change" (What We Do: Highlander Center). Methodologies that Highlander uses to serve this purpose include the following:

- **Popular education** is the process of bringing people together to share their lived experiences and build collective knowledge. Popular education learning informs action for liberation.

- **Cultural organizing** celebrates and honors people's spiritual traditions and cultural expression in the work to shift policies and practices.

- **Language justice** recognizes language as an essential part of empowerment in collective learning and strategy-building. It creates spaces where people from different places, different cultures, and different dialects/languages can come together and understand each other, without forcing themselves to communicate in a language that is not native to them.

- **Intergenerational organizing** brings together the collective wisdom of ancestors, elders, young people, and all those in between to envision, strategize, and take action for a better future.

- **Participatory action research** recognizes information as power. It is a collective process where people investigate a specific issue or question to inform organizing, strategy, and solutions.

- **Land, legacy, and place** builds strategies to nourish and tend to our relationships with our histories, places, communities, and environments that support our collective thriving (Mission and Methodologies: Highlander Center).

Between Grundtvig's tenets and Highlander Center's translation of those concepts, there is much to consider for building justice in the realm of school. At the center, these concepts help confirm it *is* possible to "do school" based on relationships and learning as opposed to competition and production. Although there are few Folk Schools[6] within the United States that act as full-time education systems for young children and adolescents, their core belief system is noteworthy: Folk Schools serve as a model for how to enact collaboration and nourishment within our community. They help us to see and to understand how to build school that is human-centered and spirited; carefully reflecting along the way. All these components work together to help us spread joy and justice in more mainstream schools.

Where *can* and/or *do* the tenets of Folk School ideology live within mainstream schools in the United States?

Here, I want to demonstrate where the tenets of Folk School ideology *do* live and *could* live within mainstream schools. I know that reading parts of Grundtvig's core philosophies and Highlander Center's methodologies might feel completely incongruous to the goals of public schooling, re: "The school should be free of government control, and there should be no tests, grades, or certificates of competence given (Borish, in Eiben 2015)." However, the goal is *not* to scrap the foundation of school entirely, or walk into your next scheduled grade team meeting and craft a brand-new credo. Rather, the purpose of this work is to gain clarity on what social justice *can look like* and, in some schools, *does look like* in action when tethered within the needs

---

6   The ones that *do* exist, however, are fascinating, albeit somewhat inaccessible for all people. Aside from Highlander Folk School, which has a vast network of diverse peoples and is run by majority BIPOC folx working specifically toward the rights of people in Appalachia and the South, I've noticed that many Folk Schools (who have categorized themselves as a Folk School) are characteristically white, but not necessarily centered in dominant culture. For an example, read more about Center for Belonging Folk School in Iowa at https://www.centerforbelonging.earth/ . There are other learning experiences that majority BIPOC kids do experience that have tenets of Folk School ideologies, but are not named as such. For an example, read more about Nikolai Pizzarro's blueprint for a school called Liberatorium: A Neighborhood Permaculture-Forest School & Learning Space based in Atlanta at https://linktr.ee/raisingreaders.

of community as opposed to a larger, disconnected agenda (usually rooted outside of kids' learning experiences).

Even though this might feel far away from where your school is at, or what your community believes in, or what you are ready for, I encourage you to do a little dreaming here. Let's say that something in one of the fields in Table 3.1 feels impossible given the constraints of your current school community. Imagine your life in school if those constraints didn't exist. What if it were possible to build workable versions of the kinds of positive, constructive components described in Table 3.1? I encourage you to take notes or flag in the margins what appeals to you.

TABLE 3.1 Spaces for spreading joy and justice in schools.

	Spaces for Joy and Justice in Schools
Popular education/The wholeness of the individual is experienced only in the context of community.	<ul><li>Community circles.</li><li>Restorative circles.</li><li>Group work/Flexible grouping structures.</li><li>Socratic seminar/Class congress.</li><li>Recess.</li><li>Lunch.</li><li>Thought sanctuaries (start with libraries, teachers' lounge, dedicated classroom spaces).</li></ul>
Participatory action research/The purpose of education is to respond to the needs and struggles of people.	<ul><li>Formative assessments.</li><li>Inquiry-driven, co-created curriculum.</li><li>Interviews:<ul><li>Inter-class interviews (teacher-student/student-teacher/student-student).</li><li>Intra-school interviews (student-principal/AP/student-students in different classes/student-parent/caregivers).</li><li>Audit trails.</li><li>Multiliteracies.</li></ul></li></ul>
Cultural organizing/Education should embrace the heart, mind, and body. "The school should be for life, for the spiritual, and for that which is of the heart" (Grundtvig, in Borish 2005, p. 196).	<ul><li>Culturally relevant teaching and learning (in the classroom, in professional development, in family engagements).</li><li>Representative texts and meaningful literature.</li><li>Social-emotional learning.</li><li>School-supported playdates.</li><li>Field trips.</li></ul>

(Continued)

TABLE 3.1 (Continued)

	Spaces for Joy and Justice in Schools
Intergenerational organizing/ Education must consider the nature of children and youth and their needs.	<ul><li>Student-led conferences.</li><li>Family engagement series.</li><li>Literacy and math workshops.</li><li>Needs assessment gatherings.</li><li>Social gatherings designed to foster intra-school connections.</li></ul>
Language justice/The living word, (oral culture) is central.	<ul><li>School communication translated in all the languages spoken in the community.</li><li>Translation services provided for real-time meetings.</li><li>Value is placed on oral literacies within curriculum (storytelling, chatting with peers, collecting oral histories), as well as AAVE and other forms of the English Language.</li><li>Translanguaging.</li><li>Language goals are woven into the curriculum and high-quality ELL services are provided.</li></ul>
Land, legacy, and place/Students must be given time to develop the capacity for feeling before learning facts, and appreciation before learning skills.	<ul><li>Place-based pedagogy.</li><li>Walking tours.</li><li>Somatic literacy.</li><li>Community elders invited as guest speakers.</li><li>Appreciation circles.</li><li>Teachers, students, and families view each other from capacity orientations versus deficit perspectives.</li></ul>

After reviewing Table 3.1 of possible spaces to spread joy and justice in schools, think about which component/s you may want to work on building in your own school community. At this point, it will be more helpful to play around with multiple ideas rather than commitment to just one plan. This is meant to be a generative thinking spot in the book; later, we'll clarify some of the components that might be unfamiliar to you. Each space for spreading joy and justice is expanded upon in different areas of this book. As you read, you'll gain more clarity on what this work entails in connection to your role, your positionality, and the needs of your community. Additionally, you also may want to spend time doing research in connection to what excites you!

Work Along: Generating Joy and Justice within the Collaborate-Nurture-Build-Reflect Framework

In this work along we combine our knowledge of human-centered practices displayed in our study on Folk Schools and generalized knowledge on how schools operate and connect it directly to *your* life in school from the roles you occupy (parent/caregiver, teacher, principal, assistant principal, social worker, school psychologist, paraprofessional, student teacher, teaching assistant, etc.).

1. List what spaces for spreading joy and justice interest you from Table 3.1. What component of human-centered teaching practices are they connected to? How might they live within your school?

Human-centered teaching practices of interest	Where do they live in your school and/or *how* might they live in your school?

2. Surface Collaborate, Nurture, Build, and Reflect in Your School

Use this note catcher to jot down actions or characteristics from your school community that show evidence of collaboration, nourishment, building, and reflection.

Collaboration	Nurture	Building	Reflection

3. Now, consider the following:

- What about your school shows social justice? Joy?

- What about your school might be disconnected from social justice and joy?

- Is your collaboration/nurture/building/reflection robust or sparse? Which column was easier to unpack than others? What column was most difficult?

4. Make two working goals:

   a. What part of your CNBR Framework will you place emphasis on for further development and why?

   b. What components of joy and justice will you place emphasis on for further development and why? (Think about Table 3.1: What activities, mission language, or community connections could live within your school spaces? Your classroom? Your interpersonal relationships?)

> ### Historical Underpinnings: We Might Know Our *Now*, but Do We Know Our Legacy?
>
> Part of knowing your stuff is knowing your history. Educators, students, and their families comprise the institution of school; without them, it doesn't exist. However, as we go about unpacking injustices within that institution, it's important to understand the root causes of various forms of oppression, injustice, and harm that have disproportionately affected groups of people with distinct characteristics and identity markers. Without treating the root cause of a disease, we are only treating the symptoms of a system that harms so many. At this juncture, I offer an historical trek within the institution of school that works to unravel injustice in the name of moving toward radical hope and joy: https://www.kassandcorn .com/teachingfiercely/.

Gentle Notes on Learning: Rituals and the Beginnings of Our Thought Sanctuary

I know this work is hard. I know there are times where your current school environment will feel unhealthy, and where you will feel like an alien within it. There will be moments when your peers or your friends will disappoint you, where people you thought were aligned with your teaching goals are actually mismatched to your inner self's awakening, or your stance on what it means to be in community with people in school. There will be space and time where you feel like no one is listening to you and nothing is getting "done."

This is where I offer my metaphorical shoulder: I encourage you to treat yourself, to pause, and to take a breath. As educators, we have been programmed to operate within a deep sense of efficiency, at the cost of our well-being and general functionality. This climb toward efficacy isn't always healthy, and oftentimes educators have a tendency to think with their heads rather than their hearts as a coping mechanism. The phenomenon is the mind and body's stress response working as a warning system when we perceive an experience as a threat (T. Woon, personal communication). We avoid that warning system by shutting off our emotions.

Many teachers I'm in connection with find great solace with the simple gifts of space and time, and I hope that with these reflective moments, as you read alone, with a partner, or maybe even in a book club, you, too, are able to carve out those things.

I also offer you this gentle note on learning: reflection is where we remember, where we process and progress. It's the space where new ideas are formed, shaped, and find a place to stick. Even when we plough through new information and ideas with the greatest intentions, when we do so with a lack of thoughtfulness, then we are robbing ourselves of the kinds of learning we seek to build within our classroom communities: learning that is just, nourishing, student-centered, and community-oriented. How can we implement an experience within our learning spaces that we have hardly experienced ourselves?

Part of our work in reconstructing our mental models for spreading joy and justice in schools is by developing rituals that build the muscles for collaboration, nourishment, building, and reflection. With practice, these muscles become reflexive, forming a new mental model that sustains our health, our spirit, and our livelihood—especially when it feels like the world is crashing down all around us.

As I am sure you've noted, throughout this book, we'll be reflecting together, like, *a lot*. The primary goal of our work together, reader, is for you to have a documented journey of your own teaching journey as I parse through mine. To move forward, we've got to look back, and, first and foremost, we've got to start with ourselves.

First we'll consider how to develop our long-term abilities to reflect by considering (a) how we are taking care of our bodies by becoming more in tune with how our biology impacts our mental state and (b) what other social needs we need to feel and experience when we are working toward joy and justice in community.

Somatic Literacy

To sustain frequent and deep reflection, it's important to work on developing our *somatic literacy*. The first piece of this term, somatic, means having to do with the body and how it is interconnected with one's mind. And literacy, this catch-all term for so many things in our edu-world, simply put, means the ability to read and write. So, in short . . . we're going to work on reading our bodies!

I can almost feel the eye rolls! It's okay, I get it. This is new. This is different. It might feel strange. But hear me out. Developing somatic literacy is newish for me, too. Sometimes it makes me feel weird, sometimes it makes me feel great—but the overriding piece of knowledge that makes our time well spent on the endeavor toward building our somatic literacy is this: so long as our minds and hearts are separated from one another in the schools we teach in, in front of the students and families we love, it is highly likely the classrooms our students learn in will replicate the same systems that harmed us. So, humor me here; the risk is too great.

Our first practice round will be short. As you become more experienced with reading your own body, you'll be able to do this with future groups of learners yourself.

Work Along: Somatic Literacy Body Inventory

The point of a body check-in/inventory is to practice identifying the sensations our body feels in the moment.

1. Review the list of sensation words in Figure 3.1 created by Meenadchi from the Non-violent Communcation Center. Note: these are not emotions, or feelings; they are *physical* sensations.

2. Consider a lesson you taught to a group of people that resonates with you. Jot down a brief anecdote that describes your memory.

    Example: I'm remembering some of those first experiences I shared from the beginning of my teaching career. During one of the lessons I taught to a group of eleventh and twelfth graders during the America Speaks project I designed, I remember creating an identity chart for America with my students. It was wild: kids were talking out of turn and I certainly hadn't developed a strong sense of "management"—but our conversation was so vibrant. It was charged and full of passion. Few students agreed on what America was or who it claimed to be, but I remember noting their fervor—and for me, with them, it opened up a landscape of possibilities for how and what we would learn together.

3. Keeping that teaching experience in mind, refer to the list of sensation words in Figure 3.1. Which words most accurately describe the physical sensations you felt during that teaching experience? Identify every sensation you remember feeling.

    Example: Electric, pulsing, spacious, tense.

4. Reflect. Do the physical sensations you named for question three inhibit or enable you personally? Do the sensations you named open up possibilities for positive feelings? Or do they feel more captive, disabling a sense of innovation or freedom in your work?

Example: For me, the pulsing and electric sensations were incredibly enabling for my high-energy, somewhat open-ended instructional practice with older learners. The sensations fed me, and helped me feel a sense of renewal in my spirit, like what I was doing was important, even special. The spacious and tense sensations produced multiple pathways for me. The spaciousness led to almost too many possibilities for how the curriculum could go, or sometimes I worried I was straying too far away from what I was "supposed" to teach. The sensation of being tense, or tightness, is all too familiar. As a person with a diagnosed general anxiety disorder, "tense" is a

FIGURE 3.1 Body sensations list (Meenadchi 2020).

constant in my physicality. In some ways, it allows me to be incredibly productive, but other times, that tightness is restrictive in that I may squash a possibility or a dream because it takes too long or makes me feel lost.

What our body experiences on a physical level impacts how we feel on an emotional level. And how we feel, holistically, matters for how much, to what degree, and with *whom* we are able to learn. Now that you've had this short experience in reflecting somatically, we'll put this practice in our pockets for now. We'll keep our practice warm, though. Because as we imagine building our pedagogies—really figuring out what is justice, what is joy, why does it matter, and how does it look—we have to be able to identify these things within ourselves. And that starts with the most basic recognition of what our bodies feel in real time.

To Remember Is to Feel a Collection of Tensions with Elements of Joy

Earlier, I mentioned what pains me. To remember, to reflect, is to feel a collection of tensions, a sprinkling of joy, and depending on how long you've been alive, a cobbling together of emotions and experiences that have somehow painted the path on which we stand today. In many schools, Western culture dominates,[7] especially within the United States. Students, teachers, and school leaders are taught to remove their emotive capacity from decision-making, to stick with "the" agenda, and carry on, despite whatever may be happening in the world that surrounds them. In fact, one of the human body's greatest physiological coping mechanisms is to shut down one's capacity to feel when things get hard; our bodies work instead to evoke an adrenaline response that equips the body to move robotically throughout the day, to get by, to enable us to eat and drink, and, yes, to teach. But that same response makes it really, really hard to *learn*.

Here, I pose that we allow ourselves to feel. That we commit our whole selves, our whole body experience into the classrooms we share with our learners. I know there are many barriers[8] that disallow many of us to fully exist on both macro (big, institutional) and micro (small, personal) levels, that inhibit our motivation to even try to *be* fully in a classroom space. As an empath, for years, and many moments in between, I have certainly willed myself to ignore my emotions to simply get through the day. If I didn't embark upon my adrenaline response, removing myself from an immersion of tears and angst in the face of school's injustices like having to teach a packaged curriculum to students with varying abilities, receiving a teaching assignment outside my licensure, and being ignored and silenced from different parts of power-laced hierarchies would have swept me out of this profession a long, long time ago.

To create any sorts of shifts in the paradigms we occupy, we must be vulnerable with ourselves and one another. If we want to enable people to show up as their whole selves, feelings and all, we have to practice with ourselves first.

---

7   Dominant cultures are the ways of life from groups of people who share similar identity markers that demonstrate the most power, and are the most deeply considered within systems. For example, in the majority of schools within the United States, Christian culture is dominant, and deeply impacts structures created such as a school's academic calendar and acknowledgement of holidays within the community at large.

8   Macro-level and micro-level barriers will be addressed throughout the text, but right now, we're focusing on you!

Personal Needs and Feeling Better—Even *Good* in a Learning Community

Recently, I worked with a group of educators to build multi-literacies and culturally responsive practices over the course of a four-day summer institute. Teachers who participated had just finished teaching through the 2019–2020 school year, one of the most unpredictable academic years in the history of school. My partner and I knew we had to create the safest, most nourishing learning environment possible—exhausted teachers were *choosing* to spend their time with us, and we wanted them to feel nourished before, during, and after.

We put our heads together and surfaced our previous histories in learning environments of all types, from our adolescent lives all the way into grad school. We asked ourselves: *In what spaces did we feel best about ourselves? In what spaces did we feel good? Where did we feel smart?*

Perhaps you won't have too many school-based learning environments that make you feel great. Maybe, like me, you'll identify that the learning environments that felt best were the ones closer to home, like your grandmother's davenport, or your mother's kitchen.

When I'm working to build community in spaces where people have experienced collective trauma, or when people's humanity has been dishonored, typically I look to our foremothers for answers. In this case, I looked to Gloria Ladson-Billings. In her book *The Dreamkeepers* (1994), a seminal text for educators everywhere that provides the groundwork for Culturally Responsive Education, she says: "My teacher was a woman who told us how much fun we were each going to have and how much she expected us to learn. Our school was safe and clean, with people who cared about you: again, a lot like home" (p. 3).

To do the hard work of transformation—of self, of community, of classrooms, and/or of school—educators must think hard on what it means for their learners to feel at home in their learning environment. The following activity is something I experienced in one of my few school-based spaces that made me feel good about myself, not just as a learner, but as a human being.

I had just left my job as a classroom teacher in an elementary school in Sunset Park, Brooklyn, and had accepted a new position working with one of my mentors, Celia Oyler, to support The Inclusive Classrooms Project at Teachers College, Columbia University. As we carved out a plan for documenting the important work our partner teachers were doing in their classrooms with one of my new colleagues I had just met, Celia, with her infinite and fervent warmth, abruptly stopped our meeting agenda after we had already started and insisted we work on building our "documentation community," which was, at that point, three people.

Her experience and wisdom compelled her to print out a "Needs Inventory," provided at no cost by The Center for Nonviolent Communication. She instructed both my colleague and me to think about what we needed to feel good about ourselves in the space in which we were meeting, which was her faculty office at Teachers College. She gave us a few minutes to think, circle three needs, and then invited us to share with one another what our needs were and why those things were important for us to feel good. We shared, she documented. She also shared, and added her needs to the list. From then on, every time we met, we had a list of needs to serve as our North Stars for optimal learning.

After that experience, I realized something. I'd often been asked questions like, "What do you need to do to be successful?" or "What do you need to complete this project by the stated classroom goal?" But a question as simple as "What do you need to feel *good* here?" . . . I'd never really had an experience with a question like that in a school—especially not in a space like a university, which can feel especially stifling!

I had always loved meeting with Celia, but after that experience, I loved meeting with her and my colleague even more—I felt at home in her office. And as for my three needs, I had identified *authenticity*, *joy*, and *to be seen*. And sure, those things were present in many ways before we did that exercise, but naming those needs was especially affirming. That helped me feel seen. Ensuring my needs were met, as a community, helped me feel safe, which is a necessary undercurrent to enable a need like *joy*. And the posted list of needs served as a note of accountability for all of us as we created goals, made plans, or worked through our ideas.

So, as we worked to cultivate a safer learning environment for a group of teachers who were giving a lot to the community by simply being present, we chose to begin our community build with a similar activity. As you think about cultivating or recreating a learning community in your own space, I encourage you to try it out! I've included a lesson below. By no means should you feel as if you have to replicate this as written; it is simply a suggested roadmap to get closer to the original objective, which is collecting needs from a group of learners to create safety and warmth, and serving as accountability through the duration of time spent together.

Feelin' Good: Our Needs Lesson Plan

Objectives:

- Surface community needs to cultivate safety and warmth within a learning environment.

- Develop an accountability touchstone for ensuring community needs are met throughout time.

Learner audience: Ages 4 to 100! This activity is kind of like the card game Uno. It can be adapted for almost any age group.

- For kids who are emergent readers, or early elementary, consider using the needs inventory with visual vocabulary support. Children can draw their needs, and tell you orally while receiving help to label their pictures. You could also do this activity during a morning meeting, and make it a shared writing experience where children dictate their needs out loud and grown-ups list the needs in real time.

- Older kids or grown-ups may wish to explore their needs on a deeper level independently before sharing with the rest of the community. For example, they could collect photos from various life experiences or geographical spaces that demonstrate their needs, and write long about how those visuals evidence their needs. The class could then create a communal bulletin board that serves as visual accountability for all participating in the learning space.

Materials: Needs Inventory List (available free online from The Center for Nonviolent Communication); optional: maker materials.

Connection: Share a story with your learning community about a place or experience that made you feel good, at your best, and/or smart. Invite them to add places and/or experiences that made them feel those same ways. List their comments on a visual chart.

Teaching point: *Explicitly state the objective.* Something like: "Learners, today we are going to think hard about what we need to feel good about ourselves in this learning space. It is my goal to work with you to make sure everybody has what they need to feel good here. We need to feel good about ourselves to feel we can learn!"

Mini-lesson: (This is super mini . . . like five to seven minutes.) "When we feel good about ourselves, usually that means our needs are being met. For example, when our bellies are full, we're not hungry. We're satisfied, so we're able to talk about our daily activities, like playing with friends, walking in the park, or reading a book. But when we're hungry, and don't

(Continued)

have enough food to eat, our needs aren't being met. All we can do is think about our stomach rumbling. It's hard to focus, and we feel yucky. Our emotional needs are similar! (Show the class the **Needs Inventory**.) This is called a **Needs Inventory**. It's a list of needs a lot of people have named "important" to feel good about themselves in a learning community. Not everybody has all those needs. Most people have two or three that are *really* important to them. For example, one of my greatest needs in a learning community, especially one like ours, is joy. Joy is something that makes me feel like I'm having fun, that gets rid of my headaches, that makes me smile when I'm around people. Without joy in our learning space, it's hard for me to be clear, and I feel funny when I have to say things out loud. For me, I am going to name joy as one of my really important needs."

Active engagement (in communal learning): "I want you all to think to yourself for a moment. What's something on this list that seems really important for you to feel good about yourself? (After a moment): I want to invite you to share with the person sitting next to you the need you named. Try to explain why that need makes you feel good. (Listen in to learners talking.) (Share a few experiences you heard kids talking about.) (Invite one or two kids to share their needs with the rest of the class.)

Independent practice: On your own, I want you to think even more deeply. Think about places in your life, and experiences you've had, that make you feel really good. Then, use the list of needs to try to match those feelings you had. Which of your needs were being met that made you feel so good? Circle all the needs that make sense for you. Finally, think about what's *most* important for you. Star the three most important needs.

More active engagement: Invite learners to work with a partner or in a small group of three or four people. This time, they are sharing the needs they named, and they are working hard to be clear about why those needs are so important to them. There are many options for documentation of needs. Here are a few:

- Learners work together to create a visual demonstration of their needs; include the needs along with symbols, diagrams, or pictures to demonstrate why those needs are so important to them.

- Learners work together to list their needs, sharing their "why" and then are invited to access a box of maker materials to create an abstract interpretation of their needs.

Sharing: Each group or partnership is invited to share, visually or orally, with the rest of the class. You may wish to do a "gallery walk" where the class visits each chart or creation for a few minutes at a time, noticing needs, and collecting thoughts and reactions on sticky notes. The most important component of sharing is that the collective needs inventory can live in a space within the classroom environment that can be frequently revisited and seen to serve as community accountability.

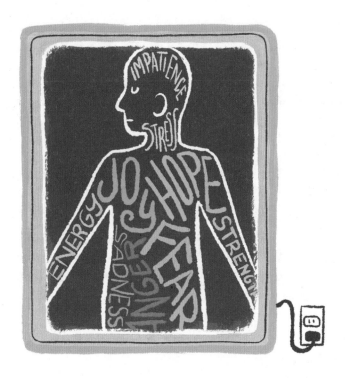

Chapter 4:
Pursue Joy by Thwarting Injustice: Develop Teacher Agency Through Reflective Practice and Collaboration

As a newer teacher in the early 2000s, I wouldn't have predicted just how deeply I would dive into the ecosystem of school over the next 15 years, how much I would delight in collaborating with other teachers and families, and how career sustaining I would find curriculum-making to be. Certainly a major ingredient in the movement toward student centeredness and teacher agency is the love educators like myself and so many others have put forth in reclaiming their intellectualism and curriculum-making as part of our profession.

However, within that love, teacher intellectualism, and robust curriculum-making lay major tensions in terms of how various leaders, families, and even educators themselves perceive the role of *teacher* in a school community.

In the first section of the book, we talked about how important it is for educators to engage in seeing and feeling the pressure of injustice to be an agent of joy and justice within their school community.

In this next section, we will practice unpacking some of those tensions that lay within the questions: What is the role of a teacher in terms of what they should teach and how students in their classrooms should learn? How can teachers reclaim their role through reflective practice? How does joy live within this pursuit?

2006

In the mid-2000s, New York City, along with a few other major urban centers in the United States, had robust campaigns calling twenty-somethings and other career-changers into their chronically sparse teaching forces. These campaigns were everywhere: digital posters plastered AOL message boards, and analog posters slathered college campuses, beckoning folx from all facets of life with four-year degrees to "fill a critical need" and to "share knowledge and experience with youth!" In turn for teaching in said urban centers, these alternate routes to teaching certification paid for your graduate tuition and helped you along the road to getting your teaching licensure through the state. The catch: schools were located in far-out neighborhoods, special education and science were the only teaching licenses for your choosing, and you had to teach full time while earning your degree and license.

When I began my graduate studies in education to pursue teaching kids, the concentration in which my license was earned wasn't so important to me. I had just spent the last two years of my life living on the South Side of Chicago, witnessing the types of injustice that many white and other privileged people only read about. I had learned, or maybe more accurately put, *I had become aware of* the vast gaps in my brain and in my body re: knowing anything about urban education, and had begun to develop a keen understanding of how essential community and connection were in the realm of searching for hope and humanity within the context of schools that had been named "failing."

The only thing I knew for sure was that I wanted to work with kids in schools, that it was absolutely necessary for me to learn how to be in community with their families and my future colleagues, and that I did not want be in debt over $50,000 for a career that was far, far away from that sort of financial return. It made perfect sense to me to accept whatever position in whatever school with whichever group of kids through the New York City Teaching Fellows (NYCTF).

I applied to, and was invited into, the NYCTF group-to-individual interview process a few weeks later. At the time, my salary, working in an educational nonprofit housed at the University of Chicago, was meager; in short, I was poor. My financial status served me rich self-sustenance; two buses and a train? No problem, free sight-seeing. A 20-pound bag of groceries and a two-mile walk? No problem, free gym time. Four weeks for the used textbook to come? Got it, I had been meaning to renew my library card anyway. So a trip from Chicago to New York City with less than $250 to my name was simply another string of logistical challenges to be worked out.

For $224, I flew to New York City from Chicago, headed straight to the Barnes and Noble located on 17th street in Union Square, practiced my teaching lesson, whispering to myself, near the YA books (I remember my lesson involving something about M&Ms and counting . . . it was *very rudimentary*), and did the four-hour interview process at Washington Irving High School just a few blocks away. My "lodging" for the evening included a jaunt in the West Village for a post-interview after party. Late into the night, I headed back to La Guardia Airport, slept for a few hours in the airport, and was back in Hyde Park for another day of work schlepping along the route of schools I worked with as a tutoring program supervisor.

Memories of my first six weeks preparing to be a teacher are very fuzzy. I was at Brooklyn College, there was a lot of chatter around learning disabilities, and most of my time was spent commuting between Penn Station and Flatbush, Brooklyn, and to Jamaica, Queens, and back, daily.

I used to think my first day of teaching in Brooklyn was in September 2006, but it was actually June 2006, during my summer school placement (counting as my first in-service teaching hours) at a giant fortress of a school in Jamaica, Queens, which is no longer open. From my studio sublet in Chelsea,

I had to get up at 4:00 a.m. to make it to this giant school in Queens by 7:45 a.m. Of the 36 children enrolled in class, about eight showed up regularly. It was some sort of social studies make up credit class. The teacher was animated, but she barely acknowledged my presence. I wasn't really sure what to do, so I mostly observed and took notes verbatim. This was my preparation, New York State told me, for teacherhood.

My undergrad credentials didn't reflect enough math and science credits to work toward teaching science in any official capacity, so I was earmarked for a teaching certification that no longer exists: Transitional B Certification for Middle Childhood Special Education Grades 5 through 9. Ironically, my very first "official" teaching placement, in Brooklyn, was in a . . . wait for it . . . 12:1:1 special education science class to a group of eleventh and twelfth graders, who ranged from age 16 to 21.

My first day of full-time teaching in Brooklyn was illuminating for me, while completely predictable for my students. I was a 23-year-old white woman teaching a group of Latine kids and Afro-Caribbean Black kids, two to three years my junior, who found me amusing at best, irrelevant at worst. At one point in time, I was compared to the chef in the film *Ratatouille*. Another time, a game of dice erupted in the corner of my classroom and dollar bills were most definitely exchanged. Had my first days of teaching inadvertently turned into a summer block party?

In this 12:1:1 self-contained special education science class, the young people and I existed in one of the most restrictive classroom environments in a community school. I had never taught a day in my life, and yet here I was, given full jurisdiction over a group of people who were two to three years my junior. The school had yet to finish a round of painting and cleaning by the time the first day of school rolled around, so I spent the first two days of my teaching life in the auditorium, followed by an extended lunch and a really long recess in the school yard.

My roster was not official yet, but other special educators who had been working at the school had the students' backs. They made up a sort of schedule/agenda for us, and we mostly survived.

It was on the second day of school that I understood I would be a *science* teacher: for the eleventh/twelfth grade self-contained bridge class, in addition to the ninth grade Integrated Co-Teaching[1] (ICT) life science class, and the tenth grade ICT Earth science class. Because I was working with ninth grade and tenth grade teachers who were actually certified in the teaching of science, I sailed along in those classes, finding spots of momentum in developing projects that were somewhat UDL[2]-esque and accommodating to the many, many kids who were otherwise disinterested. But for that eleventh/twelfth grade class . . . I was on my own.

I asked the special education department chair if there was a particular curriculum I should follow, or perhaps a textbook the students should have. I remember looking back at her, and understanding what her glance and her sigh communicated that her words couldn't, or didn't have the energy or heart to tell me: there was *no curriculum* to follow for an eleventh/twelfth grade group of students who weren't interested in reading, for a teacher to follow who had only high school science and a brief overview of chemistry and biology in her undergraduate days.

So then, I began to lean on a different sort of curriculum-making journey: one that was messy, one that was riddled with mistakes; but also one that was student-centered and communal. My curriculum-making journey eventually found its way toward a sound research base, and it greatly impacted my growth and my students' growth, both academically and personally. In the following parts of this chapter, we'll unpack that journey starting with points of reflection not just in my teaching, but, more importantly, in yours!

Points of Reflection

When I work with fledgling teachers at the university level, one point of reflection I leave them with at the end of the semester is to write a letter to their future selves; the teacher they hope to become and the teacher they think they will be (Figure 4.1).

---

1   In New York State, Integrated Co-Teaching, widely known as ICT, is a component of the spectrum of special education services wherein two teachers—one general educator and one special educator—teach in a class to provide accommodations and specially designed instruction within a general education classroom. Up to 12 students, or 40% of students in the classroom community, may have IEPs.

2   Acronym for Universal Design for Learning.

:Padlet

themonorcollective · 1m

Letters to Your Fture Self

Write a letter to your future teaching self. Include your hopes and dreams about what kind of teacher you hope to be and how you would like to usher children to literacy.

Letter to Miss Adrianne

Dear Miss A,
I heard that is what your students call you. Teaching children is your destiny. It is the exemplification of your most authentic expression of self. The experience that you will gain when you become a fulltime teacher will be so fulfilling that you won't want to give up on your dreams. When you are initiated into the field, you will gain the opportunity to utilize the skills you accumulated throughout the years. Keep going. Your students are going to love you.

Sincerely Adri

Dear Future Me

I know you're like old now but I hope you're still pretty cool in some sense. I'd like to think that you have it all figured out now, not like when you were younger. It was hard getting there but you deserve it. I hope that you're a teacher that students feel comfortable with, a teacher that they feel they can go to whenever they are having troubles. Be inspiring to your students. I dream that you can teach children how to love reading and writing even though you hated it when you were younger. Use what you larned and you'll be fine. Remember it's not about the destination, it's about the journey.
-Younger you, Mandy Liang

I hope that all my students can trust me and know that I will be there to meet their developmental, emotional, and academic needs. I want to be that patient, nice, and fun teacher that kids will love :) Most importantly, I want my students to feel confident in themselves and to never feel like they can't do anything.

ni Sarah

12/15/2021

Dear future Iris,

Hi there! I REALLY hope that you decided to stay in school. I know there was a big bump and that one stressful situation, but I hope the passion you have for teaching is enough to give you the motivation you need to keep going. I hope you achieve your goal of becoming a second-grade teacher and inspiring the students in your classroom. In the first few years of teaching, literacy will not be an easy topic to teach. However, if you stick to your plans, you'll do great. Be someone who is caring, understanding, and wants the best for her students. Set them on a path of success and allow them to share their intelligence with you. And by also enabling the students to take part in their learning, you are allowing them to become independent thinkers. Being a teacher isn't going to be easy, and it'll require so much patience and understanding. And I'm hoping that you still want to make a difference in your community. At the end of the day, I hope you still have the passion and drive for teaching and the ambition to achieve these goals and dreams.

Dear shaima,
one of things that I have always dreamed about, is to become a supportive teacher for my students. I hope that the lesson plan I will do would benefit all the students. I would love to assist my students with learning literacy by doing fun activities. I love engaging activities or educational games in the classroom. I hope you still passionate about learning. I hope you that you achieve your dream about integrating arts in the classroom. when you are stressed, do not quite, you will be a great teacher.

Dear Victoria Chen-Fan,

I hope to be that one teacher who is like the cool aunt at family gatherings. Don't make students scared of you but make sure they respect you cause you won't get paid enough to babysit. I hope to find a fine line between strict and easy-going. I'd like to think you usher children to be literate beings by making reading and writing fun to them and encouraging creativity in the classroom. I dream to be the favorite teacher of many students. I hope you're a pretty good teacher that parents also love during the year and traveling the world during the holidays and summer. You better be thriving in the future!

L- Love, your past college self

FIGURE 4.1 Letters to Your Future Self, featuring the work of undergraduate students in my integrated literacy methodologies class at Brooklyn College in the Department of Childhood, Bilingual, and Special Education: Adrianne Payne, Mandy Liang, Sarah Peter, Victoria Chen-Fan, Shaima Elsayed, and Iris Ofray (2021).

In this reflective space, I find myself in conversation with my past self, almost as if I am in Charles Dickens's *A Christmas Carol,* with the current version of myself taking up the role of the Ghost of Christmas Past, but replace Christmas with teaching and London with Brooklyn.

In the first scene, I envision my older, seasoned self encountering my younger self: twenty-something, semi-shell shocked new teacher Kass surrounded by students who were used to their teachers failing them. I'm ill-equipped with useless tools like outdated textbooks with their matching prescribed curricula that were completely unsuitable for the teaching and learning experiences my students and I longed for.

My old self wants to hug and nourish young Kass, give an *it's okay to slow down* pep talk, and bring something life-giving, like a gigantic sandwich and big bottle of water to compensate for the meager yogurt and donut lunches of yesteryear; and, more importantly, the exhaustion that surfaced from the trial and error and classroom chaos that threaded my first years of teaching together.

In the second scene, I go back to the vignette I started earlier in this chapter, the part where I began my curriculum-making journey. Borne out of necessity, it started with listening to and observing the students I taught. I remember it was the young people in my classroom who were both my toughest critics and greatest teachers.

For example, my old ghost self-ushers this young Kass toward the joy (and the jokes!) that came with resurrecting parts of Al Gore's *An Inconvenient Truth* and my attempt to create a "fun" text pairing with film shorts from Dr. Seuss's[3] *The Lorax*. The students in my class erupted in laughter as soon as the ridiculous striped forest from *The Lorax* showed up on the TV screen! I suppose I thought showing 17-year-olds Dr. Seuss cartoons was a legit form of instruction in their environmental science class because of my fabulous teacher preparation during my six weeks spent "learning how to teach" during summer school. The students I taught never let me hear the end of those terrible curricular decisions.

But their laughter and their jokes helped me learn that more than anything, I needed to create meaningful learning activities that were linked to their lived experience, their learning needs, *and* the learning standards.

Later that same year, I remember extensive research on food deserts, field trips to the grocery store, significant meal planning, and even meal sharing with one another. Those curricular experiences were cocreated between me,

---

3   Given what I now know about Dr. Suess's racist and harmful imagery displayed in texts he authored and illustrated such as *If I Ran a Zoo*, where Black characters are portrayed as monkeys as Asian characters march with armed white men behind them (just one example of several of his publications that dehumanize Black, Indigenous, and other People of Color (Gatluak 2021), I would definitely choose a different text to match with a film about climate change. In the later years of my teacherhood, I built curricular units on climate change with young people, and we chose to use Spike Lee's documentary on Hurricane Katrina, *When the Levees Broke: A Requiem in Four Acts*.

the students I taught, and some of their families. In short, it was relevant, and it was also a curriculum that was connected to Living Science.

And finally, I visit the harder scenes with my young self. As I see this past, my whole body winces and my stomach turns. However, these are the moments that are especially important to share, because despite what the Educational Industrial Complex (see sidebar) tells you, *nobody* is infallible.

What is the Educational Industrial Complex?

The term *Military Industrial Complex* was coined by President Dwight Eisenhower during his farewell address in 1961 when he spoke of his concerns regarding how capital and those in corporate power influenced the growth and might of the U.S. military post-World War II; and ultimately, how the U.S. military would influence decision-making at the governmental level (National Archives n.d.).

The term Educational Industrial Complex was borne from that same thinking. The Educational Industrial Complex, known as the EIC, is all the different entities that are part of the education system (Brightman and Gutmore 2002). It is a vast network of personnel, products, services, and places including:

Where students go to receive their education:

- Pre-K centers, public schools, and charter schools at elementary, middle, and high school levels.

- State, community, and private colleges, and online degree programs.

Various materials that are sold for profit that purport to help teach such as:

- Curricula.

- Texts.

- Classroom supplies like desks, rugs, and white boards.

- Technology like Smartboards, tablets, and computers.

The services and programming provided by people and technology sold both for profit and not for profit to support education:

- Coaching and consulting provided by learning organizations and other institutions.

- Standardized testing.

- Data and assessment companies.

- After-school providers.

(*Continued*)

Additionally, the EIC encompasses the food provided in school cafeterias and products sold in vending machines.

While many of the aforementioned components are absolutely necessary to provide adequate educational experiences for teachers, students, and their families, what's concerning about the EIC is that all those different parts are in competition, as opposed to collaboration, with one another.

Competition isn't always bad, but what makes the EIC dangerous is that the source of competition is usually driven through the commodification of education, creating more money and power for some, while the learning and growth of people in school communities in real time is a lower priority.

Earlier I said "despite what the Educational Industrial Complex tells you, nobody is infallible." I say this because the EIC positions very few people as experts or thought leaders in the realm of teaching and learning. For those who are positioned as "experts," typically a bit of a hero narrative is woven around their teaching and learning story, and their personhood and teaching choices are commodified.

Part of what I'm working toward in this book is to provide a stronger platform for more teachers and other types of educators to share their experience and stories in effort to create avenues for community-based learning, thus relying less on outside entities to provide direction.

Certainly parts of the EIC are working in positive ways. For example, great books aren't hurting kids or teachers. However, it's the idea that only *some* books or curricula or experts are the be-all-end-all to a particular subject area, and that to access that magnificent thing, you have to spend money.

Of course, I realize this book in and of itself is part of the EIC because it is a product that is sold. However, it is designed with thoughtfulness and care that promotes teacher agency, rather than stymies their process.

I remember all the times I just pushed through class so it would be over, ignoring students' needs and centering on my own instead. I remember all the times I called the dean because students refused to take their hats off. I remember attempting to create a reading intervention experience for a group of tenth graders without really planning or understanding the foundational literacy of what I was trying to do, and how ridiculous the group of students thought the whole ordeal was, how ridiculous they thought *I* was. I remember how I used to participate in a school-wide mandate that sent students home because they weren't wearing their uniforms properly.

I'm taking deep breaths now . . . there were parts of those years that were terrible for me, yes, but even more so for those students who were the recipients of my errors.

So yes, there are a lot of gifts I wish I could grant to my new teacher self that would have made things less terrible, more joyful, more just. For example, I wish I had understood the power of community that comes with making time for enduring conversations with students *while class is in session*. I wish I had a better teacher preparation experiences to build more impactful foundational literacy and numeracy skills with my students. And more than anything, I wish I would have been more present, less focused on paying bills and finishing grad school assignments.

Had I been equipped with those gifts earlier in my career, I'm sure my school life, along with my students', would have been quite different. Perhaps I would have been more present, more slept . . . more prepared.

But this is the part of the Dickensian story where all the reflection pauses, and the characters are left with only their present: that's me, that's you, it's us, and it is our *now*.

It is in the collective journey where you find the answers. A fancy, more academic term for this work I'm suggesting is *long-term locally derived inquiry*. That is the story of my teaching career, it is the path I've not veered far from, and it is the justice work I am suggesting now. Here is what I mean.

As is with all learning, the deepest kind is one that is curiosity-based and human-centered, where those seeking the information are the most instrumental parts of the knowledge-*making* journey.

This is where individuals ask questions about the needs of the people they are in community with, note what they don't know and what they need to learn, and, together, they work to explore, find, and try various experiences, texts, and learning activities that fulfill the needs that were identified originally.

Needs evolve and time continues, and the community works together to evolve as such.

So, as much as I would have loved to enter years one and two and three in my classroom teaching life just *knowing,* I very much understand I wouldn't be who I am today had I not experienced the trials and errors along the way. However, I do know that both me and my students would have been much better off had I been granted more time to collaborate and think with my colleagues, or reflect on what I was learning in grad school to build curriculum with my school community more deeply and clearly in ways that were more deeply impactful for the student community.

Within those first years of teaching, I'm not sure having "known" would have been as well-received had I not discovered them through my own questions along with students' experiences and my colleagues' care. I firmly believe one cannot enter into a community of people—whether they are very new or very experienced—and simply *know* what that community needs. Time spent with people you are put in a position to teach matters.

The Nature of a Curriculum-Making Journey

Curricular path.

Herein lies the just nature of a curriculum-making journey, a primary component of an educator's justice work:

1. We do the inner work of understanding who we are, where we've been, and what it is we're trying to do. In other words, we develop a more powerfully reflective practice.

2. *We prepare ourselves by doing the study and practice piece of teacher preparation that helps us understand how to teach,* developing a strong base of knowledge that underscores brain-based learning, culturally responsive pedagogy, and developmentally appropriate foundational literacy and numeracy skills.

3. We work to deeply understand the communities in which we work; that is *who* we are teaching and *what* we are teaching.

4. We care for ourselves, and we care for our community.

First, let's continue our curriculum-making journey by developing a more ritualized reflective practice.

This is the reflective component that is woven through the text. While it is absolutely a series of intentional exercises, reflection works most powerfully when it is practiced habitually. It is also essential that we consider the development of agency for individuals within the field of teaching. Many of the reflective exercises we've worked through thus far in the text have called us to dig through past school experiences, including:

- Journaling about our experiences as students in the early years of our schooling.

- Thinking about the beginning years of our teaching careers (like we did earlier in this chapter).

- Considering the legacy of different laws and policies on different groups of people throughout the history of schooling.

Daily reflective practice looks different. This is the ritualized reflection we build into our lived experiences each morning or afternoon or night. The *time* in which ritualized reflection happens is not so important. Whether you choose to reflect independently or within a group is not so important either.

What's important is that you make space in your mind to think about your decisions and actions in connection to the community you teach and learn with, both honestly and consistently. This ritualized reflection helps to ensure you are in alignment with your community's needs and that you are moving toward shared learning goals like state standards, tiered objectives, and/or IEP goals.

Collaborate: Build Your Reflective Practice, Together

The following practices and rituals demonstrate ways to do this work in collaboration with other stakeholders in your school community.

Create Consistent Spaces for Reflection: Schedule Time with Colleagues That You Look Forward to (Like Lunch!)

There were, and still are, quite a few reflection rituals that make a tremendous difference in my teaching and learning life. Some of the deepest connections I've made with other humans happened during shared lunches with other teachers on my grade team.

When I was teaching elementary school in my later years of classroom life, I came to know this space as the most authentic one for my development—both personally and professionally. Every Thursday, a teacher who had been teaching for 20-plus years hosted lunch in the classroom she shared with her co-teacher, a newer teacher who brought great energy, curiosity, and humor to our shared table.

In this space, members of our fourth grade team would rotate in and out each week of the open invitation, always with at least four to five people present. Here, in conjunction with sharing interesting snacks and trading recipes, we asked each other questions we didn't necessarily feel comfortable surfacing in front of the entire teaching staff (we were in a group of approximately 100 teachers serving nearly 1,000 students!). Together, we learned skills and strategies that were more emergent and directly connected to our student community.

For example, I remember working through a new math curriculum with lots of "rich tasks" that were new to many of us. For some of us, the lessons would go terribly. We reported to our colleagues about students rolling around on the rug, or the students who would show expressions that mirrored our confused teaching.

I remember telling my colleagues how the new lessons "went" in terms of what I thought students left understanding (not a whole lot . . . was it possible that they left the math lesson at a deeper state of confusion than in which they started??). I'd ask how their students responded to similar work, or how they worked through the same problem set or task.

My colleagues' feedback was candid because after meeting every week for months (and, for some of us, *years* as we had been at the same school and grade team for quite some time), we trusted one another. This honesty came from the alchemy of teachers' genuine yearning to be better at their craft mixed with authentic sharing from people who worked toward similar goals.

We all wanted the student community to have better, more joyful, and more impactful learning experiences. We were all deeply interested in creating stronger pedagogy where students became more proficient in their foundational math, literacy, and critical thinking skills while staying true to their identities along the way.

Work Along: Trying out Lean Coffee

Creating bonds with colleagues and sharing fruitful meals that end with satiated appetites and minds doesn't happen magically. The key to initiating conversations with teachers and colleagues you work with closely lies within trusting relationships first and foremost, and, secondly, having some kind of shared goal in mind.

When bonds between colleagues exist, the shared goal is more of a subtlety in conversation; it's present because you've known each other for a while, you've witnessed each other teach, and, in general, have shared lots of experiences in school together.

For newer teams of teachers, it's essential to center your shared time on building relationships; that is to focus on having fun and developing stronger bonds. Using shared meal times to strategize and learn from one another is a more explicit endeavor.

To ritualize shared meals as a consistent space for reflection where people learn and grow together, use Lean Coffee as an organizing mechanism for your meet-up. Lean Coffee is a "structured yet agenda-less" meeting. It began in Seattle in the early 1990s as a way to bring people together to participate in shared knowledge-making, but without the cumbersome paper trail, endless committees, and pre-planning of agendas.

One of the most powerful components of Lean Coffee is the ability for all in attendance at the meeting to democratically generate a list of things to talk about. In effect, people who are involved don't feel like an agenda is being pushed upon them; rather, the agenda is relevant to their experience, and directly connected to their community's needs.

Here are steps to begin structuring meet-ups that are centered in a space of reflection using Lean Coffee with your colleagues:

1. Find a consistent time and location to meet that is already built in your schedule (like lunch!).

2. Open invitations for teachers you directly work with are most powerful in creating impact for communities of students. So, if you are a fifth grade teacher wanting to initiate this reflective space, send an email to all teachers working on your grade team, not just the people you hang out with after school.

3. Don't feel as though you have to rush the meeting space into the Lean Coffee agenda; it's important for people attending to know the meet-up is a space where they can feel relaxed and enjoy themselves. If lunch starts at 12:15, start the Lean Coffee structuring at least 10 minutes into the period. Give people time to get their lunch and organize themselves.

4. When at least three or four people are present and have transitioned into lunch, begin Lean Coffee. It's really simple!

(Continued)

a. **Each person is invited to identify a few topics they'd like to discuss.**

b. **The group then votes on which topics they are most interested in discussing,** and one person from the group keeps track of the votes. A simple way to do this is by putting a mark on each sticky note for each vote. Each person is allotted two votes.

c. **The topics are then prioritized according to votes, and the group discusses them in that order.** If stickies are used, you can remove the stickies from the board when they are done being discussed. If there is a sense of urgency around a lot of topics, you may wish to name time limits on the number of minutes spent talking about each topic. However, restricting time when there is a lot to say or feelings felt about whatever the topic may be doesn't lend well to feelings of safety and/or group bonds. That said, it's okay to "go off script."

5. When the meet-up is coming to an end, be sure to close with some kind of appreciation. This doesn't have to be a formal round of appreciations, but do make sure to say goodbyes and thank-yous. While those things might seem obvious, too often, meetings at school end abruptly and people go to the next thing without any sort of connection. Simple words like "thank-you" and "bye" go a long way in the connectedness people build and maintain with one another.

Just remember: the goal of this structure is to evoke a sense of reflection and collective growth while building relationships, not necessarily to "get stuff done." (For more information on Lean Coffee, visit their website at leancoffee.org.)

Establish Routines and Rituals with Colleagues: Purposefully Work Toward Shared Vision and Illuminate Individual Strengths

Another powerful component of reflective practice I developed throughout my teacherhood was the ability to develop a shared vision with my co-teachers. This manifested through a series of ritualistic daily check-ins, weekly planning sessions, and even frequently attended happy hours! Throughout my teaching career, the relationships I've developed in the many classroom spaces is one of the most important markers of my pedagogy. The camaraderie and fellowship that my fellow teachers and I cultivated had a profound impact on the families and students we served. It also changed our ability to sustain and grow the kinds of goals we had for our teaching and learning lives.

This work does not happen automatically, and it is different than a teaching friendship. Cultivated camaraderie and shared vision grows from intentional and meaningful planning from teachers who share a school community. It doesn't happen overnight, nor does it just happen when teachers share a hallway together or sit next to each other at staff meetings.

This is where rituals and routines come in: they are a key element for developing a collaborative reflective practice. For example, in the teacher groups I have worked in, we used a variety of protocols to surface our personal needs, cultural orientation, and values. As we got to know each other and our students, we spent time cocreating shared visions for our classroom communities, including individual strengths and students' interests. Additionally, we took great interest in developing our place-based pedagogy and how the world was positioned around us.

Our vision for our classroom was cocreated with our students and their families as well.

Place-Based Pedagogy: A Deeper Dive

Place-based pedagogy is a dynamic part of curriculum-making to consider as you are creating a vision for your classroom community. Essentially, place-based pedagogy asserts that where you are teaching and learning matters. This is another building block to creating a more just foundation.

For example, if you are attending a school located near the Plains in the Midwest, your experience will vary greatly from someone attending school located in northern Ohio near the Great Lakes. Or consider the experience of someone who attends a private religious school in comparison to someone who attends a public school within the same vicinity. Even though their schools are in close proximity to one another, their experiences will vary because the school environments are quite different.

For example, a Jewish Day School can be on one side of the street while a public school with predominantly Latine and Chinese students can be on the other. The same is true for more rural spaces or suburban spaces; if your town is near an ocean or a lake, the ways in which you might consider marine life might be significantly different that someone who lives in the middle of Kansas surrounded by fields of wheat, and vice versa.

When we consider place as part of our teaching and learning structure, we also consider the cultural expressions that are soaked into our lived experience as we cross the street and see Hebrew words on a storefront, or find a snack at the Chinese bakery, or see stretches of land with few houses as far as our eyes can stay on the horizon.

How the neighborhoods, countries, villages, cities, parkland, and farmland are constructed creates a roadmap for students' questions and curiosities, signifying the importance of the world that surrounds them within their everyday classroom conversations.

(Continued)

For further reading on place-based pedagogy, I recommend starting with Emelina Minero's article, "Place-Based Learning: A Multi-faceted Approach" featured in *Edutopia*. From there, you can read more extensively on place-based pedagogies in the book *The Power of Place: Authentic Learning Through Place-Based Education* by Tom Vander Ark, Emily Liebtag, and Nate McClennen. Also include "Land-Based Learning," as a search term to focus and center contributions from Indigenous voices.

The rituals and routines we established allowed for us to not only work toward shared understanding, but also to name what wasn't going well, concerning practices, and/or parts of a lesson that triggered pain points for individuals or groups of people. Below are suggested steps that support building a more collaborative reflective practice and establishing routines and rituals.

Determine in which context you'll be collaborating. This could be within a grade team, a subject-area department team, or perhaps in a smaller context such as a partnership within a co-teaching environment. Maybe it's just a friend who you enjoy working with who shares the same students, or students who are similar to those in your class/es. Whomever you choose to collaborate with, they should be a person or people who you are working with in a similar school or the same school community. You should also be able to schedule meetings with them regularly (preferably baked into your teaching schedule already!).

Agree to document some reflective experiences beforehand. For example, before you begin spending any kind of significant time together, spend time doing inner work by developing an identity map and/or zooming in on a few moments within your personal school history timeline (see Historical Underpinnings section online). While it will not be necessary to share your reflective artifacts fully during your first few meetings, it will be important to have the foundational mindset of *who you are* in place. The inner work of identity mapping and timeline pedagogy in the context of personal history of school allows you to consider your identity markers and how they matter in your teaching and learning life.

Schedule a first meeting during which you state your beliefs and values for the work you do. See the lesson plan in Chapter 3 for surfacing needs and values, which is the perfect protocol to do this work.

Another example of this work is featured below: documenting a team's Values-Practice Connection by sharing anecdotes that demonstrate their foundational values. There, you will find examples of story snippets that match the values of a team during one of their initial collaborative reflective sessions.

The Values-Practice Connection

This team began with the short, poignant question that defines *an educator's everything* in terms of how they operate in school communities: "What are your values?". This team surfaced their values through story, strengthening their core collective belief system within their community. The Center for Nonviolent Communication has an excellent resource to support people in naming their values available on their website, called the "Needs Inventory".

Later, each individual worked to clarify their values in alignment to their practice (as a verb!), especially when working toward the shared goals of the team's community. In Table 4.1, find the shared value set created during this period of time. We call this the Values-Practice Connection.

TABLE 4.1 Values-Practice Connection examples.

Values	Practice
Sportsmanship	<ul><li>Cocreated expectations.</li><li>Giving and receiving critical feedback.</li><li>Understanding and building more than one way of "winning" re: success in school.</li><li>Self-accountability, maintaining commitments to your "team."</li></ul>
Love	<ul><li>Developing a teaching practice that is underscored by Gary Chapman's *Discovering the 5 Love Languages at School*.</li><li>Interacting with others from a space of gratitude and reverence.</li></ul>
Authenticity	<ul><li>Sharing your stance on teaching and learning publicly and consistently.</li><li>Following up on goals based on real-time data.</li></ul>
Communication	<ul><li>Generating weekly updates, sending happenings of all kinds to the community (not just when something "good" or "bad" happens.</li><li>Honoring multi-modal communication (messaging through email, oral communication, paper fliers).</li></ul>

Move Away from Static Meeting Agendas: Complicating What We Mean When We Say "The Work"

Embracing multiliteracies like *talk story* is an important component of teaching and learning methodology, especially through the lens of engagement. In many classrooms, administrative meetings, and other professional learning experiences, the idea of "chit-chatting" or passing along stories orally is seen as separate from "the real work," the Work with a capital "W." As I've grown my own pedagogy in partnership with many students, teachers, and families over the years, I've had lots of opportunities to witness how both low stakes (e.g., a description of what one ate for breakfast) and high stakes (e.g., a description of a conflict one personally experienced in school) oral storytelling takes a powerful role in shaping learners' growth.

As a teacher who has grappled with, explored, and taught through multiple forms of literacy experiences, I'd heard of and practiced oral history projects with students. We learned about folktales and griots. Even as a kid, when I sat around the campfire (literally) and listened to my family tell ghost stories, I walked away a changed person.

To this day, with each community of learners I have worked with as a classroom teacher, whether they were in my elementary school classroom, high school advisory, or graduate class sitting with me at Teachers College, we built community circle time together to share parts of our stories.

Sometimes, the sharing would be something basic, like what students were looking forward to in the week. Other times, it would be something more emotive, like an appreciation about a specific peer. There were also times when the sharing was more restorative, like when members of the class experienced a problem or crisis together.

It wasn't until I started working with two different groups in a professional context that I learned just how powerful and important *talk story* is to a group's ability to grow and learn from one another. First, my partner, Cornelius, and I have worked with a wide network of teachers in Kapolei, Hawai'i, to support them in building their literacy practices. Second, I worked with a group called Breaths Together for Change (mentioned in Chapter 1) with the goal of ending racism through white racial reckoning.

While I could go on for a very long time about the potency of my learning in each context, my goal here is to underscore what those two groups had in common that lent themselves to not necessarily just my own personal growth, but, more importantly, the connectivity within the group and a stronger version of collective purpose.

To *talk story,* or *mo'olelo* in Hawai'i, is to pass wisdom through the spoken word. It is a pidgin phrase that comes from the *'Ōlelo* language, a tradition that comes from an Indigenous knowledge-base, and, to this day, is part of the daily life in Hawai'i and other Pacific Islands.

Rosa Say, author of *Managing with Aloha,* describes the concept of talk story:

> Our Hawaiian ancestors did not pen a written history of our islands. Information was passed generation to generation orally, with the 'Ōlelo (the language and spoken word) and in storytelling. Today there is much effort in our Hawaiian renaissance to record what we know about our past history before the kūpuna (our elders) forget and can no longer tell it to us. Still today, for us to communicate and dialogue is to "talk story." There is so very much I personally have learned from the 'Ōlelo form of teaching, perhaps most of all that anyone who speaks has the potential to be my teacher. I only need listen as well as I can, quieting the voices in my own head (Say and Fiske 2019).

My favorite part of Rosa Say's description of talk story is the part when she says that anyone who speaks has the potential to be her teacher, so long as she is able to listen. Talk story offers us an important frame to situate ourselves when we sit down to learn in the educational spaces we work within.

In Breaths Together for Change, each meeting was centered around participants' personal stories in connection to meditations we listened to. In the Hawai'i educator group Cornelius and I facilitated in partnership with educators from the community, we adopted a similar approach that was heavily influenced by mo'olelo, or talk story, as modeled by our Hawai'i education partners.

In any group I have led or been a part of, the creation of space for the telling of stories served as impetus for not just change, but also for the hope of creating something better. Creating space for the telling of our stories is a proclamation of joy, and while storytelling might feel like a subversive thing to do in a professional learning experience (and maybe in some places or institutions it is), it as an important step toward learning that impacts communities on both personal and professional levels.

The Six-Word Story

Not everybody will feel comfortable with sharing their stories. Some might even think it inappropriate in the workspace. If you aren't sure how storytelling will be received in the space you're creating for teaching and learning, the six-word story is a great place to start.

The first time I experienced six-word stories was with fifth grade students during a memoir-writing unit. I had been gifted a small book of six-word memoirs, which inspired an internal excavation of other six-word story websites and generators. I shared several six-word stories with the fifth graders, and then challenged the students to write a story about themselves using only six words. At first, they were delighted, especially the students who typically groaned after writing their third sentence. However, soon after the activity started, they grew pleasantly weary . . . encompassing yourself in so few words is hard!

That's the beauty of the six-word story. Rather than bucketing energy in grammar, long sentences, and expressive language, the locus of energy is instead put on finding just a few words to describe an experience, event, or even oneself.

I smiled at that memory when I experienced six-word stories in the Breaths Together for Change adult learning space. At the end of every single session, after we spent almost the entire time talking story, we were asked to document our learning experiences from the session through a photo, captioned with a six-word story in an online archive.

Throughout the year, we met each month. During our last meeting, we had the opportunity to view the trajectory of our growth, as well as others in the group, by reading through a year's worth of six-word stories matched with photos in the online archive we created. Some people captioned their photos to further illuminate the connectivity in their stories to their experience.

Typically, when learning is deep and emotional, human capacity for downloading new information decreases. Capturing the essence of learning in fewer words matched with visuals is a more practical and precise way to synthesize individual and group experiences as opposed to reading lengthy testimonials. It is also more practical from a time constraint and/or scheduling point of view.

To use the six-word story as a storytelling device that promotes learning and growth individually and collectively, consider the following moments and goals to implement this practice:

1. **Opening up a meeting with students or other colleagues:** Use a six-word story to describe your morning/how you are feeling today/what you are looking forward to today/what's not going well today.

2. **Assessing a learning experience:** Use a six-word story to describe your learning today. Optional: use a photo that connects to or represents your six-word story. For groups meeting consistently over time, consider including a six-word story with a photo after each meeting. Some people may wish to expand their story, captioning their photo with a descriptive connection.

3. **Envisioning a more just and joyous space:** Use a six-word story to describe what a more just and joyful space would be like for you. Optional: include an image that represents your story. Also, consider weaving the six-word stories together to create an amalgamation of stories that reflect a collective vision. Post this work somewhere public and visible to hold one another accountable for maintaining and building that shared vision throughout time.

Below, see six-word story examples from educators in Kapolei, Hawai'i, that exemplify a year's worth of their learning in literacy professional development with my organization, The Minor Collective. This group was accustomed to talking story, and my partner, Cornelius, and I actually learned how to refine this teaching and learning craft from the participants in this group.

On our last meeting date of the year, we (Cornelius and I) first invited them to talk story in small groups. We used the prompts in Figure 4.2 to catalyze their story telling.

After the group of educators engaged in talking story in small groups using the prompts from Figure 4.2, we then invited them to document their stories using the six-word story device with a representative photo and connective descriptions (option 2 from the earlier goals). In addition to the photo, we also asked them to write a small connective paragraph between their photo and their story to further expand on their thinking. We gave them approximately

FIGURE 4.2 Tell the story.

15 minutes to work independently. Following are some of their six-word stories. Find a template to create six-word stories with your community at https://www.kassandcorn.com/teachingfiercely/.

Six-word story: Keep up the fight, good work!

This relates to the conversation I had in breakout groups. Working with incoming Freshmen this year, students have missed out on that growth period within the middle school environment due to being out of school for nearly two years. So students have had to go from an elementary mindset to a high school mindset so quickly. My six-word story relates to us teachers and students keeping up the fight. To keep going and persevere in such crazy times.

—Teacher, Sophia Carba, Hawai'i

Six-word story: An inclusive future needs us all.

Earlier this year, an elementary librarian sent me a book that she felt was inappropriate for an elementary library. The book *Heartstopper Volume 2* is a YA graphic novel featuring queer characters that is being turned into a Netflix series. All 35 of my students in my Gender Sexuality Alliance Club borrowed and read that 1 book in only 2 weeks.

They all shared that our library doesn't have any books about LGBTQ+ folks, and they can't even check out books. Our community library isn't supportive of students spending time there either. Seeing how much the students loved the book, I wrote a DonorsChoose grant to get the full series, books 1–4 and they arrived yesterday. The kids were instantly in love and instead of a GSA meeting, they just wanted to read and share the books together.

I'm not an ELA teacher anymore, so to have kids all over my room sharing books, like they might have in pre-COVID times, felt special. For an inclusive future that's better for everyone, kids need to see themselves in literacy. When they can't see themselves in books, it's our job as teachers to help them find access to diverse reading material.

I'm also acknowledging that these books are NOT welcome everywhere in our nation, so it's critical that kids know an inclusive future is possible. I've been scared for the mental health of my LGBTQ+ students, and I need them to know a better world is coming, because teachers like us will help build it.

—Sarah "Mili" Milianta-Laffin, Teacher,
Ilima Middle School, Kapolei, Hawai'i

Cocreating a Shared Vision

Sometimes when we collaborate, we are only working with one other person. They might be a "teacher bestie." Or maybe they are the person you've been matched up with by your school administration, and you are teaching in the same classroom with the same group of kids every day. No matter if you are best friends or complete strangers, these shared reflective practices are important. The students you teach will be able to read your connection or lack thereof. Whether or not you are on the same page is very clear to the children you teach, and when there is dissonance between the grown-ups they rely on for safety and community, they will absorb that dissonance, resulting in confusion, chaos, or worse.

The Shared Vision exercise shown in Figure 4.3 is one way to initiate powerful collaboration, surfacing not just fundamental teaching philosophy beliefs,

Shared Vision Planning Page

Establish a strong foundation for your team by sharing your views on learning, and then combining them into one shared vision for the year. Each teacher should write their response to each of the key questions. Post this shared vision in a place where it can be revisited throughout the year so that you may strengthen your co-actions and stay on track.

	Teacher:	Teacher:
Name a few variables that support students' learning.		
What is your view on the optimal classroom learning environment?		
What talents do you bring as a teacher that you know can maximize the learning process for your students?		
What is the best way to address students' learning differences?		

Shared Vision:

FIGURE 4.3 Shared Vision planning template, adapted from Elevating Co-teaching Through UDL, Elizabeth Stein.

but also, what you imagine and hope to practice in your instruction, and in developing your classroom community.

Whether or not you are self-initiating this collaborative reflection for your own teaching or facilitating it with others, it's a powerful exercise to frame an integrated source of strength that can evolve throughout the year, serving as a point of reference for who you are, what you believe in, and what you are working towards.

In Figures 4.4 and 4.5, see examples of similar work that was facilitated during a co-teaching institute by myself and my former colleague, Dr. Katie Ledwell, with the Teachers College Inclusive Classrooms Project.

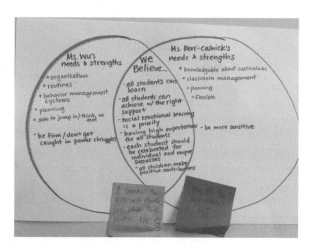

FIGURE 4.4 Chart displaying teacher's shared co-constructed vision on their shared classroom community.

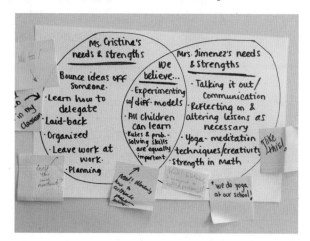

FIGURE 4.5 Chart displaying teacher's shared co-constructed vision on their shared classroom community.

Determine a weekly time you will meet. This is really important. At the beginning of the school year, a lot of excitement is generated with fresh starts and new people, but as the year moves on, people tend to disconnect and meet less frequently. Choosing a weekly time that you and your partner/s will commit to is integral for a routine to become ritualized, that is, marks of your collaboration that you and your partner/s begin to embody.

Mark the times on your calendars during the meeting. I personally *love* a shared Google calendar because it allows all people involved to see the event, share attachments and links easily, and also notify meeting participants of any changes in meeting time, place, or structure.

Hot tip: Google has an excellent "Workspace Learning Center!" Whenever I can't figure out how to do something on Google, I go to support.google .com, and explore the very user-friendly interface. In Google calendaring, they have helpful tutorials like "What can you do with Calendar?" and "Share your calendar with someone."

Other popular web calendars like Apple's Ical are also great, but they tend to be less accessible, especially for those who aren't using an Apple device. Google calendar is available and free on all devices.

Establish a planning routine. When I wasn't able to stay at school past 3:30 p.m. due to grad school classes in the evening or having to pick up my kids from daycare by 4:00 p.m., my planning routines with my colleagues got *really* real. If I didn't use my time wisely during the school day, it meant I would be staying up after hours, way past my bedtime, to finish planning and/or preparing for the next day. After one too many late nights, I began to get a lot more intentional about how I spent my teacher prep periods.

These habits have been long-lasting, even as my discretionary time evolves.

At the beginning of each meeting with my collaboration partners, I began to ask what we wanted to accomplish during our time together. After we named those components, we then prioritized what was most important to work on together, and what could be done individually if we ran out of time.

After that, we did the important work of discussing parts of our shared vision; we weren't just pontificating about our hopes and dreams or hashing out our frustrations because we could talk a good game, or because venting felt pleasant.

Rather, our conversations were rooted in the daily lived experience of classroom life, including noticings and wonderings we had based on kids' contributions within class, or their worrisome silence. We'd surface current events in light of the curricular themes we had planned on building, and change course if we needed to. We'd take stock of various strategies we were trying, and determine what was working and what wasn't by looking at artifacts and evidence like student work, or family and caregiver's feedback.

In Figure 4.6, find an example of a co-planning routine I developed that helped me and my teaching partners organize our thinking, prioritize tasks, and build ideas intentionally while considering the needs of our classroom community. I created this routine when I was working in several co-teaching relationships, that is, every day I taught with these teachers at the same time in the same classroom.

Embracing Teacher Intellect: Changing the Narrative About Teachers

Next, and perhaps the part of teachers' curriculum-making journey that is most widely understood as "important work," is the study and practice piece of *how* to teach re: how learning works between teachers and students. This is where teachers learn how to teach students foundational skills and strategies like reading, critical thinking, and numeracy. This is also where they learn to develop content knowledge on things like scientific processes and parts of history that are underscored in state curricular standards.

Throughout a teacher's career, they will be tasked with threading those knowledges together in conjunction with the students they teach and the standards and curricula their state/district/school uses. To facilitate this work through the lens of justice and joy, the goal must be to weave a curricular experience that serves their community of young humans in their classrooms from year to year along a continuum of change.

Co-planning Routine for Teacher Partnerships

This template was designed for teams who meet for approximately 45-60 minutes 2x a week. However, some teams may not have that kind of planning time. Feel free to copy this template and revise it in ways that best suit your partnership and community of learners.

5 min: Task Management: What needs to get done during this time? Prioritize tasks that will give more opportunities to execute the shared vision (i.e., looking at student work together to form strategy groups, crafting a project that exercises UDL practices, redesigning a unit of study based on your students' learning profiles)
☐
☐
☐
☐

5-7 min: Reflection: What's been working, what hasn't? Some of what you reflect on here can be addressed at another time, or you may choose to delegate some responsibilities.

What worked:	What didn't:
First step:	First step:

7-10 min: Child Study: Think about a few kids who raise questions for you at this point in time. Spend some time talking about what you've noticed, what might need to be addressed, and some initial ideas for support.

Child	Noticings	Hunches	First Step

20-30 min: Looking at Student Work/Instructional Design: Research shows that more opportunities for access and full participation are created when the students we teach are centered in our instructional design. In order to do that, ongoing assessment and reflection on the work students generate is necessary. During this time, chart out tiered learning objectives for the week, create flexible small groups to target specific goals, or even plan opportunities for learning outside classroom walls, like field trips or outdoor walks.

5-7 min: Delegating Responsibilities: Who will do what in terms of preparing materials, designing small group instructions, choosing texts, and identifying and procuring appropriate technology, parent outreach, etc.)?

Teacher 1:	Teacher 2:
Other:	

FIGURE 4.6 Co-planning routine for teacher partnerships.

However, student-centered curriculum is somewhat of a rarity in schools for a variety of reasons.

It's not easy, this complex fabric of curricular experiences teachers are tasked with weaving. Too often, the young humans are left out of the fabric construction when curricula is packaged and mandated to be delivered in very specific ways. Additionally, those aforementioned important knowledges essential to the foundations of learning are skirted over in university-based teacher preparation programs, and/or are scarcely revisited during the time in which teachers are connected to young people in schools. Think about the scant teacher preparation I described in the beginning of this section—after a mere six weeks I was granted full jurisdiction of teaching several groups of students by myself.

The Educational Industrial Complex also poses a threat to the ways in which teachers are positioned to creatively adapt the curriculum they are given to implement. State legislation, local policies, and the oversight of classroom-based decision-making from various school boards and other parent /caregiver groups challenges teachers' work even further.

I put important work in quotation marks earlier because prescribed and packaged curriculum is an affront to holding teacher knowledge valuable or something worth investing in. When we strip vital decision-making pro-cesses away from the people who spend the most time *with* and are in clos-est proximity *to* young learners in school, it is an injustice to both teachers' and students' humanity.

(I want to reiterate here: this is not teachers' fault. This is another example of how deeply rooted and multifaceted injustices have spread throughout our schools.)

The general disregard of teacher intellect in the United States has been gen-erated by public rhetoric, multiple news outlets, and social media. For exam-ple, *Time* magazine featured a series on teachers in America in September 2018. It showed multiple magazine covers with exhausted looking teachers sitting in empty classrooms, forlorn expressions on their faces, looking into the distance. One photo's tagline read: "I have a master's degree, 16 years of experience, work two extra jobs, and donate plasma to pay the bills. I'm a teacher in America" (Reilly 2018). Also published in Fall 2018 was a *New York Times Magazine* issue featuring multiple articles on teaching and education, with its cover plastered in bold, protest-style font: "TEACHERS JUST WANT TO TEACH, BUT THE CLASSROOM HAS BECOME A BATTLEGROUND."

While it is absolutely true that teachers are underpaid, overworked, and, most of all, underappreciated, this narrative constructed by American media and the general public paints a bleak, underwritten, depressing, and incom-plete picture of what being a teacher is like and who teachers are.

This is where multiple truths are important to hold.

It is also true that schools, government, and families have dangerous tensions brewing over myriad issues regarding what's best for kids, what's best for teachers, and what is and what is not in the realm of administrative responsibilities.

What's more is that the teacher shortage, a long-time issue in rural and urban centers, has been exacerbated by the COVID-19 global pandemic and within the coming years is projected to grow even larger. In Fall 2022, there were reportedly 570,000 fewer educators working in public schools, with roughly 40,000 teaching vacancies (Lowrey 2022). Current trends show that by 2025, schools in the United States will be understaffed—with up to 200,000 teacher positions unfulfilled (Jacques 2022).

And . . . there is so much more to the story of teachers, what it means *to teach, to learn,* to the full, whole, beautiful, brilliant people, who, for most of us with children, thank our blessings they are in their care for six hours every day.

Where is the part that tells the story about teachers who are present, or those who are serving the children in their communities outside of the classroom or beyond? How despite all the challenges teachers are faced with, and the minimal love American culture pushes their way, more than 3 million teachers across the United States (National Center for Educational Statistics Data n.d.) *still remain committed to the work.* And some of those who have left their school communities remain committed to kids' learning in different ways.

"Committed to the work" is a phrase I would use to describe many teachers I know, and many of whom I don't know personally, but have read or heard about and appreciate from afar. While teaching in primary and secondary schools, there were times I used to feel unstoppable in the classroom, like "The Force"[4] lived within me. There was nothing a student brought to me that I didn't try to figure out. I learned each one of them. I integrated a group of fourth and fifth graders with the thickest IEPs in the whole school into the greater school community; they participated on field trips, they created spoken word performances, they created beautiful works of art, they

---

4   Yes, "The Force" as described in *Star Wars*! The one that runs through you and gives you energy to move boldly with your instinct, your mind, and your heart!

studied the world that surrounded them. They left our classroom space with stronger literacy and numeracy skills, they developed more powerful emotional literacy, they were proud of themselves, and their peers and parents were in awe of them. And I know I didn't do this alone. I had a whole team of people working in community for the young humans who attended our school to get the kind of education they deserved.

But I left the classroom space because I felt like it started to restrict my growth. The hierarchies embedded with in the school system—such as the idea that teachers should ask permission to try something differently, or professional learning should be facilitated so specifically—to me felt suffocating. There were times I felt like my creativity was getting me in "trouble." I felt like the teacher agency developed from the learning communities I was a part of wasn't always appreciated and, perhaps worse, may have even felt threatening to some people in my community.

Whether or not that weight I felt was real or in my head, nonetheless, it pushed me out of classroom teaching and into a different role, that of coach and documentarian for TCICP at the time. Even though my creativity felt subdued, my ambition and commitment to building the bedrock of just schooling and joyful curiosity remained. Leaving the classroom wasn't an easy decision. Six years out, it is the one space I continue to long for no matter where my educational journey takes me. It is also the space that informs my current work along my educational journey.

My role now is to support teachers like my former self in the classroom, and also those educators who are far away from feeling any sort of agency. It's important to not feel as though leaving the classroom into a coaching role is "moving up." I want to flatten hierarchies that school communities uphold, and I want to create lateral circles of leadership for teachers and students and families to participate in and be proud of.

In my post-classroom teaching days, I often ask myself as a coach: Who did I need, what did I need, and what did my coworkers and students need? What knowledge and experiences were we missing? The thought sanctuary I described in Chapter 3 is paramount. Countless experiences as teacher and as coach have continuously shown the need for teachers to sit alone, sit together, and be provided with ample time for soaking in the days' experiences in order to plan for tomorrow's learning.

Historical Underpinings: Gauging "Smart"

As we consider the injustice and justices regarding the narrative on teachers, here, we pause to venture back in time to see the linkage between how we value our own intelligence, as well as our students', and standardized testing: https://www.kassandcorn.com/teachingfiercely/.

Chapter 5:
Moving Toward Joy: Student-Centered Experiences in Standards-Based Classrooms

I often think about the importance of instructional stance upon the curriculum-making journey. I remember a moment in time when I was working with the New York City Department of Education and the Teachers College Inclusive Classrooms Project (TCICP). We were working to develop space and time for teachers, across the city, to come together, share ideas, and make curriculum for students they were teaching presently; not a hand-it-to-me, read-from-the-script situation, but a real, kid-centric, accessible work of curriculum where kids learned in delight, within the realm of a classroom space, from a teacher who owned and created a learning design that was made specially for *her* students within *her* context.

We (my colleague Dr. Kara Gustafson Hollins and project directors Dr. Celia Oyler and Dr. Britt Hamre) successfully designed Curriculum Design Teams, where three groups of 25 teachers came together once a month and worked through several frameworks like UDL and Understanding by Design, tons of Gloria Ladson-Billings's work, as well as Inclusive Design Principles that had been created by Celia and Britt and shaped by TCICP staff Anne Palmer, Erika Hughes Hooper, Kara, and myself, as well as teachers on TCICP's advisory board.

On the TCICP website, we worked with participating educators to publish their curriculum to be shared with the larger educator community—for free—in hopes that folx would learn and share with one another in a communal style. Our idea was that the curriculum would serve as a mentor text for all educators working to make a curriculum special, that was designed by them in partnership with their students and their students' families. We didn't tell people what to do—rather, we served as facilitators, shapers of group knowledge, sounding boards, resource distributors, and curators of experience.

A year later, we did the same thing. But we ran into a wrinkle: in the New York City DOE UFT[1] contract, there is a clause that states teachers who are part of the teachers' union in New York City (this is the majority of the city's educators) cannot be subjected to "extensive amounts of paperwork." Union representatives across the city categorized making curriculum as an inordinate amount of paperwork.

Nevertheless, we changed the name of the teams from Curriculum Design Teams to Inclusive Instructional Design Teams, but our goal remained the same: in partnership with teachers, we sought to build and create inclusive, kid-centric spaces where all people attending school and shaping classroom-based learning designs had the power to be seen and heard, access *joyful* learning to the highest degree possible, and experience instruction in ways that were capacity-oriented rather than deficit-based. This

---

1   United Federation of Teachers, aka the teachers' union in New York City.

time around, the DOE reduced our funding. Three teams were reduced to two, and there was funding for only one staff developer, myself, to lead the project.

That year, the work was just as powerful as the first and educators responded; the planning space, for them, was an oasis from the toxicity involved in curating joy and justice within policies that don't always make sense for teachers and kids. Notions of "achievement" and "product" were put on the back burner, replaced with ideation and creation around "access," "process," and "projects." Certainly, there was no grand subversion intentionally taking place, but inside, I experienced what I now know as the duality of justice work—the simultaneous current of heartbreak and joy.

We had gotten to this place where teachers were naming that school was a place where they had a hard time planning, dreaming, or being creative, *especially* in their instructional design and curriculum-making, because of the mandates, surveillance, and product-oriented environment woven in the rhetoric that surrounded them.

The teachers I worked with designed some beautiful curriculum, and kids responded in powerful ways. More kids were participating, growing their communication skills through experiences that were underscored by inclusivity, UDL, multimodalities, and culturally relevant teaching principles. Learning outcomes, albeit beyond the traditional notions of benchmarks and standards, were made visible, and a wider group of people started to understand that growth means more than numerical data points. Teachers' actions within the classroom, spurred from the thoughtful sanctuary they experienced once a month in those design teams, served as a refreshing beacon of light for their colleagues, a posit of what could be, not just for the kids in their classroom—but for everyone.

Not surprisingly, the DOE in New York City (like many other learning institutions), pivoted their goals and wanted something more specific, something more "special-educationy,"[2] so they put their funds elsewhere after year two. However, since then, and, really, since the beginning of my career, I've

---

2   Special-educationy is a term used to show the narrowness in people's thinking around what can be called professional development to support students with special needs. For example, they might consider appropriate work in the special educational realm to be IEP goal development, or progress monitoring, while they might consider curriculum development, or racial literacy work, inappropriate.

worked to create the oasis for teachers to do the thoughtful planning work; ideate and create, to figure out communal pathways within, and even outside of their curriculum, understand the depths of self-awareness and empathy required for social justice work, and, also, the research behind theoretical foundations on literacy learning. This is when I first understood how powerful the concept of thought sanctuary was.

This chapter is an inroad for teachers to experience a similar peace that was created during those design teams to develop justice through the *tenet of human-centered care* by placing students at the center of their instructional decision-making, and evoking a sense of joy by building a curriculum that makes sense for their communities. For educators who seek to rediscover, continue, or even initiate a robust orientation to how they create not just curriculum or instructional design, but, really, the kinds of experiences and memories communities of children look back on when they're asked, How was school? *To be the teacher children cite as memory is the ultimate credential.*

Here is a sweet sojourn for teachers to experience where they work toward and create kid-centric, accessible, and socially just curriculum. In conjunction with our exploration of the historical underpinnings of school, ourselves, and the community that surrounds us, here, we will consider what this means for the curricular and instructional decisions educators make.

It is also where we prepare ourselves to do the study and practice piece of teaching and learning that helps us understand *how* to teach; developing a strong base of knowledge that underscores brain-based learning, culturally responsive pedagogy, and developmentally appropriate foundational literacy and numeracy skills.

Big Idea: Nurture

- Thought sanctuaries for teachers support joyful curiosity!

- Educators need thought sanctuaries to develop the kind of change that social justice movements in school require.

- Intentionality and follow-through are required to create these types of protective spaces in partnership with your school community.

To Teach Fiercely Requires Teacher Agency

There are many, many parts that encompass the whole of teaching fiercely; not just the title of this book, but teaching fiercely as a whole *pedagogy*. I hope you are finding those parts—all the activities, passages, and food for thought—as supportive mechanisms as you and/or your community engage in developing these capacities.

If I could, I would spend days with everyone who chooses to read this book, because to teach fiercely requires deep levels of experiential work, as well as the finer-tuning of our internal shelves. One of the most important components that activates teaching fiercely is teacher agency. There was a point early in my career where I felt like I didn't have any kind of real decision-making power, when I felt like I was just working in a system that positioned me as a cog in a wheel that keeps turning to produce the same outcomes no matter what lay in its path. Thankfully, that period didn't last very long. When I began working in partnership with families, attending meaningful professional learning experiences with my colleagues that were local and teacher-driven, and cocreating curriculum and community with students, my teacher agency blossomed. I had strong convictions about what I was doing and why I was doing it because I positioned myself as a learner.

What is teacher agency?

Like almost everything else we talk about in this book, teacher agency means a lot of different things to a lot of different people. I want to name what it has meant for me and for the communities of teachers I have been a part of as both teacher and as coach, as well as clarify how it is defined academically.

Defined anecdotally, I offer the prologue of this book . . . Anthem for a Teacher, where I say: *To teach fiercely is to be in community with your students and yourself; it's stepping outside yourself and looking into your soul. And not just your teaching soul, but your* soul *soul, because those two things aren't separate.*

This is where you are able to show up in your classroom space as your whole self, where your decisions are informed by the subtleties you feel and see from your surrounding community. You are able to pick up on subtleties because you've committed yourself to ongoing inner work and you've taken inquiry and justice as your teaching stance. Unpacking and applying foundational literacy practices and building knowledge through equitable learning is part of your pedagogy, it's ritualized in your school, and you do not work alone.

Academically defined, teacher agency is the capacity of teachers to act with intention, purposefully and constructively to direct the growth of their students' learning, as well as contribute to the growth of themselves and their colleagues' learning (Calvert 2016). Essentially, when characterized through this definition, *teacher agency is evoked when teachers are given opportunities to formulate goals for themselves and with their students in ways that are determined through their experiences and needs.*

This type of agency is also grown from a strong knowledge base in foundational literacy, and other types of literacy learning such as print-based, numerical, social, emotional, cultural, and racial literacy (think multiliteracies as described in Chapter 1). Teacher agency is fostered in spaces that position teachers as intellectual beings, change agents, and community leaders. It is also nourished by communal connections that are maintained within the school itself, as well as various entities it is connected to.

This is when teachers have real decision-making power in terms of the types of learning experiences they are a part of and have access to that are connected to developing those goals. It also means that when they and their students' needs change, those who are in administrative positions, or those who have specific roles to support and develop professional learning experiences, *listen* to their feedback. Moreover, the listening and feedback informs how the plans will be revised to support the community's evolving needs.

Before I move on, take a moment to self-assess (Figure 5.1). What level of teacher agency would you give yourself? (If you're a different type of educator, just replace the word "teacher" with "educator.")

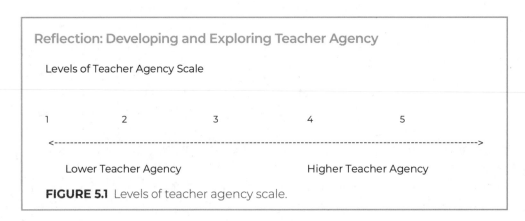

FIGURE 5.1 Levels of teacher agency scale.

TABLE 5.1 Unpacking levels of teacher agency.

1
- Read scripted lesson plan word for word.
- Students read from preselected texts or basal readers.
- Punitive action is taken when teacher does not use the lesson script.

2
- Use scripted curriculum.
- Students read exact same texts that are indicated in the curriculum.
- Punitive actions are sometimes taken when teachers stray from the curriculum.

3
- Provided curriculum is adapted.
- Students read texts available to them in the classroom or school library.
- When straying from the provided curriculum, teachers' actions are questioned.

4
- Adapt curriculum provided by the school or of your own choosing.
- Students read texts within the classroom and/or school library, and other outside sources, relevant to their identities, needs, and experiences.
- Teacher actions are sometimes questioned, but only if students' families are contacting the school administration regarding the classroom content.

5
- Create and cocreate curriculum for and with students, adapt curriculum provided by the school and/or your own choosing.
- Students read texts relevant to their identities, needs, and experiences, and those texts come from multiple sources. Classroom libraries are modified according to your current group of students.
- Teacher actions are sometimes questioned, but usually only in the case when there is concern students are being harmed.

In Table 5.1, you'll find characteristics of varying levels of teacher agency, starting with lower teacher agency (Level 1) and moving toward higher teacher agency (Level 5). Use the descriptions to consider the following reflection questions:

- What aspects of your personal teacher agency are most clear to you? How might others, such as school leaders, peers, students, and their families view your teacher agency?

- What barriers hinder your teacher agency?

- What strengthens your teacher agency?

Make a small goal for yourself in regard to developing your teacher agency. Think about what you need in relation to this goal. What are the necessary conditions for your agency to be empowered?

Creating Necessary Conditions for Teachers to Thrive

Although most people working in education agree that teachers should spend time developing their foundational understandings of brain-based learning, culturally responsive pedagogy, literacy and numeracy, a lot of their actions say otherwise. Those who are making decisions about how teachers spend their time across the school day inhibit teachers' ability to grow their pedagogy in ways that most directly impact their students. For example, in the United States, many elementary school teachers are contracted to work 38 hours a week, with 32 hours dedicated to instructional time. Secondary school teachers, on average, spend 30 of 38 hours instructing students over the course of the week (NCES 2012).

Since COVID-19, schools have been impacted in myriad ways. Particularly, being short of staff has had one of the greatest impacts on teacher well-being. The time teachers spend covering their colleagues' classes or even classes with teacher vacancies adds up. In short, teachers are overworked. This leaves them little time to reflect, rest, think, collaborate, download new information, and/or give input to the ever-evolving shifts in post-pandemic schooling, let alone enough time for creating authentic and rich curriculum. This constant grind contributes to the lack of teacher agency in determining instruction and what kinds of learning experiences are most appropriate for students in schools.

While it is absolutely important to create necessary conditions for teachers to thrive, I am not suggesting this labor should be centered on any one group of people in a school. School leaders are often blamed for teaching time constraints. However, there are many factors that are beyond school leaders' control that can be acknowledged in the pursuit of creating more nourishing teacher spaces that foster teacher agency. In fact, creating conditions for teachers to exercise their agency is most impactful when the whole community pours into creating that kind of environment (more on that later!).

First, let's complicate the school leader's role in providing space and time for teachers. In recent years, especially since the COVID pandemic, I've witnessed school leaders stretched in ways that were beyond their control, mostly due to the aforementioned staff shortages and policy bombs.[3] In many cases, school leaders and those making scheduling decisions have a deep desire to create space and time for teacher nourishment, but are

---

3   In reference to the daily briefings school leaders received during COVID-19 with new health and safety procedures, attendance tracking requirements, instructional delivery methods, and more.

working in systems that disable their ability to provide for their people in ways they hope for. This ethical dilemma school leaders experience is best described by Meira Levinson's (2015) term *moral injury*.

Dr. Lakisha Howell introduced Levinson's concept of moral injury to me one afternoon as we developed ideas on how to support teachers across various school landscapes. I named my shift in thinking regarding the role of school leaders and the inner turmoil I was witnessing as their budgets, staff, and student bodies continued to get smaller. Kisha told me that what I was witnessing was a form of moral injury, wherein people who are trying to run schools ethically are forced to work within systems that are not aligned with their ethics (Levinson 2015, p. 1). The term moral injury resonated with me, and I explored it further.

Levinson (2015) describes moral injury more specifically as "the trauma of perpetrating significant moral wrong against others despite one's whole-hearted desire and responsibility to do otherwise" (p. 1). While the wrongs that are perpetuated in schools are sometimes located in big events, more commonly they are parsed out in bite-sized pieces, accumulating over time. The experiences that attribute to educators' (namely school leaders) moral injury over time include delivering frequent coverages to teachers' already packed teaching schedules, mandating disconnected professional learning experiences that stem from top-down officials' directives, hiring unqualified teachers for students because they are the only people available for the job, following racist school disciplinary codes,[4] the inability to protect teachers from inappropriate demands given by parents and caregivers, and not being able to provide adequate supplies, materials, and texts, amongst other things.

I remember sitting (on Zoom) with a group of principals Cornelius and I had been working with for a few years before the pandemic. Like many other people working in schools during the earlier part of the pandemic, we shifted quickly, meeting virtually every month and flexibly working toward school leaders' needs. I remember Cornelius and I leading a conversation we called "Between a Rock and a Hard Place: Exploring Tensions, Considering Relief" during a learning series that had originally been designed to build equitable feedback and assessment structures. Shortly after we began one of our first workshops in Fall 2020, we were in breakout rooms discussing intellectual versus emotional labor leaders experienced while trying to keep their schools running. The principals and assistant principals, in smaller

---

4   Remember Monique Morris' book *Pushout* mentioned in Chapter 2?

groups, were more visibly weary, and also more revelatory in sharing what was really happening in their schools. One principal's statement pierced me. It went something like this:

> It's hard to engage. I'm dealing with a lot right now. This morning, a teacher called me to tell me she couldn't come in because her dad was in the ICU with COVID. Four more teachers were already out in quarantine. We still haven't been able to reach a number of families who are on our remote learning roster. One AP is also in quarantine. There are no subs available. The last thing I did before I left school yesterday was attend a citywide health and safety meeting, where every school leader has a story similar to mine. This is just one day, but it is like this almost every day. I'm so busy trying to keep people alive that finding any space to consider curriculum, instructional methodology, or simple, everyday learning needs feels extraordinary.

I'm not sure how many people understood the levels of management, emotional labor, and completely new skill sets that were required to keep people safe during the pre-vaccination part of the pandemic. I remember that my and Cornelius's goal during that workshop was to hold space for naming tensions and to provide strategies for relief. However, the weariness and pain I witnessed from those school leaders drew a new well of empathy I'd not yet been equipped with. We held space for school leaders to name tensions, but at that point in time, relief felt unreachable.

Although this anecdote is from Fall 2020, the residual impact of COVID-19, amongst other national epidemics like inflation, school shootings, racism, anti-Gay legislation, book banning, and centuries-old racism, has led many school leaders to continue to experience the moral injury of not being able to provide for their people because they have not been given the tools, resources, or blueprints to do so. I had known that teachers were in a state of deep exhaustion, but a new layer of frustration was unveiled to me when I learned that school leaders' daily responsibilities impaired their ability to adequately care and provide for their people.

"Community Up": Communal Responsibility for Cultivating Teacher Agency

Earlier, I mentioned how important it is to distribute equitable responsibility within the community to nourish teachers with time and space for planning, thinking, reflecting, and collaborating (yes, this is a thought sanctuary!). When this labor is centered on one entity, like "school leadership" or "grade team leaders" or even one person like "the principal," the likelihood that an authentic and intentional thought sanctuary for teachers will come into fruition is minimal. One way to think about this movement is through the concept of "Community Up," meaning that community growth is connective, lateral, and moves upward, together.

The Cylindrical Model (Kills First 2021) shown in Figure 5.2 is an example of a community up model, and supports organizing within a school community. Like Circles (First Nations Pedagogy n.d.), it is based on Indigenous wisdom. Many educators are familiar with Circles, where classroom communities meet together in a circle formation to initiate, build, and/or restore community. While Circles are usually referred to in the restorative context, Circles also are used as an instructional methodology wherein communities learn together, cocreating knowledge. Importantly, the community of people participating sit within a circle shape so all members are able to see each other, and no one person is centered. All people within the circle are equally visible. Usually, an item referred to as an "object of power" (First Nations Pedagogy n.d.) is held to indicate a person is the speaker, and is passed around for turn-taking.

The Cylindrical Model builds on Circle ideology; it is used to symbolize a flattened hierarchy, where no one person in the community is more important or more capable than another. As the circle of people in the community contribute and learn together, the circle grows upward, transforming into a cylinder, showing equitable growth for all (Kills First 2021).

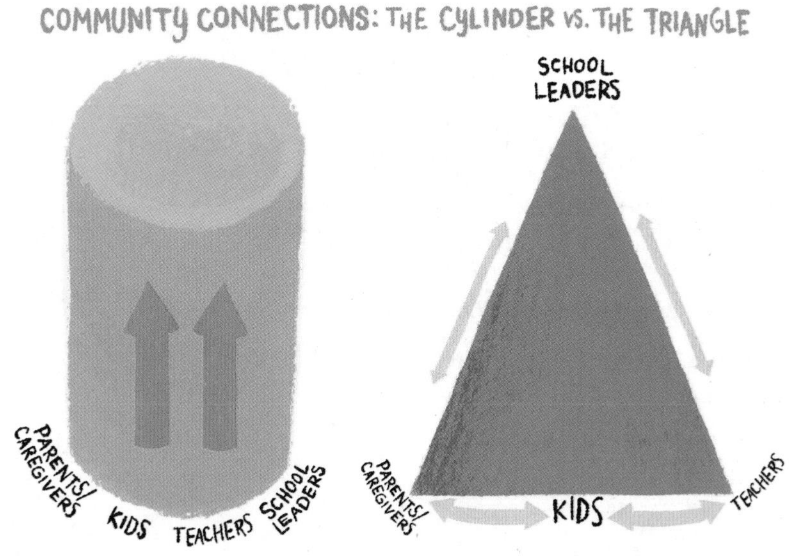

FIGURE 5.2 Community connections: the cylinder vs. the triangle.

To the right of the Cylindrical Model in Figure 5.2, notice the Triangle.[5] The triangle is a more typical representation of how power and agency flows through a school.

- At the top, school leaders are positioned with ultimate decision-making power. Their vision, guidance, and leadership (or lack thereof) significantly impacts how all people experience school.

- On the right bottom angle of the triangle, you will find teachers. The yellow arrows shown between teachers and school leaders demonstrate how connected they are as well as their relational power dynamic. This is significant: school leaders are almost always positioned above teachers.

- Kids are placed on the bottom side of the triangle, representing their lack of power within the school, as well as the people with whom they are connected to: their parents and/or caregivers and their teachers. They also serve as a conduit for how teachers and parents and/or caregivers communicate with one another. That is, what kids say happens during their school day is interpreted by parents/caregivers in ways that shape their perspective on their child's teacher. This can either hinder or strengthen teacher agency.

- Finally, you'll see the left side of the triangle connecting parents/caregivers to school leaders. This connection varies across school, but this body of voices has the power to heavily influence the ways in which school leaders strategize and make decisions.

Work Along: Considering the "Community Up" Model for Your Community

Take a moment to explore which model best represents your school community.

1. What components of each model are present in your community? Which components are absent?

2. What are the benefits of the Cylindrical Model? What about the Triangle?

3. How might teacher agency be strengthened and/or inhibited in these models?

4. What barriers do you anticipate in working to implement a more communally based model like the Cylindrical Model?

---

5   With permission from Cinnamon Kills First, I imposed the categorization and labels to the shapes she presented at the Fifteenth Annual Leadership Institute: Evaluating Student Voice Through Teacher Leadership conference.

The Cylindrical, or "community-up," Model allows the entire school community to contribute to the needs of school communities, enabling more space and time for teachers to plan, collaborate, and be thoughtful when developing curriculum and making instructional decisions based on the needs of their students. Potentiality for community contributions is vast, and, again, looks very different depending on school demographics, resources, and perspectives.

Below are a few examples of distributed community contributions.

- One community I worked in solicited parent volunteers to serve as substitute teachers so their teachers on staff could participate in professional development together with me. Many parents and caregivers volunteered; however, this community was affluent, mostly white and East Asian, and many volunteers had jobs with flexibility that allowed them to contribute their time during the school day.

- Another time, a principal I worked with liaised with a community sports group to spend time with children in the gym so teachers could curate their classroom libraries more thoughtfully together, rather than covering each other's classrooms and doing the work in isolation. In that case, the community was predominantly immigrant and BIPOC, disadvantaged economically, but advantaged in that they had a long-term commitment to building cross-community relationships.

- I've also seen students contribute to nourishing teachers' agency. One school I worked in regularly invited students to attend curriculum-making sessions with teachers, acting as thought partners with their teachers to ensure their learning was relevant to their experience. These experiences were built across their advisory program, so when curriculum meetings happened, students were prepared to contribute in meaningful ways. This particular school served economically disadvantaged students and was racially and economically diverse. Significantly, they were led by a visionary school leader with a strong, diverse school equity team who were equipped to actionize various learning structures they learned through workshops centering students, equity, and racial dynamics as part of their school experience.

The Teacher's Role in Developing Teacher Agency

This is really hard work. Remember in the introduction of this book, where I introduced the idea that spreading joy and justice requires us to face multiple truths regarding the role of teachers in school? How teachers are amongst the most overworked, exhausted, and underpaid group of professionals in the country, yet hold the most potential power to create a substantial transformation in the ways students experience schools? Well, that power only works if teachers' agency is strong, hovering near Levels 4 and 5 on that Likert Scale (Figure 5.1).

If we are to build that structured generator of hope that was unpacked in Chapter 1, one of the most important ingredients is teachers' conviction in their ability to make decisions that enact justice and enable joy within their communities for their students, and with them. One of the ways teachers can do that work is by honing their craft, delving into learning processes, developing a student-centered curriculum, and cultivating community, all through the lenses of sound research, joy, and justice.

Assessing Teacher Agency and Instructional Delivery

First, let's assess the landscape of instructional delivery and how teacher agency is connected to one's ability to realize joy and justice within schools.

Here are important notes as we engage in this work:

- Curriculum is *what* we teach.

- Instructional delivery is *how* we teach.

- *Your* pedagogy includes all the components in your teaching and learning practice (your choices, your curriculum, your style of community building, etc. (We unpacked this a lot in Chapter 1.)

While curriculum is a large component of teaching and learning in the classroom, it is an individual's pedagogy that shapes how curriculum is implemented. Moreover, pedagogy is formed by the level of agency teachers feel and enact. How much or how little teachers are involved in curriculum development impacts the kinds of decisions made and options available for the instructional delivery that students experience.

There are infinite ways to teach children, but some types of instructional delivery are more prevalent than others based on educational policy, parent/caregiver involvement, and the ways in which teachers prepare for the profession. Based on my experiences with hundreds of teachers in classroom spaces, there are four types of instructional delivery that are most frequently demonstrated by teachers given their current realities: prescriptive, adaptive, universal, and homegrown. Which one of those instructional delivery methods shows up in a school community, or a teacher's classroom, varies.

In Figure 5.3, you will see a continuum that shows the relationship between teacher agency and common instructional delivery models. These levels correspond to the teacher agency Likert scale shown in Figure 5.1. That said, if you identified your teacher agency on the lower side with a score of 1 or 2, that means your instructional delivery methods are most likely scripted or adapted, and often are not developed to accommodate the unique needs of your current students. Conversely, if you identified higher levels of teacher agency, Levels 3, 4, or 5, that means you are most likely adapting curriculum according to your expertise, your students' needs, and may even be writing your own curriculum with colleagues based on learning standards connected to your community, location, students, and world events.

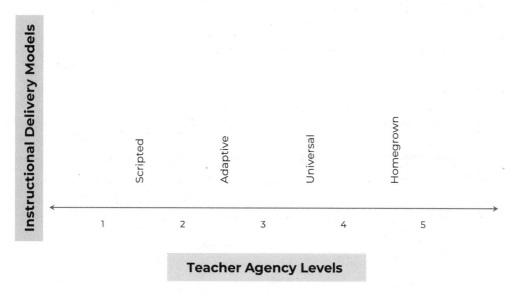

FIGURE 5.3 Community Connections: The Cylinder vs. The Triangle.

Four Methods of Instructional Delivery

Here, I will describe those four methods of instructional delivery and how they permeate school culture. Later, I will also give examples of how those instructional delivery models are situated in schools to either grow or stymie students' learning and community well-being through the pursuit of joy and justice.

Scripted Instructional Delivery is where teachers follow lesson plans that were created by someone else (usually an outside curriculum producer) and follow the lesson plan to a T. For example, if the curricula says, "Say to the students: 'Today we are going to discuss the role of Anansi in West African trickster tales,'" the teacher will say exactly those words to the students. This kind of instructional delivery comes from packaged curriculum in boxed sets from many different players within the Educational Industrial Complex. Most curriculum can be delivered according to some version of a script; although, in many cases students will be disengaged if their teacher is "delivering lines" as opposed to engaging them in authentic conversation.

- Corresponds with lower levels of teacher agency.

- Most common in school communities where the school has received sanctions for low test scores, low attendance, and/or high disciplinary referral rates *or* when teachers do not have time to plan or prep lesson plans or other curricular materials.

Adaptive Instructional Delivery is where teachers use a curriculum that was created by someone else, but adapt it according to the needs of the students they currently teach. A variety of assessments, including interviews, surveys, observations, reading fluency practice, free-form writing, and numerical fluency exams all inform their instructional adaptations. Examples of curricular adaptations include visuals, multimodal experiences like audio books and/or speech-to-text apps, peer groupings, graphic organizers and other note-taking mechanisms, more repetition in teaching concepts, slowing the pace of lessons, and giving students more time to learn concepts and work on various tasks and assignments.

- Corresponds with varying levels of teacher agency.

- Common in schools that work to support teacher planning time, and/or have the capacity to provide coverages or appropriate prep periods to teachers to create adaptations.

- Teachers decide on curricular adaptations, but the curriculum itself, is typically chosen by a school district, or school leadership team.

Universally Designed Instructional Delivery is based on principles of the Center for Applied Science and Teaching's (CAST) Universal Design for Learning (UDL). To deliver instruction through the lens of UDL, one must first consider the goals and objectives that are at the base of the unit, and think about how to create goals that allow all types of learners to access the teaching and meet said goals. One way to think about opening goals to create more accessibility is through the "learning to fly" example: When teaching a person to fly, the goal is originally written as "Students will learn to fly using their arms." To widen the goal for accessibility, the goal is rewritten omitting the latter part: "Students will learn to fly." This enables students to achieve the goal through multiple means. UDL encompasses three multiple means including representation (how information is shown), engagement (how information is interacted with), and expression (how learners communicate what they learn or know). There is a tremendous body of work regarding creating accessible curriculum through the lens of UDL located at CAST.org.

- Corresponds with higher levels of teacher agency.

- Common in schools that have heavily invested in inclusive education, sending teachers to UDL workshops, and also working to support teachers with appropriate planning time.

- Also more common in schools with stronger special education departments, as the UDL framework is widely known for creating accessible curriculum for all learners, with a special emphasis on those with IEPs, or those laying on the margins of other students' norms.

Homegrown Instructional Delivery is curriculum created by teachers and other people who are directly working with the students who will be recipients of its teaching. It is woven from the interests of the community, including its students. It centers the learning styles, identities, and various literacies they embody, as well as literacies they need support with. Formative assessments such as the ones described in the adapted instructional delivery model are regularly used. It is based on state standards and learning objectives agreed upon by the school community and is built in layers using curricular planning structures like Understanding by Design (Wiggins and McTighe 2011). Brain-based learning, foundational literacy, social science, and math research is built within the curriculum in connection to culturally relevant texts and experiences that are both cocreated and negotiated with children.

- Corresponds with highest levels of teacher agency.

- More common in secondary schools, more rare in elementary schools.

- Teachers with this level of agency work with purpose and conviction, are either highly skilled in their foundational understandings of how learning works, or they seek to find out more information to learn those understandings through workshops, their own research, or through peers within their schools.

- While planning time is appreciated by teachers with high levels of agency, they typically create their own planning experiences regardless of the school community's stance on teacher time.

The Impact of School Reform on Teacher Agency and Instructional Delivery

As stated in earlier chapters of this book, a key component of the human learning process is to build upon existing schema. For engagement to occur within a group of learners, something about the information within the curriculum must be connected to their lived experiences. In curriculum-writing practices, this is often referred to as the anticipatory set, the motivation, or the connection.

Teachers who feel empowered to recreate lessons and activities that have been pre-created by others who do not know their students work to develop relevant motivators to whet students' appetites for learning, and increase increasing their interest in the lesson's objective. Teachers who feel less empowered may feel pressure from meeting benchmarks tied to government funding. For example, in 2009, a nationwide school reform program was announced by the Obama Administration called Race to the Top (RTT). Areas this federal program sought to improve in the United States' public school system included:

- Development of rigorous standards and better assessments.

- Adoption of better data systems to provide schools, teachers, and parents with information about student progress.

- Support for teachers and school leaders to become more effective.

- Increased emphasis and resources for the rigorous interventions needed to turn around the lowest-performing schools (White House Archives n.d.).

A point system was attached to each area of improvement. States that were able to design programming inspiring growth in connection to each area of improvement were awarded points according to their program designs. The number of points states received corresponded to how much RTT grant money they were awarded. RTT, like so many other school reformation programs, was well-intentioned. However, it is attributed to very intense accountability systems centered in quantitative data. Schools now had to report all kinds of empirical data that circled back to their states' learning design to show they were informed about all the players' progress in school, including teachers, students, and administrators.

For a teacher working in underserved schools where many students are not from the dominant culture, where many families experience low-income, eroding neighborhood infrastructure, and barriers to healthcare and fresh foods, this heavy reliance on rigid data for the exchange of school funding restricts her agency, and damages the kinds of learning experiences her students have in school. Surveillance of her teaching, her students' attendance, her lesson plans, and, especially, her students' test scores infringe upon the choices she is able to make within the domain of her classroom. Her teacher agency diminishes. She is subjected to restrictive school policies that mandate lessons be taught exactly as they are written at the same time as other teachers on their grade level.

Scripted Instructional Delivery and Its Disproportionate Outcomes

Typically, students who successfully engage with scripted instructional delivery from teachers with lower agency are those from the dominant culture, usually those who are English-speaking, white, middle-upper class, reading and computing on grade level, able-bodied, have above-average executive functioning skills, and communicate orally with ease. This is not because they are smarter, rather, it is because they often have more opportunities and access to resources than their peers who do not share the same advantages.

Asian students have also shown academic success with this type of instructional delivery. For example, nationally, Asian students have higher grades and higher standardized test scores than any other racial group (Hsin and Xie 2014, p. 8416). Conversely, when students from outside the dominant culture are taught by scripted instruction that has been prescribed within packaged curriculum, their engagement decreases, impacting outcomes for their well-being and academic success.

It's also important to note that instructional delivery is deeply connected to the "what" part. Compounded with a scripted curriculum, curricular materials that are not representative or relevant to the personhood of all kids, especially those outside dominant culture are everyday acts of injustice that many kids endure on a daily basis. A 2019 report compiled by the Education Justice Research and Organizing Collaborative (EJ-ROC) demonstrated how pervasive the exclusion of people of color is within packaged curriculum and texts in wide use in schools. Their curricular audits indicated that most packaged curriculum is designed for dominant culture: nearly five times more books and curricular materials were written by white authors than all the authors from the BIPOC community combined (EJ-ROC 2019, p. 5). They audited over 1,205 books.

EJ-ROC's report builds upon Rudine Sims Bishop's work in her seminal text *Windows, Mirrors, and Sliding Glass Doors* (1990). Sims Bishop helps us understand what happens to children when we are not centering their personhood in our classroom experiences. She says: "When children cannot find themselves reflected in the books they read, or when the images they see are distorted, negative, or laughable, they learn a powerful lesson about how they are devalued in the society of which they are a part (p. 1)." As we work to build our teacher agency in community with others, we work to enact justice for all students. How do we work to ensure students both see themselves as full, belonging members in their classroom community *and* have a joyful time in that pursuit? How do we enact justice by building multiple literacies, ensuring they walk away from school with a moral complexity that allows them to both analyze print and media *and* deal with life?

While it is challenging to find space and time to care for yourself and for your students, to muster enough energy to authentically collaborate with your peers, it is important to increase teacher agency that allows, at the very least, for curriculum to be adapted, at best, universally designed and/or even homegrown within your school community. When students' personhood is considered in relation to their learning needs, culture, preferences, and interests in tandem to the ways in which curriculum is built and/or adapted within their classroom community, all children benefit, not just those who came to school with all the tools in the first place.

Building Your Curricular Inquiry: The Nuts and Bolts of Curriculum-Making Is Important in Social Justice Conversations

Sometimes, the nuts and bolts of curricular and instructional planning are left out of the conversation in educator social justice circles. I remember attending a workshop that was created for teachers who were working toward social justice during my last few years of teaching. By then, I had learned a thing or two about teaching literacy, and I thought about how different my former high schoolers' lives would have been if I had known more about the foundations of reading instruction when I taught them. The teachers who attended the workshop were going to try out some recently developed curriculum created by teachers who actively work toward social justice and often publish their curriculum and their experiences in relation to teaching it.

After spending time getting to know one another, the curriculum was introduced to us, and we were going to act as students while the workshop facilitators were the teachers. The lesson was robust: its objective was to teach students about social movements through the Black Panther Party's Ten-Point Program. After a brief overview of the Black Panthers and their Ten-Point Program, we then received specific roles, and were instructed that we were going to participate in the "tea party" protocol, where students adopt the role and characteristics of the person's profile they have been assigned and engage in a discussion with other students who adopted different roles. In this case, we were assigned various members of the Black Panther Party.

First, I was alarmed at being a white person asked to play a role of a Black person. Second, when I looked at the document I was handed describing the role I was to play, it was a full page, full of second and third tier vocabulary words, and, if I had to guess, was written at a college-reading level. I thought about my former eleventh and twelfth graders who would have most certainly appreciated the content within this lesson; the Black Panther's Ten-Point Program tethers seminal moments toward the Black freedom struggle in our nation's history. I couldn't help but wonder about Lexile levels, ableism, and, worse, pending educational neglect.

I knew this particular experience, being expected to navigate a complex text about a period of time many students are unfamiliar with, and then adopt characteristics in a role play experience they've just learned about with their peers, would not have landed in the high school classes I taught without serious adaptations. Attentive listening and interest probably would have transpired during the overview and introduction, but as soon as this dense print went to students who were still learning to parse out words at fourth and fifth grade levels, the lesson would have combusted.

Thankfully, we teachers were guinea pigs in this particular workshop experience, and it was noted that the print and Lexile level would be a major barrier for students, and a larger conversation for curricular accessibility opened. Many teachers had a lot to say about white people being assigned Black roles. (Note: reenactment of history in most cases is riddled with potential human harm—I do not recommend it, and when a Black role was assigned to me, I did not participate.)

Content, of course, is important. The way we teach is, of course, also important. But *how* we organize the trajectory of learning and pathways to access the learning is also important. To that end, it is essential we familiarize ourselves with research-based frameworks and other instructional strategies to accommodate and care for our student's learning needs so they may experience an education that is relevant to their human experience, and that is content-, standards-, and skills-based.

Curriculum-Making: Frameworks and Foundational Understandings

Research.

To catalyze this work, I have chosen two curricular design frameworks I've used in curricular and instructional design teams with many teachers, both with teams and individuals. We'll spend a little time exploring Gloria Ladson-Billings's Culturally Relevant Pedagogical framework (1994) as well as Grant Wiggins and Jay McTighe's Understanding by Design framework (2011)[6] to help you build a curriculum that is just, accessible, and connected to your students' experiences and needs. Additionally, to develop curricular organization, I'll also show you an exercise to unpack learning standards that I developed with Cornelius to support educators and help build strong roadmaps for working toward objectives and positive student outcomes.

The group of students, colleagues, and families you work with will impact how you are able to utilize these frameworks and strategies in your planning, and your curriculum-making might look different than what I am suggesting, which I welcome. In this work, I hope to foster human-centered innovation within the somewhat treacherous landscape educators face when planning in the spirit of creativity and care. As you work forward, I encourage you to keep in mind that the point here is to develop a planning experience that centers children in ways that are connected to their needs and are also both standards- and research-based, fueled with our desire to enact justice and joy in our schools.

---

6   If you enjoy exploring these frameworks, and utilizing them in your teacher design work, I encourage you to check out Gloria Ladson-Billings' seminal text *The Dreamkeepers: Successful Teachers of African American Children*, as well as Grant Wiggins and Jay McTighe's text *The Understanding by Design Guide to Creating High-Quality Units*.

Culturally Relevant and Sustaining Pedagogy

Gloria Ladson-Billings is one of the foremothers of Culturally Relevant Pedagogy (CRP[7]) that, importantly, has grown into Culturally Relevant and *Sustaining* Pedagogy (CR-SP). Ladson-Billings first documented CRP as a framework educators could use for curricular guidance and teaching in her seminal text, *The Dreamkeepers: Successful Teachers of African American Children*, in 1994. According to Ladson-Billings, culturally relevant teaching is a "pedagogy that empowers students intellectually, socially, emotionally, and politically by using cultural referents to impart knowledge, skills, and attitudes" (p. 20). She underscores the importance of cultural relevance by noting how the use of student culture in one's teaching has the ability to transcend the negative and harmful impact of dominant culture, that is, the erasure of students' history, culture, or background within everyday school life as well as in curriculum (Ladson-Billings 1994, p. 19).

What might this look like in a classroom? Well, CRP is vast. It looks different depending on who your students are. When I first started teaching CRP to groups of teachers, I designed an experience to develop felt knowledge: when teaching is culturally relevant, it is both explicit and subtle. For example, my last few years of teaching were spent teaching grades four and five in a huge elementary school in Sunset Park, Brooklyn. It was in the mid-2010s, when the "cups"[8] game was really popular among Brooklyn adolescents. Whenever I picked students up from the cafeteria or there was down time after school, students everywhere could be heard skillfully performing the cups rhythm with one another, in groups as large as 8 or 10 kids!

Before reading or lecturing about the CRP framework with teachers, I invited them to learn how to play the cups game in teams. I equipped them with cups and a YouTube tutorial. Two or three people learned the cups game, while the other person in their group was instructed to take observational notes on their learning processes, including the ways in which they

---

7   Not to be confused with critical race theory! While critical race theory was also being formulated by several scholars, namely Derrick Bell, as well as Gloria Ladson-Billings herself, Culturally Responsive Pedagogy is not synonymous with that theoretical framework, and should not be confused as such. However, I will point out that the acronym CRT has also been used to describe "Culturally Responsive Teaching," which is also not the same thing as critical race theory. It is mere coincidence that they have shared letters for their acronyms.

8   The "cups" game, sometimes called "cups" song, is when you use drinking cups and your hands to create a specific rhythm in unison with other people. There are many YouTube videos showing this game, and you can also see an example of it when Anna Kendrick's character demonstrates it during a performance in the movie *Pitch Perfect* (2012).

communicated, were able to perform, and their affect (the feeling demonstrated in the group—both said and/or unsaid). At the end of a 15-minute period, groups were invited to perform the cups rhythm. After a mixture of laughter, frustration, and even a little entertainment, we worked together to unpack how this experience was connected to the CRP framework we would be exploring as we worked on curriculum-making.

Teachers had a lot to say and share. When asked what skills were exercised when learning the cups rhythm together, they listed the following:

- **Persistence:** It took *practice* and multiple attempts to learn the rhythm, even when they felt like giving up.

- **Communication—oral language and body language:** To perform a rhythm in unison, group members had to discuss how they were going to stop, start, etc. When they learned how they were going to start and stop, they began to rely on body cues to maintain the same motions and rhythm.

- **Motor skills and dexterity:** A level of coordination is required to flip the cup, tap the cup on the table, and repeat the motion in a specific pattern multiple times.

- **Concentration and attention to detail:** During the activity, there was a lot of loud learning, cups banging, people laughing, and talking. The game requires specific movement and patterns, and it took increased concentration to learn each detail.

- **Cooperation and collaboration:** Not only did people need to work together to tap and flip the cups in unison, but they also had to work together to learn the rhythm and movement patterns.

After we unpacked the skills required to learn the objective of the cups game performance, the teachers and I came to a big understanding that reflects Ladson-Billings's "cultural referents" youth learn from: skills required to learn the cups game objective and skills required to learn academic curricular objectives are *not* mutually exclusive. While it is clear that youth culture is not synonymous with Black culture or Latinx culture or Queer culture, it is often a starting point for people's initial understanding into why it is so integral for educators to consider the ways in which students communicate and the interests in which they surface, in addition to their racial and cultural backgrounds—all of those things are intertwined.

As educators everywhere witnessed elementary school students and other adolescents perform the cups game with delight, high energy, and extreme skill, we witnessed a group of learning mechanisms in which students are equipped with to tap into other types of content within the curriculums we adapt and design. Consider students whose families come from collectivist, storytelling cultures. Many students outside dominant culture do. So how might we build upon their oral communication and group collaboration when learning about historical events, solving investigations in math and science, and/or analyzing a body of literature? How do we recognize that learning feels more comfortable when it is done in louder environments for students who are accustomed to musical environments, or who simply feel comforted with the sound of the TV on in the background? What motor skills matter in the types of writing, building, or exploring we do in our class-room spaces, and how are they recognized differently amongst individuals in your classroom spaces?

The application of cultural relevance expands possibilities for how we con-nect, teach, and learn with our students. CRP is both vast[9] and distinct, and knowing how to incorporate it within your pedagogy can feel somewhat nebulous if you are not accustomed to adapting or designing your curricu-lum. For clarity, I return to Gloria Ladson-Billings. In a later iteration of her original CRP framework where the word "sustaining" was added, Ladson-Billings readdresses the power of its application, saying culturally relevant teaching "allows for a fluid understanding of culture, and a teaching prac-tice that explicitly engages questions of equity and justice." (2014, p. 74). The Educational Alliance at Brown University offers clarity in consideration of the application of the Culturally Relevant and Sustaining Pedagogical framework in one's teaching life at school. According to the Educational Alliance, charac-teristics of the CR-SP framework include:

- Positive perspectives on parents and families.

- Communication of high expectations.

- Learning within the context of culture.

---

9   Definitely check out Dr. Gloria Ladson-Billings work more thoroughly, but also read newer iterations of the framework. Django Paris's work underscores the shift from not just rel-evance, but to sustainability in his book, *Culturally Sustaining Pedagogies: Teaching and Learning for Justice in a Changing World* (2017; Language and Literacy Series), and Lorena Germán situates her book, *Textured Teaching: A Framework for Culturally Sustaining Practices*, in classroom spaces.

- Student-centered instruction.

- Culturally mediated instruction.

- Reshaping the curriculum.

- Teacher as facilitator.

Many teachers and I have found it helpful to focus on these tenets when creating and or adapting curriculum that is culturally relevant and sustaining. Earlier, I referred to the nuts and bolts of social justice teaching. Part of the nuts and bolts is familiarizing yourself with pedagogical frameworks that are created through the lens of justice. Among the many other parts working toward socially just schools is the development and practice of authentically knowing and understanding the students you teach so that you may do the work of reshaping curriculum in ways that speak to the classroom community: teaching through cultural referents, centering students, and facilitating knowledge. Families of the students you teach must understand you are their partner, not a person above or below them who tells them all the things wrong with their child, or even all the things their child needs to do "to get back on track."

Finally, we are not diluting the work of teaching and learning by using cultural relevance as foundational equipment; rather, we are expanding the mechanisms we use to create access for all students, especially those who have been most historically marginalized, to achieve high outcomes.

Work Along: Finding CR-SP in Your Practice

Chances are, even if you've never heard of CR-SP or still feel like it will be a huge undertaking to adopt, I bet you have existing elements of it in your practice now. Some of you may find it is strong and present in your teaching, maybe you just hadn't been calling it as such! In this exercise, you will explore current teaching practice in relation to characteristics of CR-SP. Then, you will find areas for growing those components further, or developing components that are less present in your teaching.

1. In Table 5.2, I've charted the characteristics of CR-SP, and I've included examples of how those characteristics have lived in various teachers, as well as my own practice, in different classroom spaces. Read the examples.

(Continued)

TABLE 5.2 Examples of culturally relevant-sustaining pedagogies in schools.

CRSE Components	Examples in Schools
Positive perspectives on parents and families	Teachers engage in congenial nonperformance-related conversation regularly with families. For example, during morning drop off, a teacher asks a parent, "How was your weekend?" For example, when a student doesn't turn in her summer reading packet, the teacher says to the parent, "How are you! I'm so excited your child is in my class," rather than "Hi, I'm Ms. XYZ. It's really important that students read at home this year."
Communication of high expectations	Students are regularly exposed to clear guidelines regarding the literacy, social, and grade-level expectations. This communication is delivered in the languages representative in the community. For example, a "family curriculum night" is hosted by the school. Students and parents/caregivers attend together. The teacher shows projects from the past years that are similar to the types of work students will work on during the present year. They are invited to contribute ideas for their own learning, and goal-creation is a multiplayer experience, where students, their families, and teachers identify learning goals together.
Learning within the context of culture	Teachers and school communities honor how students experience the world that surrounds them. For example, when major world events occur, like climate change, the war in Ukraine, or Black Lives Matter, we respond to students questions, and imbue inquiry-based teaching as it pertains to their understandings.
Student-centered instruction	Children are positioned as partners in the school experience. Experiences are created for them based on authentic data collection, wherein they may explore and ask their own questions as opposed to continually being told what to think. Additionally, teachers provide compensatory interventions when needed. For example, if a child is showing distress as they are reading, appropriate literacy interventions are developed for the child to learn to read.
Culturally mediated instruction	Teachers are aware of various cultural mediums (language, racial identity) students use to understand and interpret information. For example, teachers ensure students' languages are represented in classrooms and schools by promoting translanguaging. Translanguaging is where multiple languages are used to communicate in the classroom, and English is not centered.

CRSE Components	Examples in Schools
Reshaping the curriculum	Educators adapt and redesign curriculum and instruction according to the needs of their current students.
	Considering authentic data, teachers slow down, speed up, change texts, include interventions, and spend more time unpacking various concepts according to how students receive and respond to learning experiences.
Teacher as facilitator	The teacher sees students are seen as contributors of knowledge to the classroom community.
	For example, when students ask questions, their questions are well-documented and addressed within the curriculum during class discussions.

2. Pay attention to your body, and exercise your somatic literacy. What is your immediate reaction? Do these examples of CR-SP practices make you feel stiff, relaxed, stressed, or radiant? Take a step back—why do you think you are having the reaction you are experiencing?

3. Circle the categories you feel are demonstrated somewhere in your school community. What do they look like in your school?

4. Check the categories you feel are demonstrated in your own practice. Describe what they look like. It may be helpful to write it out.

5. Star categories that are within your realm of influence. Which components of CR-SP would you like to build that are already represented in your teaching practice, or somewhere else in your school? Which components may be less present but you feel equipped to develop further?

Understanding by Design

This part is going to be short and sweet, because there are abundant tools in books that Wiggins and McTighe have already created that are better suited for more immersive learning experiences regarding the Understanding by Design (UbD) framework. However, I feel compelled to name UbD and offer the CliffsNotes version because backward planning is essential for developing a strong roadmap for you and your students' learning regarding their needs and wonderings in relation to curricular standards. According to Wiggins and McTighe:

> The Understanding by Design® framework (UbD™ framework) offers a planning process and structure to guide curriculum, assessment, and instruction.

Its two key ideas are contained in the title: (1) focus on teaching and assessing for understanding and learning transfer, and (2) design curriculum "backward" from those ends (2011, p. 1).

They also identify three stages within UbD, including Stage 1, where you identify "desired results." Essentially, these are your learning objectives that derive from state standards, where essential questions that drive your curriculum blossom. Grant and Wiggins ask: What do you want your students to know? What do you want them to be able to do? Stage 2 is based on assessment evidence. This is where assessment is a game changer for students learning and your teaching. The UbD framework is centered in this realm: How will you know that students were able to meet your learning objectives? What kinds of evidence do we agree upon that show their knowing and their learning growth? Finally, Stage 3, my favorite part, includes all the different types of learning experiences you plan for students to reach the learning objectives you named in Stage 1.

Roadmap feels a little cliche to describe UbD, but without it, we educators are literally lost, even if we haven't yet discovered that we aren't moving toward the place we thought we were going. Many curriculum units that have been prewritten and delivered to us are like the Google GPS on your phone: Google does its best to find us the fastest route, it knows the layout of the streets and highways. But what Google hasn't been able to do for us is anticipate the street closures, traffic jams, roadkill, and weather patterns that find their way into our local neighborhoods. In places that are familiar to us, we are able to renegotiate the route, changing directions. If you live in a place with other forms of transportation, like me, you might choose to park your car and take the subway for the remainder of the route. And sometimes, we find ourselves in spaces with no GPS signal at all, and we have to rely on the knowledge we hold as an individuals and communities to figure out where we are going.

This is where UbD comes in. Before we even leave for the trip, we first decide on where we are going. If we were taking a road trip with our colleagues, we would brainstorm places of interest for us. Fiji might be unreachable due to distance and fiscal constraints, but Puerto Rico might be more realistic. From there, we determine the kinds of experiences we want to have to honor the desired result of our collegial community: How do we know our relationships have been strengthened? That we have learned from the spaces we chose to visit? Maybe we decide on a mid-trip check-in, or appoint a few group leaders who will collect travel journals from the group. The group determines that pages from those journals will reflect relational learning, including shared dinners, or collaborative adventures like partner kayaking. Everybody who goes on the trip will participate in an exit interview. Finally, the group creates an itinerary that lists a variety of learning experiences and destinations that will promote community building.

This UbD road trip is quite different than journeys that are preplanned for you, and created by people outside your community. Sometimes, it's easy to just get on the plane and enjoy what you can, even if your unique needs haven't been taken into consideration. However, the types of learning we catalyze through a cocreated plan for the people we teach and learn with is absolutely unmatched.

While descriptions of these frameworks are brief in summary, the combination of CR-SP and UbD make up the good bones of a curriculum, and combined with strong teacher agency in practice, a powerful DNA that is specific to you and the learners in your community is evoked. Working in relationship together, this manifestation has the ability to enable the kinds of joy and justice we hope for in school communities: experiences that move away from dominant culture (see Figure 1.1 Structured Generator of Hope) and toward future goodness.

I encourage you and your colleagues to consider how CR-SP and UbD live within your curriculum-making already and/or the possibilities they might have in your future curricular planning in relation to your instructional stance and level of teacher agency.

All data tells a story—*and not all of it is bad!*

Collecting Information About Your Learners in Authentic Ways Informs Your Planning

This hyperfocus on empirical data is nothing new. It's been around since the Industrial Revolution, rooted in Taylorism, or "scientific management" (Lynn 2017, p. 145). This is the idea that purports complex problems can be solved through an objective approach, and that attention to nuance isn't as important as paying attention to production increased through the use of specific methods (think about how test prep is used to "remedy" low standardized test scores). While it is frustrating that the story of human growth is often incomplete and undertold due to how enmeshed data growth and funding are, it is still essential for us to embed the use of data collection in our everyday school lives so we may understand our children better to teach them well.

Importantly, there is a difference between quantitative and qualitative data, and both are of equal value when used in conjunction with one another. Table 5.3 describes characteristics of both types of data.

Although the overemphasis on quantitative data is problematic, standalone data in either category is also problematic. Isolated data, qualitative or quantitative, should always beg the question: What else do I need to know about this student to teach them better? The following work along is designed to stretch your thinking regarding the ways in which data is used and discussed in your community.

TABLE 5.3 Characteristics of quantitative and qualitative data.

Quantitative Data	Qualitative Data
■ Highlights targeted areas for teachers to grow with students. ■ Large groups of students can be assessed and results are often efficient and quick, produced by computer systems. ■ Shows implications for generalizations regarding how an entire class or grade performs. However . . . ■ Sometime creates blinders for what kids (and teachers) can do. ■ Sometimes "efficacy" diminishes opportunities for strength-based approaches to teaching.	■ Captures nuance: the parts of humanity, literacy, and growth that aren't always empirical. ■ Results are often robust and descriptive, such as information surfaced from *Kidwatching* (Owocki and Goodman 2002). ■ Show implications for teaching in the classroom, particularly around social literacy, racial literacy, and flexible grouping. However . . . Individual biases can play into the types of information that is documented, skewing data to represent what the data collector *thinks* is happening as opposed to what is *actually* happening.
Examples ■ Test scores/grades. ■ What is counted, i.e., number of times hand was raised during 30-minute period. ■ Attendance records. ■ Report card averages/grade card averages.	**Examples** ■ Observations ■ Conversations ■ Witnessing ■ Interviewing ■ Experiential ■ Photos, video ■ Note-taking

Work Along: Strength-Based Student Talk "Taboo" Game

When student data is discussed, the language used to describe their abilities, characteristics, or work is often loaded, and, therefore, important to complicate. I invite you to engage with this activity alone or with a group of colleagues. Not only is standalone data incomplete, but when educators discuss that data, it is often done so through a deficit perspective. This activity encourages viewing students through their capacity orientations through the use of strength-based language, and the omission of singular data fields and/or deficit bases.

1. Think about a few learners you've struggled to teach in the past, or who have frequently come up in staff meetings.

2. Write a short description of their learning profiles.

3. Read the following list. Cross out any language used from the Taboo Words/Phrases list.

   Taboo Words/Phrases:

   - Reading levels

   - High, medium, or low

   - Struggle

   - Can't

   - Reluctant

   - 1s, 2s, 3s, or 4s; no test scores or other ranking language

   - Title I

   - IEP kids

   - Special education student

4. Replace the language you crossed out with capacity-building language and more specific language. Capacity-building language names what skills, attributes, and behaviors learners presently possess from a strength-based perspective that can be built upon for growth. Specific language describes those skills, attributes, and behaviors with details that are based on a collection of information—in other words, data. For example, if you at first used the word "struggling" to describe a learner's reading ability, what are you actually observing? Are you noticing their excitement to explain a story their uncle told them over the weekend in morning circle? Are they sounding out word parts separately, and using different letter sounds than the letters that appear? Are they choosing other activities rather than reading a book during independent reading time? If you used the word "medium" to describe a learner's math ability, what exactly are they able to do? What skills have they mastered that you are able to build upon?

(Continued)

5. Reflect.

   - What did the learning profile you originally created reveal about the student?

   - Describe how it felt to talk about that student without using words and phrases on the taboo list.

   - Brainstorm what ways you can attain more powerful information about learners that will help you teach them.

Chapter 6:
The Joyful Work of Building Imaginative Capacities Matters: Know that Learning Predates School

To the Reader: Twilight

By Chase Twichell

Whenever I look
out at the snowy
mountains at this hour

and speak directly
into the ear of the sky,
it's you I'm thinking of.
You're like the spirits
the children invent
to inhabit the stuffed horse
and the doll.
I don't know who hears me.
I don't know who speaks
when the horse speaks.

One of the many magical parts of traversing the city via subway is the MTA's (Metropolitan Transit Authority) Poetry in Motion. Yes, it's true. Poems adorn the 150-year-old+ vessels of this grand city. The poems are situated in colorful, nuanced prints that absolutely *pop* out of the yellow-beige-orange-murky hues of the D/N/R train walls and its seats. The lyrical force of these poems stands strong, holding the beauty of the ride steadfast. The poems share that matched fortitude with their parents: ride any train in the city and you'll be embraced, lifted, and/or challenged by lines from the likes of Audre Lorde, Lucille Clifton, Marilyn Nelson, and Billy Collins.

The train ride offers a space for deep reflection for those who ride it, and after a full day of teaching, I remember a poem on a subway ride that provided deep clarification to a notion that sat in my heart, undefined, but certainly a driver to my teaching. Chase Twichell's poem "To the Reader: Twilight" popped out from the walls and lifted me. I was riding the D/N/R train from 59th Street and 4th Avenue to 4th Avenue and 9th Street from the elementary school I taught at in Sunset Park, Brooklyn, to my then-home in Park Slope, Brooklyn; neighborhoods touching, but not close enough for a quick walk. "To the Reader: Twilight" massaged my heart with an affirmation, a knowing, that until that point I hadn't yet been able to put into words:

You're like the spirits
the children invent
to inhabit the stuffed horse
and the doll.

"The spirits the children invent to inhabit the stuffed horse and the doll" was, is, probably always will be the thing I seek to protect, to nurture, to grow, name and acknowledge within all the spaces I share with children. There's nothing quite like the life a child gives to a toy, or an invented land erected from scraps of recyclables. Whether I am at home, in the classroom, or spending time with friends, I take the opportunity to reaffirm the majestic mind of children by witnessing their questions, saying "yes" to their strange materials requests, or encouraging a divergent thought.

My will for encouraging imagination within kids and young adults is so strong because I know those majestic minds of theirs are in constant threat of being scrubbed of inquisition in the name of high scores, "good" grades, or prescribed curriculum. *The spirits the children invent* names the bursting, loveful imagination that surfaces from children's minds, and the growing of these ideas and seemingly impossibilities, are sacred to our craft in teaching.

However, those lovely minds will only be fed the vivacity they deserve so long as they are not diminished by the institutions and systems and traumas that surround them. We must do everything in our power to protect, honor, and cherish those *spirits* of children Twichell names in the learning spaces we create for our students.

Work Along: Summoning Your Inner Child

This section discusses the s*pirits children invent*, giving life to their toys through their imaginations and curiosities. As a child, do you remember the games of pretend you engaged in, or the life you gave a particular item within your play? What were you curious about?

Spend a few moments reflecting on and documenting this experience. What feelings were evoked through this kind of play when you were a child?

How does this type of imagining or ideating translate within school communities, within classroom community life? Within the inner life and outer life of individuals in the classroom?

Tip: If you're feeling stuck, flip through an old photo book, or text somebody who knew you as a child. Ask: "What did I like? What was I 'into'?" It's also helpful to google "what happened in the year _____"; you'll see many references that have probably been absent from your mind for many, many years. For example: I just googled "what happened in 1994" and I had totally forgotten this was the year O.J. Simpson fled the police in his white Bronco!

Here's my reflection.

Warrensburg Middle School, Sixth Grade: 1994

It's 1994, and it's the era of talk show drama and MTV. Angie, Kayla, and I were watching three or four talk shows a week, serving ourselves a healthy dose of Ricki Lake, Maury Povich (if our parents weren't home), and sometimes Oprah. During this slumber party, we lip-synced to Ace of Base, Boys II Men, and The Cranberries; we drank copious amounts of hot chocolate; and we reinvented the talk-show circuit. Reimagining ourselves as talk show queens, we did our best impressions of the dramatic, confusing, and insatiable guests the hosts would interview.

It's hard for me to remember the made-up drama, but I do remember when it was my turn to play talk show queen, I chose Ricki Lake. I tolerated absolutely zero nonsense from the guests (Vanilla Ice and Tonya Harding) my friends role-played. Instead, I served up question after question to the ill-conceived drama these pretend guests portrayed before eventually posing a multitude of opinions followed with a quasi-solution. My fervent interview style swayed my friends, and they suggested I consider a career with MTV rather that pursue a college track.

While I clearly never landed a role on the cast of *Road Rules* or *The Real World,* I'm grateful for their feedback. I remember feeling my inner life warming through this sort of incremental surfacing of who I could be. In school, the opportunity to assert opinions on pop culture or the merit of celebrity behavior that we young people were so curious about was rare. More often, we were shushed away or had the TV remote "offed" when talk of O.J. Simpson's case was broadcast or when we wondered out loud about Bosnia.

At home, sometimes I had chances to exercise my stance on how things should be, but my parents were working a lot. Making space for me to explain the zeal behind Tonya Harding's attack on Nancy Kerrigan wasn't a priority. My parents listened to me, and my friends entertained my spirit within the safe space of slumber parties, but more often than not, I exercised my assertions in the safety of my bedroom.

It's a wonder that the spirit of the *talk show* version of myself, the one who solves problems, provokes the idea of "should," and articulates how things could go survived. From what I remember, versions of that self primarily showed up at slumber parties and moments in class where I had completed my work, stared out the window, and replayed scenarios of tackling topics within my imagination.

Upon reflection, I can't help but notice how I had embarked upon the implicit project of separating my inner life and outer world assigned to me by one of the environments I most consistently interacted with: school.

Question mark.

"Do Schools Kill Creativity?"

Humans are born curious: inquiry is our birthright. The spirit of imagination is intrinsically developed in our most early years of life through our biology, our curiosity, and our interaction with the environments and people that surround us. It is one of the most special components of humanity, a sacred part of who we are, it is what makes *us* us.

But perhaps one of the greatest tricks Western civilization has played upon itself is that school is the absolute primer for a person's most powerful learning. While school and classrooms and teachers offer great potentiality and momentous learning for students within their spaces, if we are to capture and nurture imagination, it is important for us to understand it from where it starts, from the *very* beginning.

There is a growing body of research that shows how schooling has actually *impeded* students' curiosity and creativity. The late educationalist Sir Ken Robinson brought this conversation to dinner tables around the world with his TED Talk "Do Schools Kill Creativity?" (Robinson 2006). With 73.5 million views to date, it is the most watched TED Talk of all time. In his talk, he argues two major points regarding the relationship between schools and creativity. First, Robinson says, "We don't grow into creativity, we grow out of it. Or rather we get educated out of it." Second, he says, "Creativity is as important as literacy and we should afford it the same status."

Robinson builds on these points in his later TED Talk entitled "Changing Education Paradigms" (2010), further illustrating schools and the barriers they impose on kids' curiosity. This time, he cites research from more than a decade prior to his first talk, illuminating divergent thinking present in early childhood that dissipates in later schooling by using Land and Jarman's *Breakpoint and Beyond* research (1992). This longitudinal study demonstrates the inverse relationship between years spent in schooling and creativity. Land and Jarman worked with 1,500 kindergartners with the goal of measuring creativity after every five years spent in school. In the test, students were given a paper clip and asked "What are all the ways you could use a paperclip?" At age five, 98% of those students received a creativity score on a genius level. At the age of 10, 30% of students received a creativity score on a genius level. At age 15, the number of genius-level creativity scores reduced to 12%, and at the average age of 31, scores reduced to just 2% (Land and Jarman 1992, in Robinson 2010).

There are a number of variables at play in regard to factors impacting the ability to summon creativity throughout school, especially when culture, identity, place, curriculum, and teacher agency are taken into account. I also have questions regarding environmental factors around the distribution of the creativity assessment (How long did students have to take the test? At what time of day did they take it? Who was their proctor?) as well as the assessment itself. However, there is something to be said about the massive and steady decline in scores demonstrated by over thousands of people as they spent more time in school.

So, what does the inverse relationship between students' creativity and time spent in school mean for educators? First, it's important to note that teachers and students have a similar relationship between practical, creative thinking and schooling: The more years we spend within the realm of institutional thinking, the less our sense of self and our imagination is revealed within our pedagogy. In this book, we have worked on a treatment plan to remedy "going through the motions" of school life, regaining our sense of self by digging into our past and our present. We've worked to expand our imagination toward dreaming up future goodness, and the mechanism we use to initiate that process is by both reestablishing and reimagining our pedagogy.

Creativity, Curiosity, and Childhood Development

Creativity underscores all of that work. It is an innate human process; it is how we make new ideas and fashion our thinking, our experiences, and even the materials we use in ways that are most authentic to our unique communities. Creativity is an aspect of our joy, without it, how are we equipped to work toward justice?

On the journey to licensure, teachers experience a course in childhood development to varying degrees. However, it's often before in-service teaching starts, and it's a body of knowledge that sits on the backburner for many people working in upper elementary or secondary schools. In other words, it's been separated from school-based decision-making. More and more often, we see the life of child development disappearing from curricular landscapes for even our youngest children. It makes me shudder.

It doesn't have to be this way: together, we can imbue childhood life back into school!

First, let's consider all kinds of ways and all kinds of things children learn from birth to the time they turn four years old. Each time I delve into the scores of work and research documenting the intellectual life of very young children, I am blown away at how capable they are, by *how much* they know and are able to do before they even arrive to school.

I didn't start my career in education knowing much about childhood development. Aside from the experiences I had caring for my nieces and nephew, who were school-aged during my first year in grad school, I'd not spent significant amounts of time with people four years old or younger. In fact, I taught for five years before I spent significant amounts of time with very young people, before I began to deeply explore how synapses and neural pathways and environments and caregivers coalesce with one another to inform what a child knows.

Before I considered how much adverse childhood experiences have power to shape and undo important milestones in life, or before I knew how all the funds of knowledge kids were bringing into school could be embraced and built upon, rather than straightened out and stretched toward assimilation, I was well underway teaching students in high school.

I was mothering my two very young children at the same time I began teaching fourth and fifth graders within an elementary school. They, of course, were my ultimate teachers, and it was from them that I learned much of what I now know about childhood development. In addition to my elementary school-aged teachers, I've also learned, and continue to learn, by witnessing my own children's development, reading well-known research from Jean Piaget, Marie Clay, George Land, and Beth Jarman, and reading and listening to lesser-known (but equally important) work from the advice of bloggers like Janet Lansbury and Dr. Sears, as well as all of my family members. Really, the sources I learn from are endless!

Here, I give you the CliffNotes version on all the things kids learn before they even receive any schooling, from the very beginning. Later, we're going to expand and bridge this information into the kinds of decisions we make at school to sustain deep levels of curiosity for the students we teach, allowing their inner lives to fuse with the outward experience of school.

Powerful and peer reviewed, The Center on the Developing Child at Harvard University provides succinct research for understanding "the science" behind childhood development. It's an excellent source for foundational knowledge for how humans learn and all the different ways their environment and early experiences impact the ways in which they engage with their peers, families, and school. The Center on the Developing Child's website is fueled with multimedia for taking a deep dive on the topic. In short, here are salient points regarding childhood development and learning:

1. **In the first few years of life, over 1 million neural connections are formed *every second*.** Already, as babies, humans are exercising powerful cognition! The brains of babies are strong, and with each day, they grow more complex. The very young brain is constantly revising itself, adding more details to its once simple structure. Sensory pathways for things like hearing and vision are developed first, followed by early language development, and later higher cognitive functions like using a spoon to eat with or learning to walk.

2. **The strength of cognitive development is incumbent upon the richness of babies' interactions with the humans and environment that surround them.** Genes and experience are both at play, and the idea of "rich environments"[1] is one that must be complicated . . . we don't want to adopt assimilationist perspectives! Perhaps you've heard of "serve and return"? Serve and return is the idea that if a baby makes some kind of baby-contribution to the world, like smiling, babbling, or taking a step, the baby's actions are

---

1   Rich linguistic environments are complicated through Sarah Michael's commentary on Hart and Risley's seminal but contentious work, *Meaningful Differences*, on early language development comparisons between well-resourced families and lower-income families.

affirmed by another human, ideally a caregiver, with some type of communicative warmth, for example, a returned smile, an affirmative sentence in response to the baby babble, or congratulatory steps after the walk. If the baby serves, or "contributes" to the world, and is not acknowledged for their effort, the brain's structure develops more weakly, causing gaps in learning and activating early stress responses.

3. **In the earliest stages of life, brains are most elastic, accepting, adapting, and revising all kinds of information.** This is one of the many reasons young children are able to capture and become fluent in more than one language much more easily than adults. Humans are never too old to learn new things, change their habits, or strengthen neural pathways, but as kids and adults grow older, new habits are harder to develop because the brain is less elastic.

4. **The brain does not work in compartments!** All of its parts—social, emotional, and cognitive capacities—are in constant interaction with one another. This is why it's so important to make space for children to explore a full range of emotions in all the spaces they occupy. When we ask them to push their feelings aside, essentially we are asking them to use a small piece of their mind.

So, at the tender age of two, very young children have developed a brain with millions of neural connections, they've used their brains to revise and select and grow new ideas about the world, and, for many, they've built a solid foundation for language learning they'll use throughout their lives. It's no wonder they are so temperamental! They've done an incredible amount of work to simply *be*.

Working Toward Justice: The Continued Conversation on Student Centeredness

People talk a lot about student-centeredness. It's a stance that many educators, including myself, have declared over and over again throughout time and throughout many different places. It is what my partner, Cornelius, has named "radically pro-kid." But it's more than a proclamation. It's also a deep study on learning, on development, on curriculum-making, and knowledge-growing. We've talked about some of those things already, but in reality, working toward student-centeredness, or thinking about what it means to be "radically pro-kid" is a never-ending conversation that evolves as kids grow older, or new kids enter your learning space.

You may be wondering, *Why call it radically pro-kid as opposed to student-centeredness?* In truth, I wish it wasn't such a radical thing to center children and adolescents in the work of teaching and learning. However, as we've explored the scope of kids and school since its inception, there hasn't been a moment in time where children have truly been at the center. Since Thomas Jefferson's original "Bill for the General Diffusion of Knowledge," along with other white, male intellectuals and politicians like Noah Webster, John Dewey, and Horace Mann, each iteration of schooling has been in the name of democracy and citizenship, but according to each of their *preferred social orders* (Ravitch and Vitteriti 2001, p. 9). Their ideals of citizenship scarcely include children outside their own white, English-speaking, able-bodied, and male identity markers. White, able-bodied, English-speaking girls worked until 1972 to be afforded the same rights as their male counterparts.

Arguably, even those children who were considered within the educational paradigm of Jefferson, Dewey, Webster, and Mann were still subjected to the idea that being a good citizen meant being productive, and that to be productive meant high achievement in schools. High achievement is a component of schooling that has been omnipresent in the conversation regarding "What makes a good school?" However, for me, the more important question is, "What makes a child sustain their joy and curiosity?" I argue that when you hold that question tight, when you assert that question alongside achievement-oriented policies, *that* is when you are being student-centered. Because you will almost always be doing this in tandem with policies that have eroded joy and contained divergent thinking, the radical element of this work has surfaced, hence Cornelius's nomenclature: to be student-centered is to be radically pro-kid. Therein lies another relationship between justice and joy, and how we work to spread it in our schools.

Historical Underpinnings: Notes on Spreading Joy: Expanding Notions on What Educational Practices Are and Where They Come From

Can you imagine what would happen if a school's "goodness" was measured by how much joy and curiosity ensued amongst its participants? What would have to change in your community for something like this to be the case?

Learn more about the cultural expansiveness of literacy practices to consider different possibilities for building joy and curiosity at https://www.kassandcorn.com/teachingfiercely/

Immersing Oneself in a Student-Centered Space

When I work to build student-centered experiences in a standards-based classroom, I do so by spending a lot of time in educator spaces. I keep my eyes and ears open in school communities, and pay attention to the felt knowledge I experience by watching how kids relate to, communicate with, or even physically locate themselves to teachers within communities who do the work of positioning children as the center of their pedagogy in ways that are clear and subtle, and are especially evident in the ways children react and respond in the classroom communities they have designed. Keep in mind—I'm in educator spaces in a lot of ways. Yes, I'm a coach, but I'm also a teacher volunteer at a local summer camp, and I also am the parent of two elementary-aged children. There are numerous spaces where I am watching, observing, analyzing, and sense-making the multitude of human interactions on a daily basis.

One of the most meaningful and salient observations is the way in which my youngest daughter's pre-K teacher positioned students at the center of her pedagogy. Markedly, she did so through an undercurrent of love. I wrote about this phenomenon a while ago, for no other reason than that I didn't want to forget it. I knew from the research that this pre-K year would probably be the most joyful year of her life spent in school. Below, I describe this felt experience and analysis in detail.

2018

My Daughter's Pre-K Classroom, Brooklyn, New York

Every time I walk into my youngest daughter's pre-K classroom, my heart swells. At the top of the stairs leading to her classroom, we are first greeted with a carefully constructed and kid-created three-dimensional alphabet museum hanging on the wall, on which most days we pause to find the letter "N," which is how her classroom door is labeled: "Classroom N." The walls are peppered with the work of inquisitive young minds; recently, stories of the children's families, drawn exclusively by the children, were posted alongside collages they had made earlier, including pictures of people in their lives who were important to them, with other fuzzy and shiny objects decorating the images.

Upon entering her classroom, we go through a fairly typical routine of unpacking, washing hands, and flipping her picture over on a chart to show everyone she has arrived (all the children do this). Also, similarly to many pre-K classrooms across the country, the class-

(Continued)

room has several "areas" that children are allowed to spend time at each morning with one another, including an ever-changing Dramatic Play corner (since the beginning of the school year, it has shifted from a kitchen, to a doctor's office, and most recently—a gym (with a pretend treadmill crafted out of a yoga mat and cardboard!!!).

However, not so typically, on a wall near the class's daily schedule there is a "feelings wheel," where children place an arrow alongside the feeling they are currently experiencing. They can choose to talk more about it, or not. Additionally, every Tuesday, they have what is called Friends School, where the school social worker pushes into the class and works quite explicitly on a curriculum that helps the children develop strong social and emotional skills. There is a biweekly parent/caregiver group that coincides with the same curriculum, led by the same social worker, supporting families to build those same skills with their children. Cornelius and I receive a flier in Indi's backpack every week, highlighting the activities Friends School engaged in with tips for us on how to support our child at home.

After about a month of pre-K, Indi said, "Mama, do you wanna know something?" I said, "YES!" (I usually respond pretty enthusiastically when any kid, especially my own, is on the cusp of articulating an idea that has been percolating.) "My teacher loves me," she replied, in the same tone someone would tell you a benign fact, like "The sky is blue." It was clear that in her mind there was no doubt that she was loved at her school, within her classroom, between the adults who care for her every day when her family is not with her. I asked her how she knew, and she said, "Because Ms. H told me." So, quite literally (and also implicitly through a million other kind and gentle micro-interactions taking place between teachers and children), my child is loved in school. Just as the sky is blue, it is a fact.

The comment, "My teacher loves me," was arresting, and it occurred to me that I, too, experienced a similar feeling whenever I dropped her off or picked her up at school: an undercurrent of love. A bit of salve for my fiery heart working in a big giant school system, where sometimes the softness of working with children gets lost in the harshness of a system that doesn't protect grown-ups' well-being, that maybe centers itself too much on achievement and not enough on growth and progress. This undercurrent of love so clearly carries a community of children forward because, more than anything, it centers their development and well-being as the priority of their school experience.

All I ever really needed to know I learned in . . . *kindergarten?*

Those notes, put together as an imprint for my work and to capture a beautiful year in school for my daughter to look back on, beckon happy tears: there is nothing like dropping off your child in a healthy school space where they declare evidence-based love for and from their teachers. I'm also slightly heartbroken after taking that trip down memory lane because it was pre-COVID schooling, which was not perfect, but certainly more resourced. And I'm also a little rejuvenated—we've so much to learn from the ways of pre-K!

A few years back, I worked briefly with a pre-K center on a topic-based professional development on Universal Design for Learning. When I prepared for the work, I studied the New York State Prekindergarten Foundation for the Common Core standards that the New York State Board of Regents adopted in January 2011. The *New York State Prekindergarten Foundation for the Common Core* is divided into several domains, with the first domain called Approaches to Learning. Below, find a summarized version of the foundational skills included in this domain:

Excerpt from *New York State Prekindergarten Foundation for the Common Core* domains

Engagement

1. Actively and confidently engages in play as a means of exploration and learning.

2. Actively engages in problem solving.

Creativity and Imagination

3. Approaches tasks, activities, and problems with creativity, imagination, and/or willingness to try new experiences or activities.

Curiosity and Initiative

4. Exhibits curiosity, interest, and willingness in learning new things and having new experiences.

Persistence

5. Demonstrates persistence.

(New York State Prekindergarten Foundation for the Common Core)

As I read and reread the text, never before had I seen such appropriate guidance for learning; guidance that could really work for any child within almost any curriculum. Those skills are just a small taste of the guide in its entirety, with other domains including: Physical Development and Health, Social and

Emotional Development and Communication, and Language and Literacy. There is a Part B in the document as well, including English Language Arts and Mathematics standards from the Common Core State Standards.

Comparatively, when children start kindergarten within the many states that have adopted Common Core Standards or states that have adopted their own standards in recent years, there are no standards named "foundational," rather, they are divided into Reading, Writing, Language, Speaking and Listening, and Mathematics, where children are expected to do things like:

CCSS.ELA-LITERACY.SL.K.1

Participate in collaborative conversations with diverse partners about *kindergarten topics and texts* with peers and adults in small and larger groups. (Common Core State Standards Initiative)

And:

Use a combination of drawing, dictating, and writing to compose informative/explanatory texts in which they name what they are writing about and supply some information about the topic. (Common Core State Standards Initiative)

Many children will be able to work toward those standards and participate in peer collaboration and writing with zeal. They will come to school excited, and rush to their caregivers to tell them about all the wonderful things that happened in their kindergarten class that day. Conversely, many children will experience great difficulty sitting in their chairs on the rug for many minutes, taking turns during conversations and/or during choice time, or even spending six hours of classroom time without having a tantrum, and their caregivers might unpack a note from their teacher in their backpacks requesting a meeting, or a paper that includes how many smileys they earned for the day.

It is with deep realism that many children entering kindergarten are still developing their "approaches to learning," regulating their emotions, and developing positive relationships with those who surround them. *Even more importantly, and of deeper concern, is that many students entering middle school, high school, and even college are still grappling with those same issues.* Yet—the crux of their development seems to have been left out of the core of their school experience, leading to just that—an experience where they go to school, as opposed to a *place they go to learn*.

Work Along: Wait, What Is It I Am Supposed to Teach?

Unpacking Curricular Standards

As I continue to work with teachers across elementary and secondary schools, there is a growing trend in the use of other people's curriculum. This is not necessarily a bad thing, and as indicated in the last chapter, there are many variables that shape teacher agency and school policy that can either hinder or bolster one's ability to teach the kinds of curriculum students need and deserve.

However, regardless of whether you are reading from a scripted curriculum, adapting a curriculum, or crafting your own curriculum, it is imperative teachers become familiar with the standards in which they are obligated to teach. It's hard enough working to transfer knowledge to groups of students when it doesn't feel entirely relevant to them. But the more we become familiar with the knowledge we are working to build, even if we didn't create the vessel the lessons and texts live within, the more we understand the destination, and the better we are able to steer it.

Within instructional and curricular design teams, I used the following method to unpack curricular standards so teachers could take more ownership of the learning designs their students would experience.

Unpacking Standards:

1. One way to gain clarity on what you are supposed to teach in a curricular standard is to render the skills, content, and habits within the standard.

   For example, the following is CCSS ELA, Grade 6, Speaking and Listening Domain for Comprehension and Collaboration. Highlighted within the standard are yellow skills (engage, collaborative discussion, expressing), turquoise content (topics, texts, and issues), and purple habits (building on others' ideas). They have been listed in the table below.

   Engage effectively in a range of collaborative discussions (one-on-one, in groups, and teacher-led) with diverse partners on grade 6 topics, texts, and issues, building on others' ideas and expressing their own clearly. (CCSS.ELA-LITERACY.SL.6.1)

Skills	Content	Habits
Engage Collaborate Oral communication Expression	Topics Texts Issues	Building on others' ideas

2. Before starting to plan learning experiences, or determine learning objectives within an upcoming unit, I encourage educators to spend some time reflecting about the purpose behind the standard they are unpacking in relation to the learners in the community they teach. It helps to name this in your own words to deepen your understanding and strengthen the direction in your teaching.

(Continued)

The table below helps to guide this kind of reflection. I've included a reflection in connection to the standard above. However, if you were to do this reflection with a similar standard, your reflection might be different because your community of learners is different.

What am I teaching?	In this speaking and listening standard, I am teaching sixth graders to participate in authentic dialogue with one another around specific topics, texts, and important issues we study together in class. Importantly, they will work together to express their ideas, and they must do so in a way that makes others understand what they are saying. They also have to create ideas together rather than just saying what they think. Their conversations about various texts should be a manifestation of their collective thinking, not just individual stories or narratives.
Why?	This type of speaking and listening is an important part of life that works toward creating stronger relationships through mutual understanding and thicker listening. Young children, adolescents, and adults share a need to feel seen and heard, like they matter. Engaging, collaborating, and communicating in ways that work toward understanding and supporting healthy thinking in a world where misinformation is rampant is crucial.
How?	It will be important to choose texts and topics that are relevant to the students' experiences. We'll have to choose some very specific protocols that will help along their turn-taking in conversation because they have a tendency to "wait to talk" and/or interrupt rather than really trying to understand where their peers are coming from. I know the School Reform Initiative has some great protocols, and I might try Reciprocal Reading to start with as well.
Do our learners know all this?	With the sixth graders I've worked with, text navigation isn't a big problem. Most of them are able to deduce a main idea and cite relevant evidence. However, they haven't shown they really listen to one another, and rarely do they build off one another's ideas. There will be a few learners who will need extra support in accessing the text, but for this component of the curriculum (speaking and listening), I'll be sure to include multimodal texts to increase access for those students.

3. Share your reflection with a colleague who teaches the same subject and grade that you do. How are your understandings similar and/or different? What ideas can you share with one another to support your unit planning?

While this may seem tedious, the important work is that you are revising how your brain internalizes a standard. Chunking the standard into skills, content, and habits helps us to (a) clarify the path in which we are journeying to reach objectives within those standards and (b) specify the learning experiences, texts, and instructional strategies we choose as we continue adapting and shaping our curriculum.

Below, I've included the steps from above with a "blank slate" for you to unpack standards on your own or within a team.

Now It's Your Turn! Unpack the Standard.

1. Choose a state standard for an upcoming unit of study.

2. Render skills, content, and habits from that standard.

3. Clarify the purpose of that standard using the questions below as guidelines.

What am I teaching?
Why?
How?
Do all my learners know this?

Placing Kids' Developmental Needs at the Center of Learning in Community

When we think about creating spaces of learning with schools (and I know, it's funny how deliberately we must invest in making a school a learning space), it makes sense to start at the very beginning of a child's experience with school. When children's emotional development and social skills are supported as the impetus for learning throughout the day, really, the fiber that makes the fabric of the classroom community, they feel better and their hearts and minds grow more. When kids feel better, teachers feel better.

In collaboration with teachers, I worked hard to think about what it means to develop the way children approach not just learning, but how to learn with one another. Moreover, we wanted to integrate the work of support- ing children developmentally throughout the day, not just tucking the work in on the fringes of the day into a "character education" or "mindfulness" period. We'll start with a bird's-eye view in a kindergarten classroom, taught by Rachel Sharpstein, and then zoom in, noting how this teacher's work took place over time, with perseverance, and with great care.

When I met Rachel Sharpstein, I had been working as a staff developer for the Teachers College Inclusive Classrooms Project in her school for a few months, working to build inclusive practices with several teacher teams in ICT classrooms.[2] During a debrief with the school's principal, it was requested

---

2   Integrated Co-Teaching, as defined in the United Federation of Teachers contract: *Students with disabilities who receive Integrated Co-Teaching services are educated with age appro- priate peers in the general education classroom. ICT provides access to the general educa- tion curriculum and specially designed instruction to meet students' individual needs.*

that I support one of their kindergarten teachers working in a general education classroom, mostly teaching by herself, who was feeling overwhelmed and particularly challenged by a few children, and very challenged by the whole class's general dependence on her for everything. The principal suggested I might help create classroom stations, or centers, with her to decrease the amount of whole-group learning.

As an educator who seldom taught alone, I knew I had to enter this space with great empathy: a 27:1 kid:teacher ratio is rarely easy. I first had an opportunity to visit her classroom. Before I meet with teachers, I usually request a low-stakes classroom visit to get a sense of their community vibe, to witness and collect important micro-interactions and other subtleties taking place between kids and kids and teachers and kids, and, also, to note how the room set up affects communication. Then, I engaged with her one-to-one, channeling all my active listening skills.

I firmly believe in teacher agency, and one way we can work together to reaffirm teacher agency is to invite teachers to our platforms and include them when we talk about different ways to enact justice and joy in our classrooms. To that end, I invited Rachel to be included in this text. Below, you 'll find her voice sharing the journey we embarked upon, underscoring the choices we made to improve both her and her students' experience.

Featuring Rachel Sharpstein: A Teacher's Anecdote

Starting the school year, I was faced with many challenges from my students. There was a general dysfunctionality within our small learning community. A few of my students required significant support to engage in school safely and productively (were in a state of crisis), and overall there was a general dependency and lack of self-awareness displayed by most of the other students. The classroom felt chaotic and students expressed not feeling safe at times. They (almost) all turned to me to help them solve even the smallest problem that would occur. I wasn't able to teach the curriculum that I had taught successfully for the past four years. Whole-group lessons couldn't be done, small-group work always ended in arguments and hurt feelings or bodies. Sharing and communicating with others was too difficult for a majority of my students. This was a totally different beast than I ever had to deal with teaching alone.

I started to collect more specific data on exactly what problems were recurring and started associating them with lagging skills. Many of the students were lagging in executive functioning, perspective-taking, flexibility, self-awareness, ability to identify and appropriately display feelings, self-regulating, turn taking, listening . . . This list seemed to go on forever and it was even more difficult to try to create and manage structures and interventions differentiated to specific students' needs. At this point, I seemed to be juggling behavior plans, alternative or modified tasks and seating, reward incentives, extensive daily or weekly communication with parents and administration, and more. It was only a matter of time before I became completely overwhelmed.

After months of attempting to put out fires, trying interventions, collecting data, holding meetings, and exhaustive conversations, I was completely exhausted. I could not continue maintaining this level of stress and effort much longer. It was not only affecting the learning and environment within the classroom, but it was starting to impact my health. I was overwhelmed and nothing seemed to be successful. This is when I reached out to administration and asked if I could work with one of the staff developers from TCICP. I knew the program was developed to support inclusive classrooms like ICT, however, the work they did with teachers was support that I felt would benefit our class. In January, I began meeting with Kass.

During my sessions with Kass, we narrowed down the most eminent problems that had been recurring. It became clear that my students were dependent on me (adults), had low self-regulation skills, and limited ability to perspective take. To help free up some of my time and energy, we felt that our top priority was to help the students become more independent, building greater self-reliance and resourcefulness.

With the goal of students becoming more independent, we created a buddy system for problem solving. We called it Super Solvers. Each student was partnered with a classmate who would be their first line of defense in solving problems. If they needed any help at all, they were expected to ask their Super Solver to help them before coming to an adult.

The students quickly took to this structure. They would support each other without prompting from adults. It made them feel more comfortable and secure in their community and throughout their day at school. They loved taking care of each other. I noticed partnerships tending to each other in times when someone was sad. They would take initiative to ask how their partner felt, suggest and support them in using strategies to feel better. Oftentimes, I would see a partnership spending time in the cozy corner together where many of our materials and tools were for emotional literacy. They might be reading a book together snuggled up in the beanbag chair or watching the glitter wands letting their worries melt away. During unpack and pack-up times, everyone partnered up and helped each other to complete all of the necessary steps. We were able to transition more quickly into learning activities, disruptions occurred less frequently, and new friendships developed, even ones that may not have naturally occurred without encouragement or support.

(Continued)

Partnerships were arranged in a scaffolded and meaningful method. In the beginning of implementation, the partnerships remain the same for a few weeks, allowing opportunity for authentic relationships to build. Eventually, partnerships were switched every two weeks, based on skill levels and needs. I started off pairing students heterogeneously, so the most dependent students (lowest skilled) had strong supports and role models. As time went on, partnerships were chosen based on progress in skill development and personalities.

In Figure 6.1, find the materials Rachel and I developed as the Super Solvers became ritualized in Rachel's classroom community.

I want to note: Rachel and I didn't create Super Solvers out of thin air. As we brainstormed and planned together, we also read and researched together. The following articles and texts informed the learning designs we created.

- *What Is Shared Imagination & Why Is It So Important to Relationship Development?* by Michelle Garcia Winner, MA, CCC-SLP and Pamela Crooke, PhD, CCC-SLP from social-thinking.com.

- "The Importance of Educational Partnerships," Chapter 1 in the book *Educational Partnerships: Connecting Schools, Families, and the Community* by Amy Cox-Petersen.

- *Whole Body Listening* by Susanne Poulette Truesdale.

- Buddy System Tip Sheet: Teaching Tools for Young Children by R. Lentini, B.J. Vaughn, and L. Fox.

We took my field notes from Rachel's classroom that included interviews with students, analysis of student artifacts, and observations of times where children demonstrated high dependency on their teacher, in combination

SUPER SOLVERS

Two minds are better than one!
Super solvers work to solve problems together!

FIGURE 6.1 Super solvers poster.

with Rachel's direct experiences and knowledge with the kids, very seriously. Based on new understandings from our research, we named the following skills to serve as the foundation for the teams of Super Solvers.

Underlying Skills for Super Solvers:

Expressive language.

Identify feeling.

Express feelings appropriately.

Express needs.

Identify and apply resources/strategies.

Efficiency in completing daily routines.

Compassion.

Empathy.

Perspective taking.

Guidelines for Super Solver Student Pairings

From there, we developed guidelines for how partnerships would be developed. This was an important aspect in the development of the learning design. Kids showed they had a really hard time working together, so we wanted to be intentional in how the kids would be partnered. We wanted Super Solvers to be sustainable.

Super Solvers

Guidelines for Developing Super Solvers Partnerships:

- Partnerships are heterogeneous, based on development of social/emotional skills.

- Partnerships should be placed in close proximity to each other at their table seats. All other partnerships (math, line up, reading, turn and talk, etc.) should be with different people. Flexibility in partnerships helps students build relationships and confidence in interacting with different types of people within the community.

(Continued)

- Partnerships should change every two to three weeks to allow time to develop a relationship, but should not be long enough to become dependent on one person.

- Super Solvers are responsible for escorting each other to different places around the school (nurse, office, other classrooms, etc.) in times of need.

Ritualizing Super Solvers

After we figured out partnerships, Rachel worked to create a schedule where Super Solvers was consistent within everyday classroom life . . . not just something that popped up every now and then (Figure 6.2). It became a ritual, and students learned to authentically check-in with one another after *lots* of practice and explicit teaching.

	Monday	Tuesday	Wednesday	Thursday	Friday
Partnerships	**Morning Check In:** "How are you feeling this morning? Why?" **Positive Thought/ Wish:** (In mindful position with lights off and closed eyes) Send your Super Solver a positive wish or thought from your heart to theirs. **Afternoon Check In:** "How are you feeling this afternoon? Why?"	**Morning Check In:** "How are you feeling this morning? Why?" **Afternoon Check In:** "How are you feeling this afternoon? Why?"	**Morning Check In:** "How are you feeling this morning? Why?" **Positive Thought/ Wish:** (In mindful position with lights off and closed eyes) Send your Super Solver a positive wish or thought from your heart to theirs. **Afternoon Check In:** "How are you feeling this afternoon? Why?"	**Morning Check In:** "How are you feeling this morning? Why?" **Afternoon Check In:** "How are you feeling this afternoon? Why?"	**Morning Check In:** "How are you feeling this morning? Why?" **Afternoon Check In:** "How are you feeling this afternoon? Why?"

FIGURE 6.2 Sample Super Solver schedule.

	Monday	Tuesday	Wednesday	Thursday	Friday
Small Groups		**Group Games:** In groups of two partnerships, play UNO together. Talk about something that went well and something that was challenging with the whole class.		**Classroom Problems and Solutions:** In groups of two partnerships, give them a picture of a problem in the classroom and have them collaboratively come up with solutions. Share with the class.	
Whole Class	**Super Solver Solutions:** Create an ongoing list for the week that the kids can add to, recognizing ways in which their Super Solvers helped them solve a problem. Post the problem and solution. Save the charts so that you can analyze the types of problems and solutions and help push them to find new solutions or best practices.				**Super Solver Celebration:** Write your Super Solver a thank you letter to appreciate she/he for something (specific) that she/he helped you with during the week. Share with class.

FIGURE 6.2 (*Continued*)

Rachel created numerous artifacts and scaffolds for students to actively participate in the various Super Solver rituals, including Thank You Cards (Figure 6.3) and Kindness Postcards (Figures 6.4 and 6.5), where students practiced recognizing each other's helpful actions and affirming each other's presence in their community.

Rachel's development of the Super Solvers rituals had a deep impact on her classroom community. Her students were becoming more independent in their learning, and were also developing supportive social skills with one another. As we continued our work together, she became more independent herself, cocreating a purposeful, deepened core of social-emotional literacy with the children in her classroom.

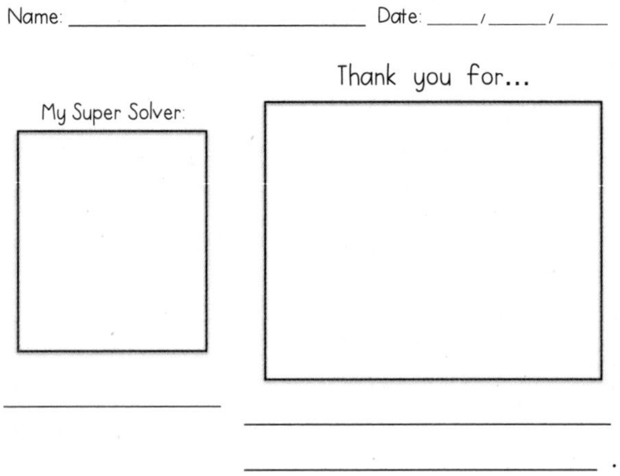

Name: _____ Date: _____ / _____ / _____

My Super Solver:

Thank you for...

FIGURE 6.3 Template used to support students in writing 'thank yous" in Rachel's classroom community (Sharpstein 2017).

SUPER SOLVER

To: _____

Love: _____

FIGURES 6.4 AND 6.5 Templates used to support students in writing affirmations to one another in Rachel's classroom community (Sharpstein 2017).

Rachel's Description of Her "Social-Emotional Literacy Centers"

Once the children had some experience in partnerships and started showing some development in social skills, we thought it was time to introduce group work. The idea of working in stations in small groups seemed like a great opportunity for them to transfer and build upon these skills.

After observing them interacting and learning, Kass and I started to narrow in on a few of the most eminent recurring problems. We narrowed down which skills were needed to effectively function in these situations to avoid having problems.

I created a continuum of social/emotional skills based on kindergarteners' development (Figure 6.6). It is a work in progress.

Emotional Literacy

Kindergarten

Every kindergartner should create an emotional literacy kit for their use to build and develop throughout the year. Resources that are introduced and child-created could be kept in the tool kit such as emoji flashcards, feelings masks, feelings chart, journal, stress relievers, timers, etc. ("Look at all these things I made! This is how I use it… This is why I use it…")

Communication:			
	Beginning of the Year	**Middle of the Year**	**End of the Year**
Meeting Basic Needs	Establishing routines to communicate basic needs such as: bathroom procedures, getting materials, snack/meal time, nurse, problem solving routine An understanding that routines, customs, and regular events can be different in other settings Teacher chosen rug/line/table spots Line walking practice School tours Lunch routine practice Introduce some classroom jobs (door holders, table captains, nurse assistant)	Students engage in routines learning and using classroom jobs, students lead some procedures with little teacher assistance. Morning meeting jobs Classroom jobs Teacher chosen rug/line/table spots	Students function at a fairly collective independent level in routines and procedures. Teacher gives minimal guidance. Student chosen rug/line/table spots

FIGURE 6.6 Sample from emotional literacy progression (Sharpstein 2017).

(Continued)

From there, Kass and I designed fun activities for the stations that would help the students develop these specific skills. There were five stations (one for each day of the week) and the category of underlying skills remained consistent as the activities would evolve over the year building on their abilities.

Stations and Corresponding Skills:

  i. Meeting Managers: teamwork, collaboration, turn taking, expressive language.

 ii. Journal Jots: Identify feelings, visually express feelings, communicate ideas.

iii. Kindness Conductors: perspective taking.

 iv. Appreciation Station: peer affirmation.

  v. Emotion Illustrators: identifying and expressing feelings orally and visually.

Figures 6.7 through 6.13 are artifacts created by Rachel Sharpstein that supported the students' participation in groups, working toward stronger social and emotional literacy.

Morning Stations

Groups	1	2	3	4	5
A	Meeting Managers	Journal Jots	Appreciation Station	Emotion Illustrators	Kindness Conductors
B	Journal Jots	Appreciation Station	Emotion Illustrators	Kindness Conductors	Meeting Managers
C	Appreciation Station	Emotion Illustrators	Kindness Conductors	Meeting Managers	Journal Jots
D	Emotion Illustrators	Kindness Conductors	Meeting Managers	Journal Jots	Appreciation Station
E	Kindness Conductors	Meeting Managers	Journal Jots	Appreciation Station	Emotion Illustrators

FIGURE 6.7 Station schedule.

This journal belongs to:

_____

This journal is a daily record of my experiences, observations, and feelings. This is a way I can process the world around me.

Things I can write about:

★ feelings
★ ideas
★ wonderings
★ things I did
★ things I want to do
★ drawings
★ respond to a book
★ write a story

FIGURE 6.8 Journal jots sample A.

Journal Jots

 How do I feel today?

I feel _____ today

because _____

_____

_____ .

FIGURE 6.9 Journal jots sample B.

**Kindness
Conductors**

1. Make a heart.

2. Write your name.

3. Write one way you can show

   kindness on it.

4. Decorate it.

FIGURE 6.10 Kindness conductors student instructions.

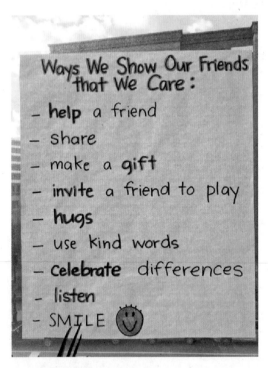

FIGURE 6.11 Kindness conductors teaching chart.

Teaching Fiercely: Spreading Joy and Justice in Our Schools

Emotion Illustrators

1. Choose one emotion from chart.

2. Write your name on the back of index card. Jack

3. Write the emotion word nice and big.  happy

4. Draw an emoji to match the emotion.

FIGURE 6.12 Emotion illustrators station.

Appreciation Station

Thank You Cards

Write a card to thank a friend for a kind thing they did for you.

How did it make you feel?

Show them you care!

FIGURE 6.13 Appreciation station.

Rachel Sharpstein had a high degree of teacher agency, and her work was supported by school leadership that built the school from inclusive principles in education. The artifacts and learning designs shown are examples of "homegrown" curriculum discussed in the previous chapter. Rachel was able to share her learning and classroom experiences with other teachers in her school during an Ed-Camp-style, locally derived, teacher-run professional learning day at her school.

Chapter 7:
Beyond the Protest March:
How to Design Justice-Oriented Learning Spaces, Experiences, and Curriculum That Is Immersed in Joy for Kids

2020: Beyond the Protest March

In the summer of 2020, the world experienced deep unrest as COVID-19 became less of a temporary mindset and more of a long-term reality. People's lives became significantly different due to the ever-changing economic markets, policy changes, and health alerts. Grocery shopping and hospital checkups, once mundane activities, became fraught events that took considerable planning and preparation.

Many families with school-age children experienced more "togetherness" than ever before when school and other activities became virtual and in-home due to quarantining and safety precautions. While dubbed "tender and fun" at first, spending hours in the same space deeply impacted the mental health of the family unit—both individually and collectively.

Kids didn't get their daily dose of friendship time, the sensory experience of school environments was diminished to corners of kids' apartments or alcoves in their bedrooms, and parents and caregivers struggled to maintain a sense of coherence in their careers as they inadvertently became their children's part-time teaching assistants.

Educators were challenged with learning entirely new teaching mediums to deliver instruction and cultivate community. Absenteeism saturated attendance rosters. Gaps between what kids used to be able to do versus what they could presently do widened.

While life became different, some old problems remained the same, if not worsened, in the United States.

On Monday, 25 May 2020, George Floyd, a 46-year-old Black man, was killed by Derek Chauvin, a 44-year-old white police officer in Minneapolis, Minnesota. (One year later, Derek Chauvin was convicted of manslaughter and sentenced to 22 years in federal prison.) Compounded with the murders of countless other Black folx[1] from policing activity and the disproportionate harm COVID-19[2] (Grace et al. 2020) unleashed within the Black community, the United States' anti-Black racism pressure cooker popped.

---

1   The BBC reports a timeline of major incidents since 2014 involving police officers that resulted in the deaths of Black Americans. The following deaths were included on the timeline: Eric Garner, Michael Brown, Tamir Rice, Walter Scott, Alton Sterling, Philando Castile, Stephon Clark, Breonna Taylor, George Floyd, and Duante Wright. Names reported were most prolific in news media channels, but do not include all of the Black people who have died from their experiences with police and/or white terrorists during that time period, before that time period, or after.

2   Black people account for 25% of those who have tested positive and 39% of the COVID-related deaths, while making up just 15% of the general population.

Although Black Lives Matter (BLM) existed in multiple iterations through different grassroots organizations prior to 2014, it became a more prominent force in public rhetoric during the protests that took place in Ferguson, Missouri, in the days and weeks after Mike Brown was murdered.

In 2014, the Black Lives Matter movement was a wave that swept across the nation.

In 2020, that wave grew into a tsunami.

This time, the undercurrent of the movement was charged in new ways, becoming even more powerful. Black Lives Matter, whether or not people agreed upon its demands, was a placeholder in nearly every dinner table across the United States, and stretched to other parts of the world as well. From the proliferation of social media's clear and painful footage of police killings that went viral, to the aforementioned disproportionate trauma that blistered from COVID-19 and to the centuries of unmet promises, Black people, along with many allies and accomplices from other racial groups, decided enough was enough.

Black Lives Matter paraphernalia flooded the market; major retailers like Target were not only selling BLM merchandise, but were also making statements declaring their commitment to racial justice. In June 2020, Brian Cornell, Target Corporation's chairman and CEO, stated:

> Target stands with Black families, communities and team members. As we face an inflection point in Minneapolis and across the country, we're listening to our team, guests and communities, committed to using our size, scale and resources to help heal and create lasting change (Target Corporate).

Target was not alone. According to reporting from *The Washington Post,* "hundreds of companies blanketed social media with statements denouncing discrimination and professing their commitment to racial justice" (Jan et al. 2020).

While companies charted their commitments using carefully designed squares on social media, individuals followed suit. Declarations that Black Lives Matter increased, and it became a common point of interest to attend various events and protests that pledged people's interest to the movement. "Are you going to the protest?" became a popular refrain for meeting people up at social gatherings.

My own family, that is, Cornelius and me, and our two Black-biracial daughters, almost every night for two weeks, witnessed the sound and energy of protest from the streets by way of our Brooklyn apartment. Regardless of closed windows, air conditioning, sound buffers—it didn't matter. When thousands of people gather on the streets in Brooklyn, there is no avoiding their sound, no matter the cause. So our children, of course, had questions.

Our older daughter (age eight at the time) thought the people who were marching were chanting "Our Justice, Our Peace!" Our younger daughter (age six at the time) was enamored with the honks, the horns, and the sheer number of people who relentlessly showed up night after night. Of course, as a mother who does her best to respond to the curiosities of all children, and especially her own, I gently told our oldest daughter that the people on the streets weren't saying "Our Justice," rather, they were saying "*No* Justice."

> Older daughter: Why Mama? Why are they saying "No Justice, No Peace"?
>
> Me: [*Heavy sigh*]. Because people are demanding safety for Black people. They are saying they won't be quiet until Black people are safe in the United States.
>
> Older daughter: Can we go out there, Mama?
>
> Younger daughter: Yeah, Mama. It looks fun!
>
> Cornelius: [*gives me a look*]
>
> Me: Me and Daddy go out there every day, but our protest just looks different. The work of protecting Black people and children comes in all different shapes and sizes. We can teach you to protest, too, but you don't always have to be in the street carrying a sign.

The website Black Lives Matter in School has created a powerful platform for educators and parents to root themselves in, with a clear path for advocacy:

1. End "zero tolerance" discipline, and implement restorative justice.

2. Hire more Black teachers.

3. Mandate Black history and ethnic studies in K-12 curriculum.

4. Fund counselors not cops (2020).

Their demands are clear and necessary, and are also in pedagogical alignment in working toward future goodness. I recommend you explore their resources to understand more about their organizing and activism at schools. Their website, www.blacklivesmatteratschool.com, includes valuable artifacts such as films, lesson plans, workshop examples, and more.

We now live in an era that is governed by matters of racial justice—for better and for worse. The "better" being that intersectional coalitions are able to gather in school institutions publicly, no longer having to meet in secret spaces to discuss race matters that impact the livelihood of all people. The "worse" part being the cognitive dissonance that happened when the news media buzz was over, when the copies of Robin DiAngelo's *White Fragility* were dog-eared and worn out, when the Black squares posted on social media months after George Floyd and Breonna Taylor's deaths later were symbolic of voided actions, when schools stopped requesting "how to talk to your kids about race" workshops because the season of BLM protesting was sort of "over."

While public proclamations, Saturday workshops, evening protest marches, and monthly social justice summits have changed the narrative regarding the urgency around justice in society and schools, they haven't necessarily changed outcomes, and they have definitely not changed the circumstances for students learning within those institutions, especially those students who are outside the sphere of dominant culture.

As I write this, in 2022, not much has changed regarding data trends for students who have been historically underserved. According to The Nation's Report Card, between 1978 and 2020, in every single category, in every single year, white students at ages 9 and 13 received the highest test scores (NAEP 2021). I will note that Asians, Pacific Islanders, Native Americans, and kids who identify as more than one race are lumped into the "Other" category in the report, so it very well may be true that one of those groups *could* have outperformed white kids. In fact, previous studies do show that Asian students outperform white children (Hsin and Xie 2014). While the achievement gap has narrowed, between the years of 2012 and 2020, statistically significant growth was not evident amongst *any* group of students, including white, Black, Hispanic, Asian/Pacific Islander, American Indian/Alaska Native, and children of two or more races parents (NAEP 2021).

Arguably, circumstances for Black, Brown, Queer, and female students have gotten worse. In the United States, several laws passed in 2021 and 2022 have worked to create a confusing landscape on what teachers "can and cannot teach" (Najarro 2022). The American Civil Liberties Union (ACLU) reports the following legal landscape deeply impacting children in U.S. schools:

- Since 2021, 10 states have passed censorship bills that restrict discussions on race and gender in school.

- In 2022 alone, 111 new bills were introduced across 33 states that specifically target K-12 schools and what they can and cannot teach (ACLU 2022).

Widespread book-banning has swept across the country through local governance and school boards. Books by and about BIPOC people, LGBTQ people, and other marginalized groups are increasingly named "inappropriate" and/or "controversial" for adolescent readers, and continue to be banned (Harris and Alter 2022). Additionally, while Title IX has worked to protect and promote gender equality in schools, the U.S. Supreme Court's overturning of *Roe v. Wade* has set a dangerous precedent for how the public will view the position of girls within society, especially institutions like schools.

Even though the foundation of schooling has always been inequitable, this inequity is further exacerbated by inhumane legislation directly impacting children. Laws in more than 30 states limit and restrict the ways in which schools can purchase curriculum, texts, and other teaching materials based on gendered and racial language, as well as which parts of history or which historical figures are represented in the curriculum (ACLU 2022). Critical race theory, developed by legal scholar Derrick Bell in the 1980s, is used to explore ways in which race is embedded in societies and systems (Cobb 2021). Since 2020, it has been distorted and co-opted by alt-right politicians for "rebranding;" in some conservative circles CRT is equated with "false history" and "Black Supremacy" (Cobb 2021). This political rhetoric has permeated school communities nationally, and has impacted the types of professional development educators have access to, the books children can read, and, ultimately, the kinds of instructional experiences kids are "allowed" to have and school leaders are "allowed" to permit (Najarro 2022).

If we are to promote authentic learning and the well-being of learners within our school communities, we must confront this legislative landscape in addition to the inequities embedded and present within our communities. Learners' shifts in experience happen in the many thousands of micro-interactions they will experience across the periods, days, weeks, semesters, and years-long classroom experiences they share with their teachers.

Certainly, folx should participate in fighting for justice in ways that feel most appropriate regarding their identities, their privileges, and their spheres of influence. However, it is part of an educator's daily work, regardless of your identity markers, to enact social justice in the school spaces we occupy, *especially* for those who are in closest proximity to students.

It is my hope that social justice protests that include a march and a sign punctuated by a string of social media posts *also* include student data, instructional know-how, representative and multi-modal texts, and responsive community engagement. I hope it means people, especially those from dominant culture, those who have more power, step back from conversations and allow space for others. I hope it means that folx are leaning into students a little more, listening to them a little harder.

Designing Justice-Oriented Learning Spaces

In a recent op-ed regarding their teaching role in social justice education, Ursula Wolfe-Rocca and Christie Nold wrote:

> Our classrooms are not sites of doom and gloom. Students are hungry for explanations—real explanations—for the world they have inherited, and in our experience, they often feel relieved to gain insight into why things are the way they are. Moreover, our curriculum emphasizes the varied, powerful and creative ways that people have resisted oppression and built justice (2022).

In my experiences as a classroom teacher, as a partner educator to many present classroom teachers, and as a student myself, I find Wolf-Rocca and Nold's anecdote to be overwhelmingly the case. When teachers work to cocreate understanding with the students they teach in regard to the world that surrounds them—and they do so from the perspective of honest, full histories, grappling with nondominant narratives, and, especially, revealing the stories of people's lived experiences—more often than not, students are grateful. Moreover, relationships are strengthened, and the classroom community grows stronger. When relevant issues are addressed and when power dynamics students seek to understand are part of the curriculum, joy exudes.

You may be wondering how teaching through the lens of social justice can be a joyful pursuit. All throughout this text, we've explored this paradigm.

There is no distinct answer except that by surfacing the truth of the world kids have inherited, by creating space for them to express their daily lived experiences, by teaching through the lens of "more than one way" and multiliteracies, we are honoring their humanity, and there is joy that goes along with that.

Pragmatically speaking, to design justice-oriented spaces with kids first calls us to define our purpose as educators: *What is it we are really trying to do?* This is another exploration we've been unpacking throughout this text. You've engaged in the inner work, you've practiced building community within thought sanctuaries, you've rediscovered what it means to nurture yourself and one another in the tension-filled political landscape of school! You've either reiterated, deepened, or rediscovered your foundational understandings of childhood development and curricular frameworks like UbD and CR-SP. You've even explored how policy decisions, both past and present, have made a difference for young people's learning and teacher's teaching.

These last sections of this text are designed for all those different components to manifest into something deep, something big, something you both know and feel. At this juncture, perhaps it feels hard to name. Even so, this feeling, "felt knowledge," is your collective wisdom at work and it defines your purpose as an educator. I encourage you to engage in this quick work along to sketch what your purpose looks like, write about it, or even just pause and have some dialogue about your purpose with a person you are close to—even a family member. The most important thing in this exercise is for your purpose to manifest outside yourself.

Thinking heart.

Feeling brain.

The Nuts and Bolts of Justice Designs

Earlier, we discussed the "good bones" of curriculum-making: the exercise of backwards planning, continued and intentional assessment, and purposeful instruction through the UbD framework. We also paired it with CR-SP, planning, assessing, and teaching, while considering the communities of people we teach and learn with authentically, imbuing culturally relevant and sustaining teaching every step of the way. The genetic makeup of how that curriculum is delivered is incumbent upon one's levels of teacher agency and their instructional stance. Those entities come from the combined force of our lived experiences—our real-life intellectual DNA. Finally, we must pay attention to the students in front of us and how the world they traverse within has impacted the past, and continues to impact their present and future.

Here, I'll start the work of creating justice-oriented learning designs with a big, broad question:

- How do we create student-centered experiences in standards-based classrooms?

That's the generic version. The one you can use anywhere and people won't bat an eye. But what I really mean is:

- How do we teach young people honestly, in ways rooted in both culturally relevant and strength-based capacities? That are also research-based?

- How do we teach young people about the world that surrounds them; things like class, gender, race, and all the other nuanced topics that are increasingly being named "taboo" . . . even when it makes grown-ups uncomfortable and in some cases . . . the legality of the text or instruction is questionable?

- What methodologies, approaches, and resources will help us teach young people about the world they are growing into in honest, developmentally appropriate ways?

Wiggins and McTighe (the UbD people) would name those my "essential questions," questions that drive the purpose of the curriculum forward.

In so many school spaces, educators struggle with how to talk to young people about the things emerging in their communities. Discussing differences and difficult histories can feel tricky. But not discussing these things gives kids a false sense of the world and who they are in it. Rudine Sims Bishops (1990) revealed this long ago, naming that children from dominant cultures experience a false sense of reality and an exaggerated sense of self when they are not exposed to the stories of people who live differently and carry different histories.

Justice-oriented teaching and learning is doing the work beyond merely expecting that kids will be the "leaders of tomorrow." This is about giving them a framework for how they—in their play and among their friends—be the leaders they were born to be today. When should they speak up, hold space, or stand back? Amongst the sea of misinformation that bombards their lives, how will they parse fact from fiction? What about their personhood matters most for them, and how do other people within their classrooms and outside of it perceive this meaningfulness? What does it mean to truly be in community with a group of people who may or may not share the same interests? (As we continue our process, I'm sure you are noticing that questions are quite prolific in this conversation. That's okay, it's as it should be. Powerful inquiry questions generate more questions. Don't be overwhelmed—it's just how it goes!)

I may have big questions, but my purpose is clear: people who work in schools will learn how to design justice-oriented learning experiences *with* children. I walk through this Earth as an able-bodied, white, cisgender woman, mother, educator/scholar in a heteronormative interracial marriage. My pedagogy is delivered through the medium of that body in connection to my centering of human care, multiliteracies, deep practice, flexibility, innovation, joy, and justice. I am here with you, in this text, and lots of other school spaces because I think transformational change is most profound in the bodies of knowledge teachers carry, learn, and deliver to and from the students they teach.

In this book, I have already mentioned that kids are curious beings and that school poses a threat to their natural disposition. Additionally, I have unpacked and offered potential approaches to make shifts away from dominant school culture and toward future goodness. This movement illuminates a form of joy that has sustained my entire teacherhood. The best part of being an educator, for me, is the privilege of witnessing the growth of people, especially kids, across a school year, when they experience humane, supportive, holistic, collaborative, relational, communal, multiliterate, and process-oriented school spaces (remember the elements of future-goodness reflected in the Structured Generator of Hope in Chapter 1?). It has always felt very special to be part of supporting and shaping that progress as a learner, as a human being.

The human condition from birth is to learn. Witnessing my own children, along with many, many others across both elementary and secondary schools has given me great insight in terms of what kinds of learning children are ready for at different stages in their lives. Throughout my own growth, especially as I transitioned from secondary school teaching to elementary school teaching, I'd no idea the gaps of growth I'd been missing in those early years of kids' lives! When I became a mother a decade ago, the phenomena of what kids are able to do, the creativity and curiosity they hold within their tiny minds and bodies, was especially fascinating. It's been beautiful to witness the spectrum of development from my own children since their births, and for other children from whatever juncture I meet them. Throughout my research and my practice with other educators, I continue to probe this idea . . . where do we take children with their questions, wonderings, and ideas about the world that surfaces in our schools?

As discussed throughout this text, there is tension in this work, between society's predetermined ideas about what school should be such as reading texts that are part of "the Canon," compliant thinking and behavior demonstrated from children and teachers, as well as product-oriented assignments re: "Is it done?" "Did I do it right?" "What do I have to do to get an 'A'?" and the kinds of authentic learning kids respond to most thoughtfully that support their well-being. I revert back to my purpose, which I hope to some extent is not so far off from yours: I am radically pro-kid. I aim to design student-centered experiences. To do that, I must find ways to respond to the types of questions, ideas, and wondering they carry. In fact, regardless of the space I am in, another teacher's classroom, the subway, the schoolyard when I drop off my kids, or even my own dinner table, I am constantly listening, mulling over, and absorbing kids' thinking. I usually write their questions down so I can keep my finger on the pulse of youth's experiences! Recently, for example, I've collected the following questions and ideas in those various spaces I occupy with youth:

- How did all these buildings get built? How did New York City come to be? Who are the workers? Why are there only boys? (5-year-old)

- If you use a ruler made in China, you'll get COVID! (9-year-old)

- Do you think 2020 was like 1968? Which do you think is worse? (10-year-old)

- I just want teachers in this building to treat me like I'm a kid. (11-year-old)

- I miss school. Playing with one friend is hard. Playing with many friends is wayyyy better. (6-year-old)

- Who has been treated worse throughout history? White women or Black men? (8-year-old)

Of course, I also witness young people ask questions that may be considered less controversial, like what people's interests are or endless "would you rather scenarios" re: "Would you rather eat a popsicle or an ice cream cone?" "Would you rather have a cat or a dog?" etc. But alongside the more banal and lighter conversations are the deeper questions kids ask, and the ideas they surface challenge traditional notions of what schooling should be, and offer a wider range of possibilities for what school could be.

How We Respond to Young People Matters

At this point, we're in the assessment phase of our backwards design process, and we are considering the unique experiences and identities of the young people we teach as we collect information about them. Here, we collect information about the kids we teach by observing and listening to them. When we consider how to center kids in our planning trajectory, the relational aspect of our work is really, really important. Remember Rita Pierson's ever-popular inspirational educator talk, where she says, "Kids have a hard time learning from people they don't like"? In my experience, this has almost always been the case, and it works the other way around too. Teachers have a hard time teaching people they don't like, another reason why it's essential educators engage in inner work as they partner with young people in their schools to build learning communities!

As educators, we have options when young people pose ideas, surface wonderings, or assert how they understand the world to be. In action research (which is what you are engaged in when you are collecting information about the kids you teach), children are the eternal other, meaning all the research is about them, but they do not often have a say in what happens within their learning experience (Hamza Constantine 2019). Decisions are consistently made for them, not with them, and this has a deep impact on the ways kids and their families review their relationship to school. As we work to develop a more open-minded community of learners, as their teachers, we have to help them unpack their rigid conceptions or their loaded wonderings about the world that surrounds them, even when we are one of the few people in our communities engaged in this work.

Where do we start? By listening. However, this simple action is difficult when everything at school feels urgent, like the class schedule, or a specific activity, or the curricular pacing calendar. Sometimes, it feels like the ideas young people bring to the light are barriers to whatever "real work" we have in our minds. There are a few different ways educators respond to young people's wonderings that I frequently encounter in schools, included in Table 7.1.

TABLE 7.1 Ways of responding to kids' wonderings.

Educator Listening Styles	Educator Response Styles
Educator doesn't listen; but waits to speak.	Kid: I wonder . . . Teacher: Yes, but, did you do your work? [Moves past child, introduces next topic, or transitions to a different activity.]
Educator listens, but passively.	Kid: I wonder . . . Teacher: Wow, that's so interesting! I'm not sure. I wonder the same thing. [Makes eye contact at first, affirms child's thoughts, does not bring up child's thoughts in class again.]
Educator listens, actively.	Kid: I wonder. . . Teacher: I want to make sure I understand you. Can you tell me more? [Gets out note-taking device, stops what they are doing, sits down and/or gets to eye level with youth idea-maker, and commits to weaving this idea into future curriculum.]

Of course, each time a young person brings up a question or an idea in class, the ways in which educators respond will be based on context. However, the more we make space for kids to say what they are thinking in ways they feel heard, the more likely it is kids will be able to express their ideas clearly, not only an essential life skill, but also a component in speaking and listening standards across many, many states! Additionally, it is at this point in kids' lives, especially between the ages of 2 to 11, where they will experience the greatest amount of plasticity in their brains than at any other time in their lives.

Young people are *really* smart. As they grow up, the ways in which they absorb information is different. Referring back to our foundational understanding in childhood development, between the ages of two to seven, learners are in the "preoperational stage," where they are beginning to use various gestures, experiences, and language to communicate their thinking in the early part of this phase, and the logic and reasoning starts to initiate toward the latter part (Piaget, in Wadsworth 2004). Kids' expressive language grows when they are affirmed and listened to by others, especially the grown-ups who care for them (Center on the Developing Child 2021). In addition, when children move through this period they develop stronger imagination, they begin to think about the future, and they learn to reflect on the past (Wadsworth 2004).

From the ages of 7 to 11, learners are in the concrete-operational stage, where they are able to differentiate their own perspective from others, begin to reason more effectively, start to organize their physical surroundings, and understand that not everything is permanent, including life. As they begin their adolescence and move toward adulthood in their later teenage years, their reasoning abilities become more systemic, and their thinking becomes more idealistic, hypothetical, and abstract (Piaget, in Wadsworth 2004).

The architecture of human learning is extraordinary, and there is not a day that goes by that I am not thinking about the many gifts children bring to us in the form of their ideas, questions, and wonderings. But paired with my awe, I am also struck with sadness. Certainly there are joyful spaces in school. There are classroom gardens, impromptu dance parties, rich picture books, and captivating discussions in classrooms all over this country. But I fear those experiences are becoming fewer and fewer as teachers feel the weight of the world on their shoulders, as well as new laws coming down the pipeline.

I cannot help but wonder what will become of our children whose ideas and questions are not honored in classroom spaces. I ask, "What happens when we keep kids busy instead of curious? What happens when ideas go unexplored? What happens when curricular experiences are rote instead of responsive?" There are centuries of research that have showed us what has happened in years past:

- Rote learning

- Literal news consumption

- Binary thinking

- Intolerance for difference

- Rigidity

- Status quo

I ask, "But what about for kids at present? What about their now?" They answer, "But Kass . . . that's *inappropriate*."

When you work to respond to young people in authentic ways, when the lived experiences of humans are part of your curriculum, chances are, you have experienced someone tell you that what you are doing is "inappropriate" somewhere along the way. Because these events are growing in frequency, it is absolutely imperative that all teachers who work to respond and center children have a strong foundational understanding in terms of childhood development, as well as a clear curricular path and purpose for the kinds of learning experiences they are building within their classroom communities. In all the spaces I occupy with my "educator hat" on, the combination of research, empathy, and relationships, have become my best friends. Not everyone feels the calling to educate grown-ups, and sometimes it feels like an incredible amount of labor, but usually I have found this teaching pivotal when developing justice-oriented learning designs.

In short, I am always working to help grown-ups who participate in schools in any way understand that there is a difference between what is considered "appropriate" versus what it means to covet "innocence." I use Table 7.2 to demonstrate this difference.

Rarely are people comfortable when I first introduce these differences. From state to state, these guidelines are different. With alarming ubiquity, legislative guidance has become increasingly oppressive. This matters for the choices we make, but the safety and well-being of the children we teach also matters.

TABLE 7.2 The difference between appropriate and innocence.

Appropriate	Innocence
Definition: suitable or proper (Oxford) In school: ■ Within a child's ZPD. ■ Connected to learning standards. ■ Supporting school's mission. ■ Representative of Respect for All campaign.	Definition: The notion of innocence refers to children's simplicity, their lack of knowledge, and their purity not yet spoiled by mundane affairs. (Oxford) In school: ■ A luxury disproportionately represented in higher SES families, and white families. ■ A right for all children. ■ What does it mean when we fail to recognize what children *have* been exposed to? What they *do* know? 　■ Protest marches 　■ COVID deaths 　■ Police brutality 　■ #MeToo 　■ Menstruation 　■ Gender

So I use the thing that has helped humans survive their discomfort since the beginning of time: stories. Vulnerability is required here. I'm not always in the mood to be transparent with people who have a very different stance from me. Even so, I summon my inner Hulk, grow familiar with my own sustained discomfort, and remind myself of my purpose. From there, my deep conviction is settled, and I know what I am about to share is vital to the well-being of children. This may not be your cup of tea, and everyone has their own level of vulnerability they are willing to embrace in their teaching for lots of different reasons. I can share what works for me in hopes it will inspire something that works for you.

Here's how it goes: people see the chart in Table 7.2. If it's teachers, usually there's a lot of affirmation in experiences. The work is not as hard. But if it's parents and caregivers, I have to work harder. Often, the argument will surface that children are "too young" to know about x, y, or z. So I ask: "Whose innocence is protected?" In Table 7.2, you'll note that this is a disproportionate luxury for kids who fit within dominant culture. And then I share my first #MeToo story from kindergarten, which I'll share in a moment. I wasn't deeply violated. I don't share all the details. It's not a trauma that has significantly wounded my life, but it is an experience that informed my life as a student, and the relationship I would have with grown-ups who were supposed to protect me throughout my schooling.

Here's my #MeToo story: When I was five years old, I gave a boy my phone number and let him kiss me so he would stop chasing me on the playground. Even still, every day for most of my kindergarten recess, he threatened to kiss me. It became part of my kindergarten life, my norm. One day he called me, and my mom was horrified that a five-year-old boy had my phone number and wanted to talk with me. She did not think it was cute at all. I was horribly embarrassed, and felt shame that somehow this boy calling me was *my* fault. The next day, my mom had our phone number changed, and the school told him to stop chasing me. I still sat next to him in class. And that was it. No further conversations.

I tell people this story to illuminate that what may appear to "be cute" or "not a big deal" in the eyes of others is actually mortifying for children. Ideas like "boys will be boys" circulate amongst adults while children suffer, navigating the situation via kid-governed play rules, teaching kids like me, and other kids who experience shame through the words and actions of their peers, that people who work at school can't, or rather *don't*, really help them.

Protect Children by Anticipating Injustice and Preventing Harm

There are so many actions that could, or *should*, have happened, from my teachers and people who worked at my school. In schools, adults have the most power. It is their responsibility to see and anticipate injustices, protect children, prevent and undo harm, and offer children ways to protect themselves, or upstand in situations where they can protect others. In this particular situation, I see three avenues adults working at my school could have taken, and I think in many schools, they could be applied in the present:

1. **Anticipate.** Educators can anticipate that children will touch each other in their play. Not all touching is bad, and touching is something that can be expected amongst young people. That being said, educators can teach young people lessons on consent as part of their curriculum.

2. **Protect and empower victims.** It is key to notice when children might be feeling uncomfortable, and especially when there may be potential harm happening, even if it doesn't look like "harm" at first. Being fully present when children are leading their own play is necessary to notice any injustices that may occur. When you notice potential for harm, ensure you are giving children tools and options to remove themselves from situations that are harmful, or may become harmful. Role play scenarios, 1:1 conversations, and even stories that demonstrate upstanding are all avenues for this kind of learning.

3. **Teach and unpack power dynamics to the perpetrator.** Even when a harmful situation feels like it is over, it usually is not and tends to play out in other ways. There is a reason why 64.4% of business leaders are men in the United States (Zippia 2022). Over time, girls are tacitly trained to become subservient, and this work starts as early as pre-K. It is imperative we partner with the families of children who are treating other children unfairly, or even harming them, to unlearn that behavior. That starts with unlearning mindsets around one's role in society. There is a lot of room in the curriculum to assemble various texts and class discussions to unlearn toxic

masculinity. This can look a lot of different ways. Perhaps it starts with a few intentional read-alouds that surface boys being emotive in positive ways. Conversations after those read-alouds can surface more questions that help children name many ways to be strong, and they don't always include the messages we see in the world.

Reflection: Protecting Your Childhood Self at Your Current School

Again, everybody has different kinds of experiences in schools regarding their identities and school locations. In this exercise, I encourage you to engage in the same exercise I just demonstrated.

- Think back to your elementary school life . . . what did you experience that didn't feel right?

- What do you wish the grown-ups around you had done?

- Imagine your childhood self was at your current school: Would your school be equipped to support you? How do you imagine the grown-ups in your community would support you?

What Matters to Children

In the pursuit toward justice for those working in education, people will often cite their Ivy League degrees, the research they've conducted or participated in, the multiple letters after their names, the articles they've written, or the years of experience they have teaching. But when it comes to centering the child in our pursuit, what really matters? Especially from the vantage point of young people . . .

Author and educator Nikolai Pizarro de Jesus reminds us to ask ourselves this very question. In a panel discussion hosted by The Bank Street College of Education, Pizarro implored the audience to take a moment to pause and consider: "What credentials matter to children?" She then cited credentials that were most important to her, saying: "My neighbor's child comes to my house to rest. My son tells me when he is scared." Pizarro served us an important reminder, and I reflected as such, this time through the lens of my former classroom spaces. Internally, I probed the broader question, and narrowed it down asking myself: How do children's actions tell me that what I'm doing is equipping them with the tools they need to grow and feel safe and feel loved and always positioning them in a space where they feel like they are a learner? Internally, I responded:

- They come to my room every morning before school starts to spend time with me.

- They bring up questions in morning circle about what they've seen or heard about in the world that no other adult is talking to them about.

- *They show their tears, their joys, their whole selves.* (I vividly remember a former student coming into the morning circle space abruptly, talking about how mad he was at his step-brother for breaking his toy. The whole class community helped him solve his problem.)

What matters to young people goes far beyond the items on our CVs or résumés, and there are great implications from those actions in terms of creating curriculum and developing community centered in justice.

Reflection: Naming Credentials That Matter

First, pay attention to your somatic literacy. What are you experiencing at this point in time as you read this text? How does your body feel?

Then, name three credentials students would name for you based on their experiences with you. If it's hard to come up with them, ask your students! You can also think about students you've taught in the past. What credentials might they name for you?

I know this all may feel very hard. Perhaps, too, it feels very affirming, or maybe you are still feeling like this is all within the realm of impossibility. Please know that I will forever be your cheerleader.

This is hard, but it's also possible. You can do this!

I offer a few general guidelines that underscore the plausibility for justice-oriented learning designs in different types of school locations:

- Know that asking questions about what's happening in the world is kids' prerogative. Having conversations about kids' questions is a natural, organic occurrence in elementary school classrooms. It's authentic inquiry when we respond to their questions in thoughtful ways.

- Federal law indicates there is a separation of church and state within schools. More often than not, standards are formulated around science and accredited research institutions. That means it is your right as a teacher, educator, or school leader to teach science, and separate fact from fiction. When people give you pushback, especially students' families, I offer the language below to families to guide their beliefs in their homes. For example:

  a. At home: "In this family we value . . ."

  b. In school: "In this school we teach from a research-based perspective. . . . We value x, y, z. If you don't agree with what we're teaching, you are welcome to have a separate conversation with your child at home. But please know, in this class, in this school, we will be discussing the world that surrounds us."

One helpful exercise for educators who are working with communities that have different stances to the type of education their children should receive is to engage in role-playing scenarios with their colleagues to prepare themselves for pushback. For example, this is when one colleague would take on the role of a community member disagreeing with content being taught, and then a teacher would practice using the language above to guide their conversation.

Chapter 8:
Negotiating the Curriculum for Your Current Students in Today's World

One way I like to begin planning for learning experiences in connection to larger ideas and goals that young people have explicitly named, situations that have come up, or even the news is to use Vivian Maria Vasquez's concept of "negotiated curriculum" (2004). According to Vasquez, the negotiated curriculum is a "process for adjusting and reconstructing what we know, naming what matters for us, situating learning in lived experiences in connection to grade level standards" (p. 1). Note this is a stark contrast to designing curriculum for kids to accumulate information and skills in isolation from their lived experience and the communities that surround them.

TABLE 8.1 Template for making curriculum relevant through negotiation.

Curricular Standards	Revised Curriculum
(Reading) Ask and answer questions about key details in a text read-aloud or information presented orally or through other media.	
(Writing) Write narratives to develop real or imagined experiences or events using effective technique, well-chosen details, and well-structured event sequences.	
(Social Studies) Recognize, analyze, and use different forms of evidence used to make meaning in Social Studies (including primary and secondary sources such as art and photographs, artifacts, oral histories, maps, and graphs).	
(Math) Understand the relationship between numbers and quantities; connect counting to cardinality.	

Loosely adapted from Vivian Maria Vasquez, *Negotiating Critical Literacies with Young Children* (2004).

I use a template like the one in Table 8.1 that has been adapted from Vasquez's work on the negotiated curriculum to organize my thinking in terms of what standards I am obligated to teach according to my contract, and spaces for connections and experiences that are relevant to kids that speak to the skills, content, and habits that are embedded within those standards.

In Table 8.1, the standards included on the left are Common Core State Standards. Again, as we are naming essential questions or the big ideas that inform our route, these ideas must be connected to grade-level standards. On the right, there is space to consider what revisions are necessary to both accommodate kids' academic needs as well as the changing tides of today's world.

To negotiate the curriculum is to create relevant learning experiences that directly speak to the needs of the students you teach. That is, it is working to promote justice in their learning and everyday being, even as they are 7- or 10- or 13-year-olds. Table 8.2 is more expansive than Table 8.1, and helps create space for the negotiated pieces, or the adjustments you make to learning experiences that may have already been written, or that you have planned quite differently in years past.

After brainstorming a negotiated curriculum that is connected to learning mandates, or state standards, the next step is to organize learning activities across a unit into different "bends." If the learning design is your roadmap,

TABLE 8.2 Planning for your current students in today's world.

Issue(s) and Data	Community Happenings/ Situational Context	Areas of Study, Including Texts, Materials, and Other Resources	Actions, Experiences, and Projects	Connected Topics and Further Areas to Study
School closure, COVID-19 global pandemic, social gaps between kids Kids' comments: ■ If you eat Chinese food, you'll get COVID! –9 year old ■ I miss school. ■ Playing with one friend is hard. ■ Playing with many friends is wayyyy better. –6 year old	After a series of varied messages from the school district regarding COVID-19 school closures, students were no longer able to see each other regularly at school. Teachers across the city were told to not address COVID-19 directly, and many students in the lower grades overheard from older kids at the school that the "germs had come from China." One child overheard another child say that if they ate Chinese food, they would get COVID. When school buildings officially closed, and all students learned remotely, first graders said they didn't like playing with only one friend. They said they liked playing with "*many* friends." Currently, there is a social gap with many kids who continued to attend hybrid learning, vs. kids who were fully remote last year.	■ Germ theory: What are germs and how they spread video. ■ How much is one million? (Five million germs live on one hand!) ■ Created a class infographic for the 3 Ws. ■ Geography lesson. ■ What are stereotypes? ■ Individual in connection to society (narrative writing). ■ Intentional peer relationship support in class/recess.	■ Self-accountability for disease prevention, school-wide handwashing campaign. ■ Science-based information sharing; PSA on family's social media. ■ Outdoor playgroup. ■ Acquiring and diversifying recess, supplies. ■ Developing explicit emotional literacy centers.	■ Identity: Who are my ancestors? ■ How do we help more classmates get to play with us outside? ■ Why didn't the president wear a mask? ■ Loss. ■ Competing ideas on what is "fact."

Loosely adapted from Vivian Maria Vasquez, *Negotiating Critical Literacies with Young Children* (2004).

the curriculum is the itinerary for the journey you embark on, and all the activities embedded within that curriculum are the different places you stop and things you experience. Eating a three-course dinner after one hour of driving wouldn't make sense, just as starting a dynamic group project on day one of the unit wouldn't make sense either. As you pace the different activities with various lesson plans across the unit, imagine the first leg of the journey, the second leg of the journey, and the third leg of your journey. What learning activities make the most sense for your students to engage in earlier? Later? What skills are you teaching along the way in addition to the content? Do your students have the necessary habits to engage in the activities you've created? What habits will you need to teach?

Unit plans take many shapes and forms, just as lesson plans do. I have lots of curricular maps and lesson plan templates I've used in the past, but, honestly, no template has made an enormous difference in my own work as a classroom teacher, or the many teachers I have partnered with. Rather, it is the style of thinking of UbD, and the adoption of a culturally relevant and sustaining framework as an operational lens, that has made all the difference (combined with teacher agency and human development, of course!). That said, I invite you to use whatever curricular planning tools and templates feel best for you in the name of designing justice-oriented learning experiences!

How does this work manifest? Are you sure students are learning literacy?

There is a common misconception that when you're negotiating or revising a curriculum with the children you teach, you're walking away from standards-based teaching, or they are missing something vitally important within a curriculum as it was previously written. This is simply untrue. By naming the skills, content, and habits embedded within the standards we are obligated to teach in connection to the questions, ideas, and wonderings students surface in school spaces, we are simply moving through an operational stance of how learning works. Additionally, when we consider the unique human experiences of individual children, and the cultural backgrounds they present within our communities, we are enhancing the learning landscape by building a pathway for strengthened relationships and a more open community of learners.

In the following sidebar are artifacts from students in New York City schools that demonstrate this sort of literacy learning.

Kindergarten-Level Personal Narratives

Mandated Curriculum: Write narratives to develop real or imagined experiences or events using effective techniques, well-chosen details, and well-structured event sequences.

Negotiated Curriculum: Develop connections between real-life current events, learning how they impact oneself and their community. For example, students may watch a news-clip about vaccine making after they express concern about getting sick during a morning meeting. Teachers will teach narrative writing using sequential order and well-chosen

Kindergarten student writing sample.

(Continued)

details, but they also will fuse the elements of concern amongst the community alongside the information they see in the newsclip.

Students developed a written narrative synthesizing their own experiences along with what they learned from the newsclip.

Disease Spread and Personal Hygiene

Mandated Curriculum:

- (Math) Understand the relationship between numbers and quantities; connect counting to cardinality.

- (Social Studies) Recognize, analyze, and use different forms of evidence used to make meaning in Social Studies (including primary and secondary sources such as art and photographs, artifacts, oral histories, maps, and graphs).

Negotiated Curriculum:

- To develop students' number sense, specifically cardinality as stated in the mandated curriculum, students explore the concept of "1 million" through the lens of how germs spread. Close-up pictures of bacteria and germs are shown to the class, along with infographics on how handwashing is instrumental to preventing germs from spreading. For example, the essential question includes, "How much is one million?," followed with a teaching motivation like "Did you know 5 million germs live on one hand!?"

- In Social Studies, the teacher has the opportunity to negotiate the curriculum by using infographics to explore information literacy, that is, how to interpret content on a primary or secondary source. To demonstrate further understanding, students could develop their own infographics in small groups, answering the question, "What are germs and how do they spread?"

Students analyzed artifacts using cardinality and other visual cues to grow awareness about disease spread. They used print-based language and visual communication to develop an advocacy campaign for personal hygiene. As such, not only are students learning skills and content knowledge within the mandated curriculum, but they also are working toward a more relevant understanding of the world that surrounds them, and tending to their emotional needs as well.

Work Along: Generate Issues Relevant Within Your Community

Practice engaging in the process of negotiating curriculum. Generate some issues that have come up recently in your community, or refer to questions, ideas, and/or wonderings from kids you documented in the work along in Chapter 7. If you are accustomed to adapting curriculum, use a curriculum that shows grade-level standards in an upcoming unit you will be teaching, or if you are developing homegrown curriculum, refer to the standards in your state. To fully grasp the standards you will work from, I encourage you to use the unpacking process (skills/content/habits) in Chapter 6. After you have documented the standards that will tether students' literacy learning, use the Negotiated Curriculum Brainstorm Template to surface learning activities and experiences that will become part of your classroom community's learning journey.

Three Paths for Considering Kids, Justice, and Curriculum Design

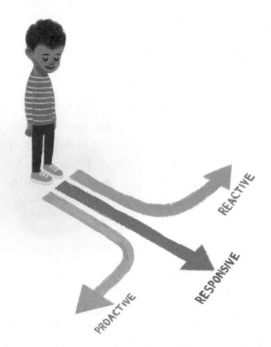

Three paths for considering justice-oriented learning designs.

We are now at the point in our curriculum-making where we have decided where we want to go, that is, we've documented our big questions, we have engaged in a variety of assessments, and we've collected information about our students to understand their personalities, learning needs, and cultural backgrounds more robustly. In stage three of Wiggins and McTigues's UbD, this is where learning experiences are planned. Some people like to think of this part as "lesson planning." And while that is true, sometimes a lesson plan template can get in the way of creative possibilities. In the end, I almost always will document a period of learning within a lesson plan format. However, before I do that, there's a bit more artistry and strategic thinking involved.

In terms of strategic thinking, the ways educators approach justice-oriented learning designs typically go one of three ways. First, and most formidable, is the proactive approach. This is when educators deeply understand childhood development, they've studied up and listened and learned about their students' families, cultural backgrounds, and learning needs, they are paying attention to what's happening in all the in-between spaces of school like the hallways and cafeteria, and it is from those areas that inform how their classroom community is built and how their curriculum goes. One of the most devastating factors during the height of the COVID-19 pandemic in schools was the inability of educators to do any significant levels of proactive planning; every moment of school changed so drastically on a daily basis, and educators were often forced to make reactive decisions.

Educators also approach justice-oriented learning responsively. This is usually the best-case scenario given the resources educators have and circumstances that most educators are situated within. This is when educators witness, observe, listen, and do all the things they would have proactively, but in the case of the responsive teacher, it's not always possible to anticipate what students need or what is going to happen. Rather, they actively listen to students' needs and either respond in the moment or design learning in the coming days to address those needs.

The third strategy, the reactive approach, is also very common. While this approach is better than not doing anything at all in the pursuit toward justice, it often comes too late, after people in the community, usually young people, have already been harmed. For example, after a series of racial epithets were drawn on bathroom stalls, teachers might begin to design learning experiences that address racial acceptance.

These approaches correspond with different ways of designing justice-oriented learning, which you will find in Table 8.3.

In this section, I will show brief examples of what each of these learning designs looks like within curriculum-making.

TABLE 8.3 Corresponding approaches to learning designs and curriculum-making.

Proactive	**Intentionality in Deepening Critical Literacy Within and Across Curriculum.** Creating systems in learning spaces that support children in moving through the world as researchers with a critical lens.
Responsive	**The Inquiry Based Model.** Kids serve you the hard information, i.e., the child brings their news/comments to the classroom.
Reactive	**When Personhood Within the Community Is Threatened.** An overt or implicit "ism" is experienced by a group of people or an individual based on their race, ethnicity, gender, or sexuality.

The Proactive Approach: Intentionality in Deepening Critical Literacy Within and Across a Curriculum

This is where you create systems in your learning space that teach children to move through the world as a researcher with a critical lens.

- Create an audit trail. An audit trail is a visual articulation of learning and thinking that is meant to be visible not only to people in the classroom, but to others in the school community as well (Hartse and Vasquez 1997).

- Make your morning meeting a space where criticality lives. For example, students can adopt classroom jobs where they have a turn to surface concerns about the world that surrounds them, such as "Class Chairperson" (Vasquez 2004).

- Reshape morning workstations (Table 8.4) that allow kids to grapple with and learn more about named issues.

  - In younger grades, this often will come from informal play experiences.
  - Upper elementary students often will cite news they overhear family talking about, or they see on social media.

- Use protocols such as Sara K. Ahmed's "In Your News" where kids sharing news, whether it be difficult, banal, or silly, is routinized in daily classroom structures (2018).

TABLE 8.4 Morning workstations revised to create space for kids' lived experiences.

Traditional Morning Workstations	Kids Experiences Are Assessed	Adjusted Morning Workstations
Traditional morning workstations in lower elementary school: ■ Word study station ■ Calendar station ■ Morning message station ■ Survey station ■ Counting jar station		Adjustments are made to negotiate learning toward justice orientation: ■ Word study station includes space for social justice vocabulary. ■ Survey station now includes data collection on issues kids care about. ■ "Talk story" replaces "counting jar" station. Station is now an exploration of a variety of texts that connect to kids' news.

The Responsive Approach: The Inquiry-Based Model

This is when kids serve you the information, for example, the child brings the news or the "tricky topic" (usually unplanned!) to the classroom. Because inquiry-style teaching is more of a stance than a "thing you can do," I've included a specific example below that demonstrates this style of teaching from my own elementary school classroom, when I was frequently served "hard news."

I was teaching fourth and fifth graders when the Pulse Massacre occurred in June 2016, and 49 people were killed at a gay nightclub in Orlando, Florida. The day after the shooting, the kids came in, and before we even sat down for morning circle, students were exclaiming: "¡Las arma de fuego!" Since it was June, and we'd been together for a full school year, the classroom community I'd cocreated with the students was strong. They knew that in our class we talked about things—even when other classes didn't. We always have options for how we choose to respond to students' questions, ideas, and wonderings. At this point in my career I was seasoned. I had strong teacher agency and a well-developed stance in terms of who I was in the world as an educator. I was able to approach this experience from a responsive, active listening space, and inquiry-based teaching was the mechanism I chose as a treatment toward justice. When kids come in the classroom space talking and saying phrases that include words like "gay," "guns," and "killing," you do not skip over that energy and pivot into silent reading. Rather, you mentally note that students have witnessed a crisis, and they need help processing the bits and pieces they've heard.

The learning trajectory I took is described as follows. (And note, although this community was in New York City, many students came from conservatively religious families.)

First, I revised the schedule to make time for the heated talk. I knew if I didn't, the kids were still going to be talking about the shootings or thinking about them in another way. I also felt my "injustice" body alarms going off: hearing the kids' confusion and dark banter about the shooting was alarming. Queer people were part of our community, and I wanted them to understand how their statements had power to hurt and harm people.

Next, we gathered in our circle space, which we did every day for a variety of reasons. On most days, we gathered to engage in community building, sharing pieces of our lives, our hurts, our celebrations. This day, I engaged in direct teaching right away to clarify terms. As I noted before, many times in social justice education, literacy learning gets lost. In the circle space, I defined the terms, *Queer*, *nightclub*, and *massacre*. Not because I thought those are the types of tier-two and tier-three words that should be on upper-elementary vocabulary lists, but because those were the words the students were saying over and over in the incorrect context, not knowing their full meaning. Kids mimic the grown-ups who surround them, and their social comprehension models intersect all facets of life—media, family circles, random strangers they overhear at stores, friends, video game chatter. They picked this language up from somewhere, and at this point, it didn't matter from where. What mattered was that they knew the meaning of the language they were using. I am not talking about the inner workings of nightclub life, I don't need to talk about the type of dances or songs people listen to at Pulse nightclub. Again, I am directly responding to the news, words, phrases, and questions kids brought into the classroom space.

Then, I created space for questions. "Time for Questions" was a pretty typical experience for kids in our classroom. It was yet another ritual we held sacred to ensure everyone understood important elements of whatever discussion we had been engaged in. In general, but especially for difficult topics, kids want to know more. They are worried and they are wondering. In this particular scenario, the Queer community has long suffered at the hands of traditional schooling norms. If we are truly working toward justice, it is everyone's job to normalize talking about Queer life in the classroom just like you would talk about married life between a man and a woman in a classroom.

This style of inquiry-based teaching isn't just like other literacy inquiry. Anytime you have an inquiry based on the nexus of one's humanity that some consider to be incumbent upon their identity markers, you will most certainly have to guard your inquiry with care. For me, I maintain that my open lines of communication with the families of the students I taught, as well as my colleagues, paired with strong foundational learning knowledge, allowed me to engage in conversations with my students that many teachers are not able to have. There was a level of trust between my students, their families, and my colleagues that ensured I was working to maintain the well-being of the kid-community. So, I invited community members in, we watched videos, and we read together. Myths about Queer life my students previously understood to be true were dismantled.

Imagine what would have happened if I ignored the heated conversation at the beginning of that day in June 2016? Queer educators often witness their humanity disregarded as their peers stay silent, as they witness books about families like their own being banned.

I haven't figured it all out. I know there are a lot of "what ifs" in regard to what's been banned, or what's not allowed. I try to live in the space of "let's try this" or "how can we work around that?"

Beyond the what ifs, most of all, I think about how this little collective of fourth and fifth graders began to grow their understanding about a group of people and moved from a space of misconception to one of empathy. That group was on a path to loving all peoples, and I felt lucky I got to be a part of that.

The Inquiry-Based Learning Model

The following steps summarize the inquiry-based learning model.

Help the young people unpack their thinking in a ritualized talk space. Ritualized talk spaces include, but are not limited to, morning circles, advisory periods, midday debriefs, closing circles, etc. If there is no ritualized space for class discussion outside of academic content, this work will be much more difficult. I recommend that whatever discussion modes have been successful with your community are resurrected and remembered by both teacher and students before engaging in charged conversation.

> **Help students process the news they've brought in without adding information that further complicates their limited understanding of it.**
>
> - Let them do as much of the talking as possible.
>
> - Use prompts like "Tell me more . . ." and "Can you say that in another way?"
>
> - Clarify terms that are important for understanding.
>
> - Allow peers to ask peers questions about what they don't understand. Also make space to "table" questions to address at another time.
>
> - Document the children's words verbatim.

But Kass, "That's inappropriate!"

My friend Phil Bildner, author and writer of several middle-grade novels that feature Queer characters, often tells his audiences: "No human being is inappropriate." That phrase has carried me a long way, not because I believe there is anything inappropriate about a person's sexual orientation, but because, unfortunately, there are many people who do. When I am in conversation with these kinds of people, I center my language in research. Table 8.5 can support your engagements when you are dealing with homophobia, or any number of other "isms" in your school communities.

TABLE 8.5 The dangers of not talking about it with corresponding research.

The Dangers of "Not Talking About It"	Corresponding Research to Support the Claims
- Not talking about tragedy when other people are in crisis is teaching kids to walk right on by when other people are in pain.	- *The Bystander Effect* (1968) by John M. Darley and Bibb Latané.
- Not talking about Queerness, Blackness, whiteness, toxic masculinity, and many other inequities harms children. It gives them an exaggerated sense of self and hyperbolizes what's "normal."	- *Windows, Mirrors, and Sliding Glass Doors* (1990) by Rudine Sims Bishop.
- Not talking about what's going on in the world has created widespread social illiteracy. - Not talking about race early in life contributes to greater misconceptions about the "other."	- *Adults Delay Conversations About Race Because They Underestimate Children's Processing of Race* (2021) by Sullivan et al.
- Children and families from BIPOC and Queer communities are often belabored with educating their peers about racism and their families. Even first graders.	- "What White Colleagues Need to Understand" by Brazas and McGeehan, learningforjustice.org. - GLSEN.org; School Climate Reports.

(Continued)

TABLE 8.5 (Continued)

The Dangers of "Not Talking About It"	Corresponding Research to Support the Claims
■ Not talking about race leaves children to make guesses rather than informed ideas about race. Children as young as six months old begin to categorize others by race.	■ "The Development of Racial Categorization in Early Childhood" by Pauker, Williams, and Steele.
■ Not talking about race with children fuels inaccurate assumptions. Explicitly talking about race with children creates more positive attitudes about people of different races.	■ Vittrup, B. (2016). Early childhood teachers' approaches to multicultural education and perceived barriers to disseminating anti-bias messages. *Multicultural Education* 23 (3–4): 37–41.

The Reactive Approach: Personhood Within the Community Is Threatened

If your school community has not engaged in self-reflective work, does not acknowledge the difference between "same" and "fair," or does not have a consistent infrastructure to address the needs of teachers and students on a regular basis, chances are that someone's personhood has been threatened. Unfortunately, this reactive approach is fairly common because there are many school communities that fit the characteristics described above. However, it is better to say something after a harmful event has occurred, as there is more danger in not saying anything at all.

The work of standing up for those who have been threatened or harmed is enabled through your sense of purpose. Let's say that our purpose is to ensure that *all* children who participate in learning spaces are able to show up whole, feel valued in their full humanity, and honor others', especially those who have been historically marginalized. While I have many stories I have witnessed in this regard, they are the stories for other people to tell, from those who have been harmed. The following story has been told and shared widely. Professor Patricia J. Williams (2021) recounts threatened personhood in one of her recent essays on talking about race:

> My son L. was invited to a neighbor's seventh birthday party. When we arrived, the neighbor child (R.) introduced L. to the small circle of other children, all of whom were white; he did so in hushed tones, seemingly so that adults wouldn't hear. "This is my friend L.," he whispered. "He's Black!"

While this scenario is not my direct experience, it is representative of a great many witnessings through my life as a former elementary school educator, current parent of Black biracial children, and an educator who visits a lot of schools with hugely diverse student demographics. The teaching and learning I recommend (in the sidebar to follow) to use in the aftermath of an event such as the one described above are, however, derivatives of my own experiences in schools.

How to React When Personhood in the Community Is Threatened

1. Move swiftly!

   - Intervene in the moment when possible. For example, tell R., the white child, "We don't need to whisper when we use race words."

   - Immediately reach out to the child (and their family!*) who is closest to harm.

   In this case, it would be the Black child, L. For example: "I know that R. introduced you to a group of people in a different sort of way. How are you feeling? I'm so sorry you had to experience that. I want to help you feel safe. Is there anything you need right now to feel better? I am working on a plan right now with your family to make sure you always feel like yourself when you're at school."

2. Know childhood development. Kids use language and behavior to test power. Before assuming the worst about a first grader and their family, create open dialogue that allows the child to say more about their language choices. Kids learn about race through comprehensive models, that is, their knowledge is a manifestation of YouTube videos, billboards, dinner table conversations, overheard subway chats, their older sibling's friends, etc. (Hagerman 2020). That said, the language they use to describe others isn't necessarily because that's the language their caregivers are using.

3. Engage in "pocket conversations." Hold smaller conversations when discussing topics that have attacked an individual in your community. Not everything needs to happen in circle time.

4. Use texts to provide layers of meaning and historical context to the situation. There are many, many picture books that are representative of all kinds of people and experiences. Additionally, text sets have been curated for educators to support them in conversations regarding race and identity, as well as social literacy and a lot of other issues that pop up in communities. Websites run by We Need Diverse Books (diversebooks.org) and social-justicebooks.org both have a plethora of resources.

---

*   Note, if you haven't established contact or any kind of relationship with the child's family, this work is going to be really, really hard. **But you'll still have to do it**.

The Continuing Journey: A Constant Preparation (Not Necessarily Fun, but Definitely Joyful)

More often than not, I am of the mindset that binaries (the either/or thinking that so many parts of dominant culture amplify and prioritize), are not always applicable or universal to everyone's situation. I've talked a lot about the "packaged" nature of what "should" be done in school spaces for teachers and students that doesn't bode well for the general wellness of people in schools or learning outcomes for students. That said, I hesitate to insert the do's and don'ts columns in Table 8.6, but I recognize that blueprints are valuable in providing direction as people figure out their journeys toward justice. As you parse through Table 8.6, I encourage you to consider your role, your realm of influence, and also legal considerations that are part of your school community. Keep in mind: federal considerations such as those put forth in IDEA supersede what various individuals or community groups may request.

TABLE 8.6 Designing for justice do's and don'ts.

Do's	Don'ts
DO: **Anticipate pushback,** and practice defending your position. Caregiver/parent to teacher: "You are indoctrinating my child." Teacher to caregiver/parent: "In this school, we teach from a research-based curriculum rooted in scientific understanding and childhood development."	DON'T: **Rely on a pre-packaged social justice curriculum to do your work for you.** Above all, this work is about honoring the humans in front of you, and helping them develop a critical, literate, moral core. *Always be wary of any reenactment situation*! Example: Pre-curated "Culturally Relevant" libraries classroom libraries might not be expansive or targeted for students in your community.

TABLE 8.6 (Continued)

Do's	Don'ts
DO: **Approach the work with care.** Work with a buddy. An affinity partner will work best in some cases. Stay connected to your students' families, and make it a point to be available and initiate consistent feedback (especially positive feedback!).	DON'T: **Consider this work a separate subject,** an exotic celebration, or a "one and done" project. Example: only teaching about Native Americans in the Fall or Black folx in February.
DO: **Underscore the difference between kids,** surfacing concerns that should be referred to a school counselor or social worker. All educators are mandated reporters.	DON'T: **Quit!** If you mess up, (and you probably will), don't stop! Keep going. Read more. Try again. Kids and families can be forgiving if you show your investment in long-term justice.

Epilogue: Redefining Ferocity

2022

We're six weeks into the school year, and Cornelius and I are facilitating the beginning of a year-long learning series with a cross-school community of teachers in our home district. We open our day with gentle celebratory conversation. Here, teachers are meeting each other for the first time. Prompts like "Who was your childhood crush" and "Go into your phone—where were you exactly one year ago today" light up conversations and the beginnings of community start to form. The positive vibes are palpable.

We're charged with developing relational equity amongst teachers, school leaders, students, and families, figuring out what it really means to live and breathe practices in schools that are human-centered, that spark intellectual curiosity, that enact joy, and that are developed through the lens of justice.

We discuss the "community up model" (see Chapter 5), and I show the teachers a chart of Gary Chapman's "Five Love Languages" that my friend

Marcus Harden and I unpacked in our earlier work on love and building literacy culture across schools. I show them Marcus's examples from his former students within the chart. We review the continuum of communication exchanges (Minor and Harden 2020). Cornelius and I give examples of our love languages, and how they differ across contexts (quality time for Cornelius, acts of service for me).

I ask teachers to identify their love language, too; that is, how they like to receive love in the context of school. There is a pause. The energy changes. Not from good to bad, but from fun and spirited to more saturated with hurt and need. A teacher then shares what maybe all the others are thinking:

> It's hard to name how I like to receive love in school because it's been so long since I've felt it. For the past few years, I've not really focused on anything but filling everyone else's cup.

Our budding community sits in a moment of quiet, swallowing the heaviness in the air.

There are a lot of different ways to describe the reality of teaching life within the context of school. Regularly, I witness the spirited quest so many teachers embark on toward joy and justice in spite of x and y and z. But the journey is draining. Teachers, educators, and just about everyone who plays a role in running a school are exhausted. The transformation we work so hard for, sometimes, feels invisible.

But remember those multiple truths I identified way back in the introduction?

> **Truth 1:** Now, more than ever, teachers have limited bandwidth to engage with the idea of re-existing in the world.

> **Truth 2:** Now, more than ever, changing the school experience for kids who are learning within that institution requires labor, instincts, and collaborative, creative critical thinking from those who are most proximate to their experience.

More than anything about school, I believe in the possibility of the relationships and learning that happens between a teacher and their students.

I continue to embrace that possibility. Whether you are a teacher, a school leader, or a caregiver, think about what it means to nourish the teaching community. The alchemy created when something like a Structured Generator of Hope is held closely within a community—prioritized, and facilitated with fidelity—has the power to actualize the joyful and just transformation so many of us have been looking for. That, to me, reader is *redefining ferocity*.

The last thing I leave you with as we press pause on our journey together, reader, are elements of my personal edu-credo. Whether you are initiating, developing, or holding *your* edu-credo more tightly, consider what it means for *you* to teach fiercely, and work toward spreading joy and justice in our schools.

My Edu-Credo

We care for ourselves, and we care for our community.

> We work to deeply understand the communities in which we work; that is, *who* we are teaching and *what* we are teaching. This also includes ourselves. What are the necessary conditions for educators to work in schools in a state of well-being?

The resistance lies in educators' ability to locate, experience, and sustain joy for themselves and their community. It also lies in their ability to identify and unpack both justice and injustice.

> We take our personal needs into consideration and are mindful of multiple perspectives on joy as it radiates throughout school communities.

Curriculum-making and developing classroom life is expansive work. Those who spend the most time with students are in the best position to make decisions about their learning life, alongside research and community support.

Justice is multifaceted. Part of our justice work is positioning youth, teachers, and families as cocreators of the school experience alongside policy makers, researchers, principals, and superintendents. Agency comes from trust, expertise, and collective work toward justice and joy.

Developing a Personal Edu-Credo

A final work along: I invite you to draft, revise, or reestablish elements of your own personal edu-credo as you work to teach fiercely, and spread joy and justice in our schools.

Works Cited

ACLU. (2022). Defending our right to learn. https://www.aclu.org/news/free-speech/defending-our-right-to-learn.

Ahmed, S. (2018). *Being the Change: Lessons and Strategies to Teach Social Comprehension*. Portsmouth, NH: Heinemann.

American Civil Liberties Union. (n.d.). Title IX - gender equity in education. https://www.aclu.org/title-ix-gender-equity-education (accessed 5 August 2022).

Anderson, M. (2016). Why are black girls disproportionally pushed out of schools? *The Atlantic* (15 March). https://www.theatlantic.com/education/archive/2016/03/the-criminalization-of-black-girls-in-schools/473718.

Anzaldúa, G.E. (2002). now let us shift . . . the path of conocimiento . . . inner work, public acts. In: *This Bridge We Call Home: Radical Visions for Transformation* (eds. G.E. Anzaldúa and A. Keating), pp. 540–578. New York: Routledge.

BBC News. (2021). George Floyd: timeline of black deaths and protests. *BBC News* (22 April). https://www.bbc.com/news/world-us-canada-52905408.

Bell, M.K. (2015). Making space. *Learning for Justice* (Summer). https://www.learningforjustice.org/magazine/summer-2015/making-space.

Berger, S. and Curato, M. (2018). *What If . . .* Boston: Little, Brown Books for Young Readers.

Berkes, A. (2009). A bill for the more general diffusion of knowledge. *Thomas Jefferson Encyclopedia* (April). https://www.monticello.org/site/research-and-collections/bill-more-general-diffusion-knowledge.

Bhagwath, A. (2020). *Sacred Alignment of Religious Structures to North Star.* doi:10.13140/RG.2.2.21834.39367/4 (20 October).

Black Lives Matter at School. (n.d.). www.blacklivesmatteratschool.com (accessed 23 May 2022).

Booth, T.T. (2010). Cheaper than bullets: American Indian boarding schools and assimilation policy, 1890–1930. In: *Images, Imaginations, and Beyond: Proceedings of the Eighth Native American Symposium* (ed. M.B. Spencer), 46–56. Durant, OK: Southeastern Oklahoma State University.

Borish, S.M. (2005). *The Land of the Living.* Grass Valley, CA: Blue Dolphin Publishing.

Bowles, S. and Gintis, H. (2011). *Schooling In Capitalist America.* Chicago: Haymarket Books.

Brightman, H.J. and Gutmore, D. (2002). The educational-industrial complex. *The Educational Forum* 66 (4): 302–308.

Brown, A.M. (2017). *Emergent Strategy: Shaping Change, Changing Worlds.* Chico, CA: AK Press.

Butler, O. (2019). *Parable of the Sower (Parable, 1).* New York: Grand Central Publishing.

Calvert, L. (2016). The power of teacher agency. *The Learning Professional: The Learning Forward Journal.* https://learningforward.org/journal/april-2016-issue/the-power-of-teacher-agency/#:%7E:text=What%20Is%20Teacher%20Agency%3F,the%20growth%20of%20their%20colleagues.

Center for Belonging Folk School. (n.d.). www.centerforbelonging.earth (accessed 13 July 2022).

Center for Nonviolent Communication. (2005). Needs inventory. https://www.cnvc.org/training/resource/needs-inventory.

Center on the Developing Child. (2020). InBrief: the science of early childhood development. Harvard University. https://developingchild.harvard.edu/resources/inbrief-science-of-ecd.

Cobb, J. (2021). The man behind critical race theory. *The New Yorker* (13 September). https://www.newyorker.com/magazine/2021/09/20/the-man-behind-critical-race-theory.

Common Core State Standards Initiative. (n.d.). www.corestandards.org.

Common Core State Standards Initiative. (2010). English Language Arts Standards. https://www.corestandards.org/ELA-Literacy (accessed 6 May 2022).

Common Core State Standards Initiative. (2010). Speaking and listening, Grade 6. English Language Arts Standards. https://www.corestandards.org/ELA-Literacy/SL/6/1.

Covert, A. (2015). Understanding information architecture. Abby Covert, Information Architect (18 September). https://abbycovert.com/speaking/understanding-ia.

Cox-Petersen, A. (2010). *Educational Partnerships: Connecting Schools, Families, and the Community*. Newbury Park, CA: SAGE Publications, Inc.

Curriculum, Assessment and Teaching Transformation. (n.d.). Constructivism. University at Buffalo, https://www.buffalo.edu/catt/develop/theory/constructivism.html#title_1308821097 (accessed 30 November 2021).

Davis, A. (1990). *Women, Culture and Politics*. New York: Vintage.

Dewey, J. (2018). *Democracy and Education*. Gorham, ME: Myers Education Press.

Didion, J. (2017). *Slouching Towards Bethlehem: Essays*. New York: Open Road Integrated Media.

Education Alliance at Brown University. (2008). Characteristics of culturally relevant teaching. https://web.archive.org/web/20211112164708/https://

www.brown.edu/academics/education-alliance/sites/brown.edu.academics.education-alliance/files/uploads/KLOOM_crt_entire.pdf (accessed 1 September 2016).

Eiben, V. (2015). A brief history of folk schools. Folk Education Association of America. https://folkschoolalliance.org/a-brief-history-of-folk-schools.

Encyclopedia.com. (n.d.). 1783–1815: Education: Overview. https://www.encyclopedia.com/history/news-wires-white-papers-and-books/1783-1815-education-overview (accessed 8 June 2022).

Erivo, C. and Barlow, P.C. (2021). *Remember to Dream, Ebere*. New York: Little, Brown Books for Young Readers.

Facing History & Ourselves. (n.d.). The origins of eugenics. https://www.facinghistory.org/resource-library/origins-eugenics (accessed 22 April 2022). Quoting in part Francis Galton (1883): 24.

Facing History & Ourselves. (2020). *Race and Membership in American History: The Eugenics Movement*. https://www.facinghistory.org/resource-library/race-membership-american-history-eugenics-movement (accessed 30 October 2022).

Facing History & Ourselves. (n.d.). School: the story of American public education. https://www.facinghistory.org/books-borrowing/school-story-american-public-education (accessed 6 May 2022).

Family Equality Council. (2017). LGBTQ family fact sheet. U.S. Census Bureau, Family Equality Council. https://www2.census.gov/cac/nac/meetings/2017-11/LGBTQ-families-factsheet.pdf.

First Nations Pedagogy Online. (n.d.). Talking circles. https://firstnationspedagogy.ca/circletalks.html (accessed 29 July 2022).

Galton, F. (1883, 1907). *Inquiries into the Human Faculty and Its Development*. New York: Macmillan. https://galton.org/books/human-faculty/text/galton-1883-human-faculty-v4.pdf.

Gatluak, N. (2021). Six Dr. Seuss books to be recalled due to racist imagery. *Iowa State Daily* (9 March). https://iowastatedaily.com/251358/limelight/six-dr-seuss-books-to-be-recalled-due-to-racist-imagery/.

Generator Source. (n.d.). How does a generator create electricity? How Generators Work. https://www.generatorsource.com/How_Generators_Work.aspx (accessed 9 March 2022).

German, L.E. (2021). *Textured Teaching: A Framework for Culturally Sustaining Practices*. Portsmouth, NH: Heinemann.

GLSEN. (2014). Key concepts and terms. Gay, Lesbian & Straight Education Network. https://www.glsen.org/sites/default/files/2020-04/GLSEN%20Terms%20and%20Concepts%20Thematic.pdf (accessed 31 May 2022).

González, N., Moll, L.C., and Amanti, C. (2005). *Funds of Knowledge: Theorizing Practices in Households, Communities, and Classrooms.* New York: Routledge.

Gordon, B.M. (1990). The necessity of African-American epistemology for educational theory and practice. *Journal of Education* 172 (3): 88–106. http://www.jstor.org/stable/42742188.

Gordon-Reed, A. (2009). *The Hemingses of Monticello: An American Family.* New York: W.W. Norton and Company.

Gore, A. and Guggenheim, D. (2006). *An Inconvenient Truth.* Uploaded by YouTube 23 May 2012. https://www.youtube.com/watch?v=8ZUoYGAI5i0&feature=youtube.

Gould, E., Schieder, J., and Geier, K. (2016). What is the gender pay gap and is it real? the complete guide to how women are paid less than men and why it can't be explained away. Economic Policy Institute (20 October). https://www.epi.org/publication/what-is-the-gender-pay-gap-and-is-it-real.

Grace, D., Johnson, C., and Reid, T. (2020). Racial inequality and COVID-19. The Greenlining Institute (4 May). https://greenlining.org/press/opinion-columns/2020/racial-inequality-and-covid-19/?gclid=Cj0KCQjw1ZeUBhDyARIsAOzAqQIRt_MURqQ03quxFn2wfS_Jr6O-ZrtlrROBH5dOjbhkxswceJ9fNtsaAkATEALw_wcB.

Green, E.D. (2016). What are the most-cited publications in the social sciences (according to Google Scholar)? Impact of Social Sciences Blog (12 May). eprints.lse.ac.uk/66752 (accessed 8 July 2022).

Gross, A., Iruka, I.U., Williams, T., Jones, D., and Pizarro de Jesus, N. (2021). Disrupting anti-Black racism in early childhood education: center, abolish, liberate, Panel discussion at Black Lives Matter at School Week Early Childhood Symposium. Bank Street College of Education in New York City (4 February 2021). https://www.bankstreet.edu/our-work-with-schools-and-communities/bank-street-education-center/center-on-culture-race-equity/black-lives-matter-at-school-week-2/.

Growe, R. and Montgomery, P.S. (2003). Educational equity in America: is education the great equalizer? *Professional Educator* 25 (2): 23–29. https://eric.ed.gov/?id=EJ842412.

Hagerman, M. (2020). *White Kids*. Amsterdam: Amsterdam University Press.

Hamza Constantine, D. (2019). Presentation at the NCTE annual conference. Austin, TX (21–24 November 2019).

Harris, E and Alter, A. (2022). Why book ban efforts are spreading across the U.S. *The New York Times* (8 February). https://www.nytimes.com/2022/01/30/books/book-ban-us-schools.html.

Highlander Research and Education Center. (n.d.). Our history. https://highlandercenter.org/our-history-timeline. (accessed 11 January 2022).

History.com Staff. (2018). Chinese Exclusion Act. History (24 August). https://www.history.com/topics/immigration/chinese-exclusion-act-1882 (accessed 17 March 2021).

Horsford, S.D. (2021). Whose vision will guide racial equity in schools? *Education Week* (17 March). https://www.edweek.org/leadership/opinion-whose-vision-will-guide-racial-equity-in-schools/2021/03 (accessed 29 June 2021).

Howard, T.C. (2020). How to root out anti-Black racism from your school. *Education Week* (3 June). https://www.edweek.org/leadership/opinion-how-to-root-out-anti-black-racism-from-your-school/2020/06.

Howe, S.G. (2017). Outgoing correspondence [Massachusetts School for Idiotic and Feeble-Minded Youth]. Massachusetts Archives. http://chc.library.umass.edu/state-archives/2017/04/18/outgoing-correspondence-massachusetts-school-for-idiotic-and-feeble-minded-youth.

Hsin, A. and Yu, X. (2014). Explaining Asian Americans' academic advantage over whites. *Proceedings of the National Academy of Sciences* 111 (23): 8416–8421. doi:10.1073/pnas.1406402111.

IGN. (2019). Lana Wachowski describes what it's like returning to the Matrix. YouTube (19 December). https://www.youtube.com/watch?v=6mkNIs2XWZU.

International Literacy Association. (n.d.). Literacy glossary. Ila.org. https://www.literacyworldwide.org/get-resources/literacy-glossary (accessed 11 December 2021).

Jacques, S. (2019). Tackle the top drivers of teacher attrition. Hanover Research (22 July). https://www.hanoverresearch.com/reports-and-briefs/tackle-the-top-drivers-of-teacher-attrition (accessed 10 February 2022).

Jan, T., McGregor, J., Merle, R., and Tiju, N. (2020). As big corporations say 'Black Lives Matter,' their track records raise skepticism. *The Washington Post* (13 June). https://www.washingtonpost.com/business/2020/06/13/after-years-marginalizing-black-employees-customers-corporate-america-says-black-lives-matter/.

Jefferson, T. (1779). A bill for the more general diffusion of knowledge. Monticello.org. https://www.monticello.org/site/research-and-collections/bill-more-general-diffusion-knowledge.

Jones, L.A. (2021). We need to keep dreaming, even when it feels impossible. Here's why. Ideas.Ted.Com (11 March). https://ideas.ted.com/we-need-to-keep-dreaming-even-when-it-feels-impossible-heres-why.

Kills First, C. (2020). Decolonize the classroom. Keynote speech at the Fifteenth Annual Teacher Leadership Institute: Elevating Student Voice Through Teacher Leadership, virtual conference (15 June 2020).

Kim, R. (2019). *Elevating Equity and Justice: Ten U.S. Supreme Court Cases Every Teacher Should Know*. Portsmouth, NH: Heinemann.

Kirkland, D. (2020). How we can center equity and racial justice when schools reopen. A Will to Love (11 June). https://davidekirkland.wordpress.com/2020/06/05/how-we-can-center-equity-and-racial-justice-when-schools-reopen.

Kozol, J. (2012). *Savage Inequalities: Children in America's Schools*. New York: Crown Publishing Group.

Ladson-Billings, G. (2014). Culturally relevant pedagogy 2.0: a.k.a. the remix. *Harvard Educational Review* 84 (1): 74–84. doi:10.17763/haer.84.1.p2rj131485484751.

Ladson-Billings, G. (1994). *The Dreamkeepers: Successful Teachers of African American Children*. San Francisco: Jossey-Bass.

Land, G. and Jarman, B. (1992). *Breakpoint and Beyond: Mastering the Future Today*. New York: Harper Business.

Lean Coffee. (n.d.). Start one in your city! Leancoffee.org (accessed 23 June 2022).

Lear, J. (2008). *Radical Hope: Ethics in the Face of Cultural Devastation*. Cambridge, MA: Harvard University Press.

Lee, A.M.I. (n.d.). What is the Individuals with Disabilities Education Act (IDEA)? Understood. https://www.understood.org/en/articles/individuals-with-disabilities-education-act-idea-what-you-need-to-know?utm_source=google-search-grant&utm_medium=paid&utm_campaign=evrgrn-may20-fm&gclid=Cj0KCQjw-daUBhCIARIsALbkjSaFl2Wo LxdXKoXH-g_uc32AHB7vjoFEPNiDk0MscUuXfl_KfEWaEDIaAr4zEALw_wcB (accessed 31 May 2022).

Lentini, R., Vaughn, B.J., and Fox, L. (2005). Buddy system tip sheet: teaching tools for young children with challenging behavior. University of South Florida. https://challengingbehavior.cbcs.usf.edu/docs/ttyc/TTYC_BuddySys-temTipSheet.pdf.

Levinson, M. Moral injury and the ethics of educational injustice. *Harvard Educational Review* 85 (2): 203–228. doi:10.17763/0017-8055.85.2.203.

Lorde, A. and Clarke, C. (2007). *Sister Outsider: Essays and Speeches*. Toronto: Crossing Press.

Love, B. (2020). *We Want to Do More Than Survive: Abolitionist Teaching and the Pursuit of Educational Freedom*. Boston: Beacon Press.

Lowrey, A. (2022). Teachers, nurses, and child-care workers have had enough. *The Atlantic* (27 September).

Lyiscott, J. (2019). *Black Appetite. White Food: Issues of Race, Voice, and Justice Within and Beyond the Classroom*. Oxfordshire: Routledge.

Lynn, A. (2017). MacIntyre, managerialism, and metatheory: organizational theory as an ideology of control. *Journal of Critical Realism* 16 (2): 143–162. doi: 10.1080/14767430.2017.1282299.

Mark, J. (2018). The Egyptian afterlife & the feather of truth. World History Encyclopedia (30 March). https://www.worldhistory.org/article/42/the-egyptian-afterlife--the-feather-of-truth (accessed 7 July 2022).

Marshall, J.M. (2012). Common schools movement. *Encyclopedia of Diversity in Education* 1: 416–417. Sage Publications. doi:10.4135/9781452218533.n131.

Mcleod, S. (2019). Constructivism as a theory for teaching and learning. *Simply Psychology* (17 July). https://www.simplypsychology.org/constructivism.html.

Me Too. (2022). metoomvmt.org.

Meacham, J. (1996). Mind, society, and racism. *Human Development* 39 (5): 301–306. doi:10.1159/000278482.

Media Literacy Now. (n.d.). What is media literacy? https://medialiteracynow.org/what-is-media-literacy/ (accessed 29 September 2022).

Merriam-Webster.com. (n.d.). Heteronormative. https://www.merriam-webster.com/dictionary/heteronormative (accessed 23 April 2022).

Merriam-Webster. (n.d.). Racism. https://www.merriam-webster.com/dictionary/racism#usage-1 (accessed 22 April 2022).

Merritt, E.G. (2016). Time for teacher learning, planning critical for school reform. *Phi Delta Kappan* 98 (4): 31–36. doi:10.1177/0031721716681774.

Miller, D. and Sharp, C. (2018). *Game Changer! Book Access for All Kids*. New York: Scholastic Professional.

Minero, E. (2016). Place-based learning: a multifaceted approach. Edutopia (19 April). https://www.edutopia.org/practice/place-based-learning-connecting-kids-their-community.

Minor, K. and Harden, M. (2020). Love as a qualifier: building literacy culture across a school. *Journal of Adolescent & Adult Literacy* 64 (2): 127–133. doi:10.1002/jaal.1091.

Moore, J. (director). (2012). *Pitch Perfect* [motion picture]. Uploaded by NBC Universal. https://www.youtube.com/watch?v=OrHLn4zuePs.

Morris, M. (2016). *Pushout: The Criminalization of Black Girls in Schools*. New York: The New Press.

Muhammad, G. (2020). *Cultivating Genius: An Equity Framework for Culturally and Historically Responsive Literacy*. New York: Scholastic Teaching Resources.

NAEP. (2021). NAEP long-term trends assessment results: reading and mathematics. The Nation's Report Card. https://www.nationsreportcard.gov/ltt/?age=9.

Najarro, I. (2022). How laws on race, sexuality could clash with culturally responsive teaching. *Education Week* (21 April). https://www.edweek.org/policy-politics/how-laws-on-race-sexuality-could-clash-with-culturally-responsive-teaching/2022/04.

Namerow, J. (2007). Justice, community, and Adrienne Rich. Jewish Women's Archive (25 April). https://jwa.org/blog/adriennerich.

National Archives. (n.d.). President Dwight D. Eisenhower's farewell address. https://www.archives.gov/milestone-documents/president-dwight-d-eisenhowers-farewell-address.

Nikolai, P. (n.d.). @raisingreaders. Linktree. https://linktr.ee/raisingreaders (accessed 13 July 2022).

National Center for Education Statistics. (n.d.). Back-to-school statistics. https://nces.ed.gov/fastfacts/display.asp?id=372.

National Center for Education Statistics. (2012). Schools and staffing survey (SASS). https://nces.ed.gov/surveys/sass/tables/sass1112_2013314_t12n_005.asp.

New York City Independent Budget Office. (2019). Admissions overhaul: simulating the outcome under the mayor's plan for admissions to the city's specialized high schools. Schools Brief. https://ibo.nyc.ny.us/iboreports/admissions-overhaul-simulating-the-outcome-under-the-mayors-plan-for-admissions-to-the-citys-specialized-high-schools-jan-2019.pdf.

New York State Education Department (2016). K-12 social studies framework. https://www.nysed.gov/curriculum-instruction/k-12-social-studies-framework.

New York State Education Department. (2011). The New York State Prekindergarten Foundation for the Common Core. https://www.p12.nysed.gov/

earlylearning/standards/documents/PrekindergartenFoundationfortheCom-monCore.pdf.

New York Times. (2018). Behind the cover: the education issue. *The New York Times* (17 September). https://www.nytimes.com/2018/09/05/magazine/behind-the-cover-the-education-issue.html.

New York Times. (2022). How George Floyd died, and what happened next. *The New York Times* (29 July). https://www.nytimes.com/article/george-floyd.html.

NYC Coalition for Educational Justice. (2019). Chronically absent: exclusion of people of color from NYC curricula. The Education Justice Research and Organizing Collaborative (EJ-ROC). https://steinhardt.nyu.edu/metrocenter/ejroc/chronically-absent-exclusion-people-color-nyc-elementary-school-curricula (accessed 7 July 2022).

NYC Coalition for Educational Justice. (2020). Diverse city, white curriculum: the exclusion of people of color from English language arts in NYC schools. https://steinhardt.nyu.edu/metrocenter/ejroc/diverse-city-white-curriculum.

Obama, M. (2021). Keynote address at the NCTE annual convention (18 November).

Only a Teacher: Schoolhouse Pioneers. (n.d.). John Dewey (1859–1952). PBS Online, https://www.pbs.org/onlyateacher/john.html (accessed 6 May 2022).

Owocki, G. and Goodman, Y. (2002). *Kidwatching: Documenting Children's Literacy Development*. Portsmouth, NH: Heinemann.

Paris, D and Alim, H.S. (eds.) (2017). *Culturally Sustaining Pedagogies: Teaching and Learning for Justice in a Changing World*. New York: Teachers College Press.

Poetry Foundation. (1998). To the Reader: Twilight by Chase Twichell. Poetry Foundation. https://www.poetryfoundation.org/poems/51102/to-the-reader-twilight.

Ravitch, D. and Viteritti, J. (2001). *Making Good Citizens: Education and Civil Society*. New Haven, CT: Yale University Press.

Reilly, K. (2018). 'I work 3 jobs and donate blood plasma to pay the bills.' This is what it's like to be a teacher in America. *Time* (13 September).

Rethinking School. (n.d.). History of bilingual education. https://rethinking-schools.org/articles/history-of-bilingual-education (accessed 4 May 2021).

Rich, A. (1995). *On Lies, Secrets, and Silence: Selected Prose 1966–1978*. New York: W.W. Norton and Company.

Rivera, G. (1972). Willowbrook: the last great disgrace (Full 1972 Special). ABC7 New York (2 February). https://abc7ny.com/11700456.

Robinson, K. (2010). Changing education paradigms. RSA Animate (11:40). https://www.ted.com/talks/sir_ken_robinson_changing_educa-tion_paradigms?utm_campaign=tedspread&utm_medium=referral&utm_source=tedcomshare.

Robinson, K. (2006). Do schools kill creativity? TED2006 video (19:12). https://www.ted.com/talks/sir_ken_robinson_do_schools_kill_creativity?language=en.

Rodriguez, N.N. and Swalwell, K. (2021). *Social Studies for a Better World: An Anti-Oppressive Approach for Elementary Educators*. New York: W.W. Norton.

Romito, D. and Freeman, L. (2018). *Pies from Nowhere: How Georgia Gilmore Sustained the Montgomery Bus Boycott*. New York: little bee books.

Rothstein, R. and Jacobsen, R. (2007). A test of time: unchanged priorities for student outcomes. Economic Policy Institute (5 March). https://www.epi.org/publication/webfeatures_viewpoints_student_outcomes_priorities.

Say, R. and Fiske, V. (2019). Talk story, any day. She Lives Aloha (17 October). https://www.shelivesaloha.com/blog/talk-story.

School of Africana and Multicultural Studies. (n.d.). About the Sankofa bird. Southern Illinois University. https://cola.siu.edu/africanastudies/about-us/sankofa.php (accessed 31 May 2022).

Sealey-Ruiz, Y. (2020). Archaeology of Self (TM). Yolanda Sealey-Ruiz. https://www.yolandasealeyruiz.com/archaeology-of-self (accessed 31 May 2022).

Senge, P., Kleiner, A., Roberts, C. et al. (1994). The *Fifth Discipline Field-book: Strategies and Tools for Building a Learning Organization*. New York: Currency, Later Edition.

Sesame Street Communities (n.d.). https://sesamestreetincommunities.org/.

Shah, P.E., Weeks, H.M., Richards, B. and Kaciroti, N. (2018). Early childhood curiosity and kindergarten reading and math academic achievement. *Pediatric Research* 84 (3): 380–386. doi:10.1038/s41390-018-0039-3.

Sims Bishop, R. (1990). Windows, mirrors, and sliding glass doors. *Perspectives: Choosing and Using Books for the Classroom* 6 (3). https://cenicregional.org/wp-content/uploads/2017/08/Mirrors-Windows-and-Sliding-Glass-Doors.pdf.

Slavery and the Making of America. (2004). The Slave Experience: Education, Arts, and Culture. WNET: Thirteen. https://www.thirteen.org/wnet/slavery/experience/education/history2.html (accessed 8 June 2022).

Smith, C.A. (2018). Cite Black Women. www.citeblackwomencollective.org.

Smith Crocco, M. and Lee, S. (2008). Teaching the levees: a curriculum for democratic dialogue and civic engagement to accompany the HBO documentary film event, *Spike Lee's When the Levees Broke: A Requiem in Four Acts*. New York: Teachers College Press.

Starmack, S. (2015). Folk tales: definition, characteristics, types and examples. Study.com. https://study.com/academy/lesson/folk-tales-definition-characteristics-types-examples.html.

Sullivan, J., Wilton, L., and Apfelbaum, E.P. (2021). Adults delay conversations about race because they underestimate children's processing of race. *Journal of Experimental Psychology: General* 150 (2): 395–400. doi:10.1037/xge0000851.

Taie, S. and Goldring, R. (2020). Characteristics of public and private elementary and secondary school teachers in the United States: results from the 2017–18 National Teacher and Principal Survey First Look. Washington, DC: U.S. Department of Education. National Center for Education Statistics. https://nces.ed.gov/pubs2020/2020142.pdf.

Target Corporate. (2020). Target commits $10 million and ongoing resources for rebuilding efforts and advancing social justice. Press release (5 June). https://corporate.target.com/article/2020/06/commitments-rebuilding-and-social-justice.

Tatum, B.D. (2021). *Why Are All the Black Kids Sitting Together in the Cafeteria?: And Other Conversations About Race*. New York: Penguin.

Texas Education Agency. (2018). Texas essential knowledge and skills. https://tea.texas.gov/academics/curriculum-standards/teks/texas-essential-knowledge-and-skills.

Truesdale, S.P. (1990). Whole-body listening. *Language, Speech, and Hearing Services in Schools* 21 (3): 183–184. doi:10.1044/0161-1461.2103.183.

United Federation of Teachers. (n.d.). Integrated Co-Teaching (ICT). https://www.uft.org/teaching/students-disabilities/integrated-co-teaching-ict (accessed 6 May 2022).

U.S. Census Bureau. (2011). Index of single parent households. https://www2.census.gov/library/publications/2010/compendia/statab/130ed/tables/11s1336.pdf (accessed 31 May 2022).

U.S. Census Bureau. (2011). Single-parent households: statistical abstracts of the United States. https://www2.census.gov/library/publications/2010/compendia/statab/130ed/tables/11s1336.pdf.

U.S. Environmental Protection Agency. (n.d.). What is Superfund? https://www.epa.gov/superfund/what-superfund (accessed 7 March 2022).

Vander Ark, T., Liebtag, E., and McClennen, N. (2020). *The Power of Place: Authentic Learning Through Place-Based Education*. Alexandria, VA: ASCD.

Vasquez, V.M. (2004). *Negotiating Critical Literacies with Young Children*. New York: Routledge Press/Lawrence Erlbaum Associates, Inc.

Wadsworth, B. (2004). Piaget's Theory of Cognitive and Affective Development. Boston: Pearson/Allyn & Bacon.

Washington Office of Superintendent of Public Instruction. (2019). Social Studies Learning Standards. https://www.k12.wa.us/sites/default/files/public/socialstudies/standards/OSPI_SocStudies_Standards_2019.pdf.

White House Archives. (n.d.). Race to the Top. The Obama White House Archives. https://obamawhitehouse.archives.gov/issues/education/k-12/race-to-the-top (accessed 7 July 2022).

Wiggins, G. and McTighe, J. (2011). *The Understanding by Design Guide to Creating High-Quality Units*. Alexandria, VA: ASCD.

Williams, P.J. (2021). How *not* to talk about race. *The Nation* (8 December). https://www.thenation.com/article/society/talk-about-race.

Wolfe-Rocca, U. and Nold, C. (2022). Opinion: Why the narrative that critical race theory 'makes white kids feel guilty' is a lie. The Hechinger Report (2 August). http://hechingerreport.org/opinion-why-the-narrative-that-critical-race-theory-makes-white-kids-feel-guilty-is-a-lie.

Xiaoqing, R. (2021). Test anxiety. *City Journal* (4 April). https://www.city-journal.org/asian-american-activists-fighting-ncy-school-reform.

Zippia. (2022). Leader demographics and statistics in the US. https://www.zippia.com/leader-jobs/demographics.

About the Author

Kass Minor is an inclusive educator and community organizer who is deeply involved in local, inquiry-based teacher research and school community development. Alongside partnerships with the University of Chicago, Teachers College Inclusive Classrooms Project, The Author Village, and the New York City Department of Education, since 2004, she has worked as a teacher, staff developer, adjunct professor, speaker, and documentarian. Along with her partner and husband, Cornelius Minor, she established The Minor Collective LLC, a community-based movement designed to foster sustainable change in schools, redefining what it means to develop affirming, welcoming school culture and instructional practice through the lens of racial justice, decolonization, and liberation. On the off chance Kass is not working in a school, you'll find her rekindling her inner child through ongoing experiments in urban gardening with her two daughters, curating numerous at-home libraries (different ones—full of tea, recipes, and, yes, books!), and designing jewelry in the company of her fluffy Siberan cat, Boris, and husband, Cornelius, in Brooklyn, New York. To connect with Kass online, or for more on Kass's work and publications, visit kassandcorn.com.

Index

Page numbers followed by *t* indicate tables and *f* indicates figures

Teaching Fiercely: Spreading Joy and Justice in Our Schools